Recent Trends in Cryptography

CONTEMPORARY MATHEMATICS

477

Recent Trends in Cryptography

UIMP-RSME Santaló Summer School
July 11–15, 2005
Universidad Internacional Menéndez Pelayo
Santander, Spain

Ignacio Luengo
Editor

 American Mathematical Society
Real Sociedad Matemática Española

American Mathematical Society
Providence, Rhode Island

Editorial Board of Contemporary Mathematics

Dennis DeTurck, managing editor

George Andrews   Abel Klein   Martin J. Strauss

Editorial Committee of the Real Sociedad Matemática Española

Guillermo P. Curbera, Director

Emilio Carrizosa   José M. Muñoz Porras
Javier Duoandikoetxea   Pedro J. Paúl
Alberto Elduque   Pablo Pedregal
Sebastián Montiel   Juan Soler

2000 *Mathematics Subject Classification.* Primary 94Axx, 94A60, 94A62, 11T71, 14G50, 68P25, 14H52.

Library of Congress Cataloging-in-Publication Data

UIMP-RSME Santaló Summer School (2005 : Universidad Internacional Menéndez Pelayo)
  Recent trends in cryptography : UIMP-RSME Santaló Summer School, July 11–15, 2005, Universidad Internacional Menéndez Pelayo, Santander, Spain / Ignacio Luengo, editor.
    p. cm. — (Contemporary mathematics ; v. 477)
  Includes bibliographical references.
  ISBN 978-0-8218-3984-3 (alk. paper)
  1. Coding theory—Congresses. 2. Cryptography—Mathematics—Congresses. 3. Ciphers—Congresses. I. Luengo, Ignacio, 1953– II. Universidad Internacional Menéndez Pelayo. III. Real Sociedad Matemática Española. IV. Title.

QA268.U49 2005
652′.8—dc22
                                                                                2008033089

Copying and reprinting. Material in this book may be reproduced by any means for educational and scientific purposes without fee or permission with the exception of reproduction by services that collect fees for delivery of documents and provided that the customary acknowledgment of the source is given. This consent does not extend to other kinds of copying for general distribution, for advertising or promotional purposes, or for resale. Requests for permission for commercial use of material should be addressed to the Acquisitions Department, American Mathematical Society, 201 Charles Street, Providence, Rhode Island 02904-2294, USA. Requests can also be made by e-mail to `reprint-permission@ams.org`.

Excluded from these provisions is material in articles for which the author holds copyright. In such cases, requests for permission to use or reprint should be addressed directly to the author(s). (Copyright ownership is indicated in the notice in the lower right-hand corner of the first page of each article.)

© 2009 by the American Mathematical Society. All rights reserved.
The American Mathematical Society retains all rights
except those granted to the United States Government.
Copyright of individual articles may revert to the public domain 28 years
after publication. Contact the AMS for copyright status of individual articles.
Printed in the United States of America.

∞ The paper used in this book is acid-free and falls within the guidelines
established to ensure permanence and durability.
Visit the AMS home page at http://www.ams.org/

10 9 8 7 6 5 4 3 2 1   14 13 12 11 10 09

Contents

Preface	vii
Cellular Automata in Stream Ciphers Amparo Fúster-Sabater	1
Linear and Nonlinear Sequences and Applications to Stream Ciphers Tor Helleseth	21
An Introduction to Pairing-Based Cryptography Alfred Menezes	47
Public-Key Cryptanalysis Phong Q. Nguyen	67
Pseudorandom Number Generators from Elliptic Curves Igor E. Shparlinski	121

Preface

This volume contains the written versions of four courses plus the one seminar talk given at the Lluis A. Santaló Summer School, entitled "Recent Trends in Cryptography", and organized by the Real Sociedad Matemática Española (RSME). One of the objectives of the RSME is to present the challenges and opportunities that the modern Information Society offer to the mathematical community. Following this objective, the main goal of the Summer School was to give an overview of some recent mathematical methods used in cryptography and cryptanalysis. There were four courses given by well-known specialists plus several seminar talks and two round table discussions with representatives of the industry, administration, and research communities. The Summer School was held at the Universidad Internacional Menéndez Pelayo (UIMP) at the Palacio de la Magdalena in Santander (Spain) on July 11–15, 2005.

The program of the school consisted of four courses taught by Tor Helleseth, Alfred Menezes, Phong Nguyen, and Igor Shparlinski. There were also talks by Amparo Fúster, Jaime Gutiérrez, Ignacio Luengo, and two round table discussions. The main topics were analysis of stream cyphers and public-key cryptography — a revolutionary idea introduced thirty years ago that has changed our lives in aspects such as the Internet and electronic commerce. All topics were of great interest for their applications to the different aspects of information security, such as authentication, digital signatures, smart cards, electronic voting, and the security of mobile phones. The course of T. Helleseth gave a very nice introduction to stream cyphers including the main mathematical aspect, such as boolean functions, and combination of stream cyphers, and algebraic and correlation attacks to such cyphers. The course of A. Menezes gave an introduction to pairing-based cryptography with elliptic curves and his main applications, such as short signatures and identity based encryption. This course presented some important developments in protocol design, Tate pairing computations, and selection of elliptic curves. The course of Phong Nguyen made a complete introduction to the mathematical techniques used in the cryptanalysis of public-key cryptosystems. It included a description of the main public-key cryptosystems, its security, and attacks. This course also presented an introduction to lattices and more advanced attacks based on them. The course of I. Shparlinski presented a survey of several recently suggested constructions of generating sequences of pseudorandom points on elliptic curves. Such constructions are of interest for both classical and elliptic curve cryptography and are also of intrinsic mathematical interest.

All this material is presented in this proceedings collection in an expository manner with many examples and references and will be very useful to graduate students and research mathematicians and engineers interested in mathematical methods in cryptography and cryptanalysis.

As organizer of the school, I wish to thank the RSME for giving us the opportunity to organize this event and also to the UIMP for their great help in its arrangement and for allowing us to use the excellent facilities of the Palacio de la Magdalena. I would also like to thank Amparo Fúster Sabater from CSIC, who did a great job co-organizing the event, and all the students and participants, whose interest and dedication was responsible for the great atmosphere of the courses. My deepest gratitude goes to the speakers, who presented very good courses and made the extra effort to write the course notes — these will be very useful for the mathematical community. "Muchas gracias" for the excellent job. Finally, thanks to RSME, UIMP, and the Departamento de Álgebra of the Universidad Complutense de Madrid for their administrative and financial support.

Ignacio Luengo

Cellular Automata in Stream Ciphers

Amparo Fúster-Sabater

ABSTRACT. A wide family of nonlinear sequence generators, the so-called clock-controlled shrinking generators, has been analyzed and identified with a subset of linear cellular automata. The algorithm that converts the given generator into a linear model based on automata is very simple and can be applied in a range of practical interest. Due to the linearity of these automata as well as the characteristics of this class of generators, a cryptanalytic approach can be proposed. Linear cellular structures easily model keystream generators with application in stream cipher cryptography.

1. Introduction

Cellular Automata (CA) are particular forms of finite state machines that can be investigated by the usual analytic techniques ([10], [17], [19], [25]). CA have been used in application areas so different as physical system simulation, biological process, species evolution, socio-economical models or test pattern generation. They are defined as arrays of identical cells in an n-dimensional space and characterized by different parameters [26]: the cellular geometry, the neighborhood specification, the number of contents per cell and the transition rule to compute the successor state. Their simple, modular and cascable structure makes them very attractive for VLSI implementations.

On the other hand, Linear Feedback Shift Registers (LFSRs) [11] are linear structures currently used in the generation of pseudorandom sequences. The inherent simplicity of LFSRs, their ease of implementation and the good statistical properties of their output sequences turn them into natural building blocks for the design of pseudorandom sequence generators with applications in spread-spectrum communications, circuit testing, error-correcting codes, numerical simulations or cryptography.

In recent years, one-dimensional CA have been proposed as an alternative to LFSRs ([2], [3], [19], [26]) in the sense that every sequence generated by a LFSR can

---

1991 *Mathematics Subject Classification.* Primary 40B05, 40C05; Secondary 68R01.

Key words and phrases. Cellular automata, clock-controlled generators, sequence reconstruction, cryptography.

Work supported by Ministerio de Educación y Ciencia (Spain) Projects SEG2004-02418 and SEG2004-04352-C04-03.

be obtained from one-dimensional CA too. In cryptographic applications, pseudo-random sequence generators currently involve several LFSRs combined by means of nonlinear functions or irregular clocking techniques (see [18], [20]). Moreover in [21], it is proved that one-dimensional linear CA are isomorphic to conventional LFSRs. Thus, the latter structures can be simply substituted by the former ones in order to accomplish the same goal: generation of keystream sequences.

The above class of linear CA has been found to satisfy randomness properties with application in the testing of digital circuits, Built-In Self-Test (BIST) schemes and self-checking [27]. The current interest of these CA stems from the lack of correlation between the bit sequences generated by adjacent cells, see [9]. In this sense, linear CA are superior to the more common LFSRs [11] that have been traditionally used as pseudorandom pattern generators. Nevertheless, the main advantage of CA is that multiple generators designed as nonlinear structures in terms of LFSRs preserve the linearity when they are expressed under the form of CA.

This paper considers the problem of finding one-dimensional CA that reproduce the output sequence of a particular LFSR-based generator. More precisely, in this work a wide class of LFSR-based nonlinear generators, the so-called Clock-Controlled Shrinking Generators (CCSGs) [15], can be described in terms of one-dimensional CA configurations. Indeed, the well known Shrinking Generator [8] is just an element of such a class. The automata here presented unify in a simple structure the above mentioned class of sequence generators. The algorithm that converts a given CCSG into a CA-based linear model is very simple and can be applied to CCSGs in a range of practical interest. The underlying idea of this modelling procedure is the concatenation of a basic automaton. Once the generators have been linearized, a cryptanalytic approach to reconstruct the generated sequence is also presented.

The paper is organized as follows: in section 2, the basic structures considered, e.g. one-dimensional CA and CCSGs, are introduced. A simple algorithm to determine the pair of CA corresponding to a particular shrinking generator and its generalization to Clock-Controlled Shrinking Generators are given in sections 3 and 4, respectively. A method of reconstructing the generated sequence that exploits the linearity of the CA-based model is presented in section 5. Finally, conclusions in section 6 end the paper.

2. Basic Structures

In the following subsections, we introduce the general characteristics of the basic structures we are dealing with: one-dimensional cellular automata, the shrinking generator and the class of clock-controlled shrinking generators. The work is restricted to CA and LFSRs with binary contents. In addition, all the LFSRs here considered are maximal-length LFSRs, that is their output sequences are *PN*-sequences and their characteristic polynomials are primitive polynomials, see [11] and [18].

2.1. One-Dimensional Cellular Automata. One-dimensional cellular automata can be described as L-cell registers [4], whose cell contents are updated at the same time instant according to a particular k-variable function (the *transition rule*) denoted by Φ. If the function Φ is a linear function, so is the cellular automaton. In addition, for cellular automata with binary contents there can be up to

2^{2^k} different mappings to the next state. Moreover, if $k = 2r + 1$, then the binary content of the i-th cell at time $t + 1$ depends on the contents of k neighbor cells at time t in the following way:

(2.1) $$x_i^{t+1} = \Phi(x_{i-r}^t, \ldots, x_i^t, \ldots, x_{i+r}^t) \ (i = 1, \ldots, L).$$

The number of cells L (numbered from left to right) is the length of the automaton. CA are called *uniform* whether all cells evolve under the same rule while CA are called *hybrid* whether different cells evolve under different rules. At the ends of the array, two different boundary conditions are possible: *null automata* when cells with permanent null contents are supposed adjacent to the extreme cells or *periodic automata* when extreme cells are supposed adjacent.

In this paper, only transition rules with $k = 3$ will be considered. Thus, there are 2^8 of such rules among which just two (rule 90 and rule 150) lead to non trivial machines. Such rules are described as follows :

Rule 90
$$x_i^{t+1} = \Phi_{90}(x_{i-1}^t, x_i^t, x_{i+1}^t) = x_{i-1}^t + x_{i+1}^t$$

111	110	101	100	011	010	001	000
0	1	0	1	1	0	1	0

Rule 150
$$x_i^{t+1} = \Phi_{150}(x_{i-1}^t, x_i^t, x_{i+1}^t) = x_{i-1}^t + x_i^t + x_{i+1}^t$$

111	110	101	100	011	010	001	000
1	0	0	1	0	1	1	0

Remark that the names rule 90 and rule 150 derive from the decimal values of their next-state functions: 01011010 (binary) = 90 (decimal) and 10010110 (binary) = 150 (decimal). Indeed, x_i^{t+1} the content of the i-th cell at time $t + 1$ depends on the contents of either two different cells (rule 90) or three different cells (rule 150) at time t. The symbol + denotes addition modulo 2 among cell contents. Remark that both transition rules are linear. This work deals exclusively with one-dimensional linear null hybrid CA with rules 90 and 150. A natural way of specifying such CA is an L-tuple $M = [R_1, R_2, \ldots, R_L]$, called *rule vector*, where $R_i = 0$ if the i-th cell satisfies rule 90 while $R_i = 1$ if the i-th cell satisfies rule 150. A sub-automaton of the previous automata class consisting of cells 1 through i will be denoted by $R_1 R_2 \ldots R_i$.

For a cellular automaton of length $L = 10$ cells, configuration rules ($R_1 = 0, R_2 = 1, R_3 = 1, R_4 = 1, R_5 = 0, R_6 = 0, R_7 = 1, R_8 = 1, R_9 = 1, R_{10} = 0$) and initial state $(0, 0, 0, 1, 1, 1, 0, 1, 1, 0)$, Table 1 illustrates the formation of its output sequences (binary sequences read vertically) and the succession of states (binary configurations of 10 bits read horizontally). For the above mentioned rules, the different states of the automaton are grouped in closed cycles. The number of different output sequences for a particular cycle is $\leq L$ as the same sequence (although shifted) may appear simultaneously in different cells. At the same time, all the sequences in a cycle will have the same period and linear complexity [17]. Moreover, any of the output sequence of the automaton can be produced at any cell provided that the right state cycle is chosen.

On the other hand, linear finite state machines are currently represented and analyzed by means of their transition matrices. The form and characteristics of these matrices for the CA under consideration can be found in [4]. In fact, such

TABLE 1. An one-dimensional linear null hybrid cellular automaton of 10 cells with rules 90/150 starting at a given initial state

90	150	150	150	90	90	150	150	150	90
0	0	0	1	1	1	0	1	1	0
0	0	1	0	0	1	0	0	0	1
0	1	1	1	1	0	1	0	1	0
1	0	1	1	1	0	1	0	1	1
0	0	0	1	1	0	1	0	0	1
0	0	1	0	1	0	1	1	1	0
0	1	1	0	0	0	0	1	0	1
1	0	0	1	0	0	1	1	0	0
0	1	1	1	1	1	0	0	1	0
1	0	1	1	0	1	1	1	1	1
⋮	⋮	⋮	⋮	⋮	⋮	⋮	⋮	⋮	⋮

matrices are tri-diagonal matrices with the rule vector on the main diagonal, 1's on the diagonals below and above the main one and all other entries being zero. Every automaton is completely specified by its characteristic polynomial, that is the characteristic polynomial of its transition matrix. Such a characteristic polynomial can be computed in terms of the characteristic polynomials of the previous sub-automata according to the recurrence relation [4]:

(2.2) $$P_i(x) = (x + R_i)P_{i-1}(x) + P_{i-2}(x), \quad 0 < i \leq L$$

being $P_{-1}(x) = 0$ and $P_0(x) = 1$. Next, the following definition is introduced:

DEFINITION 2.1. A Multiplicative-Polynomial Cellular Automaton is defined as a cellular automaton whose characteristic polynomial is a reducible polynomial of the form $P_M(x) = (P(x))^p$ where p is a positive integer. If $P(x)$ is a primitive polynomial, then the automaton is called a Primitive Multiplicative-Polynomial Cellular Automaton.

The class of binary sequence generators we are dealing with is described in the following subsections.

2.2. The Shrinking Generator. The shrinking generator is a binary sequence generator [8] composed by two LFSRs : a control register SR_1 that decimates the sequence produced by the other register SR_2. We denote by L_j $(j = 1, 2)$ their corresponding lengths with $(L_1, L_2) = 1$ as well as $L_1 < L_2$. Then, we denote by $C_j(x) \in GF(2)[x]$ $(j = 1, 2)$ their corresponding characteristic polynomials of degree L_j $(j = 1, 2)$, respectively.

The sequence produced by SR_1, denoted by $\{a_i\}$, controls the bits of the sequence produced by SR_2, that is $\{b_i\}$, which are included in the output sequence $\{z_j\}$ (the *shrunken sequence*), according to the following rule P:
  (1) If $a_i = 1 \Longrightarrow z_j = b_i$
  (2) If $a_i = 0 \Longrightarrow b_i$ is discarded.

A simple example illustrates the behavior of this structure.

EXAMPLE 2.2. Let us consider the following LFSRs:

(1) Register SR_1 of length $L_1 = 3$, characteristic polynomial $C_1(x) = 1 + x^2 + x^3$ and initial state $IS_1 = (1, 0, 0)$. The *PN*-sequence generated by SR_1 is $\{1, 0, 0, 1, 1, 1, 0\}$ with period $T_1 = 2^{L_1} - 1 = 7$.
(2) Register SR_2 of length $L_2 = 4$, characteristic polynomial $C_2(x) = 1 + x + x^4$ and initial state $IS_2 = (1, 0, 0, 0)$. The *PN*-sequence generated by SR_2 is $\{1, 0, 0, 0, 1, 0, 0, 1, 1, 0, 1, 0, 1, 1, 1\}$ with period $T_2 = 2^{L_2} - 1 = 15$.

The output sequence $\{z_j\}$ is given by:

- $\{a_i\} \to 1\,0\,0\,1\,1\,1\,0\,1\,0\,0\,1\,1\,1\,0\,1\,0\,0\,1\,1\,1\,0\,1$ .....
- $\{b_i\} \to 1\,\underline{0}\,0\,0\,1\,\underline{0}\,0\,1\,\underline{1}\,0\,1\,0\,1\,\underline{1}\,1\,\underline{1}\,0\,0\,0\,1\,\underline{0}\,0$ .....
- $\{z_j\} \to 1\,0\,1\,0\,1\,1\,0\,1\,1\,0\,0\,1\,0$ .....

The underlined bits $\underline{0}$ or $\underline{1}$ in $\{b_i\}$ are discarded.

In brief, the sequence produced by the shrinking generator is an irregular decimation of $\{b_i\}$ from the bits of $\{a_i\}$. According to [8], the period of the shrunken sequence is

(2.3) $$T = (2^{L_2} - 1)2^{(L_1 - 1)}$$

and its linear complexity [20], notated LC, satisfies the following inequality

(2.4) $$L_2\,2^{(L_1 - 2)} < LC \leq L_2\,2^{(L_1 - 1)}.$$

A simple calculation, based on the fact that every state of SR_2 coincides once with every state of SR_1, allows one to compute the number of 1's in the shrunken sequence. Such a number is constant and equal to

(2.5) $$No.\ 1's = 2^{(L_2 - 1)} 2^{(L_1 - 1)}.$$

Comparing period and number of $1's$, it can be concluded that the shrunken sequence is a quasi-balanced sequence.

In addition, it can be proved [8] that the output sequence has good distributional statistics too. Therefore, this scheme is suitable for practical implementation of stream ciphers and pattern generators.

2.3. The Clock-Controlled Shrinking Generators. The Clock-Controlled Shrinking Generators constitute a wide class of clock-controlled sequence generators [15] with applications in cryptography, error correcting codes and digital signature. An CCSG is a sequence generator composed of two LFSRs notated SR_1 and SR_2. The parameters of both registers are defined as those of subsection 2.2. At any time t, SR_1 (the control register) is clocked normally while the second register SR_2 is clocked a number of times given by an integer decimation function notated X_t. In fact, if $A_0(t)$, $A_1(t)$, ..., $A_{L_1-1}(t)$ are the binary cell contents of SR_1 at time t, then X_t is defined as

(2.6) $$X_t = 1 + 2^0 A_{i_0}(t) + 2^1 A_{i_1}(t) + \ldots + 2^{w-1} A_{i_{w-1}}(t)$$

where $i_0, i_1, \ldots, i_{w-1} \in \{0, 1, \ldots, L_1 - 1\}$ and $0 < w \leq L_1 - 1$.

In this way, the output sequence of an CCSG is obtained from a double decimation:

(1) The output sequence of SR_2, $\{b_i\}$, is decimated by means of X_t giving rise to the sequence $\{b'_i\}$.
(2) The same decimation rule P, defined in subsection 2.2, is applied to the sequence $\{b'_i\}$.

Remark that if $X_t \equiv 1$ (no cells are selected in SR_1), then the proposed generator is just the shrinking generator. Let us see a simple example of CCSG.

EXAMPLE 2.3. For the same LFSRs defined in the previous example and the function $X_t = 1 + 2^0 A_0(t)$ with $w = 1$, the decimated sequence $\{b'_i\}$ is given by:
- $\{b_i\} \to 1\ \underline{0}\ 0\ 0\ 1\ \underline{0}\ 0\ \underline{1}\ 1\ 0\ 1\ 0\ \underline{1}\ 1\ 1\ 1\ \underline{0}\ \underline{0}\ \underline{0}\ 1\ \underline{0}\ 0\ 1\ 1\ 0\ 1\ 0\ 1\ \underline{1}\ 1\ \underline{1}\ ...$
- $X_t \to 2\ 1\ 1\ 2\ 2\ 2\ 1\ 2\ 1\ 1\ 2\ 2\ 2\ 1\ 2\ 1\ 1\ 2\ 2\ ...$
- $\{b'_i\} \to 1\ 0\ 0\ 1\ 0\ 1\ 1\ 0\ 1\ 1\ 1\ 0\ 1\ 0\ 1\ 0\ 1\ 0\ 1\ 1\ ...$

According to the decimation function X_t, the underlined bits $\underline{0}$ or $\underline{1}$ in $\{b_i\}$ are discarded in order to produce the sequence $\{b'_i\}$. Then the output sequence $\{z_j\}$ of the CCSG is given by:
- $\{a_i\} \to 1\ 0\ 0\ 1\ 1\ 1\ 0\ 1\ 0\ 0\ 1\ 1\ 1\ 0\ 1\ 0\ 0\ 1\ 1\ 1\ 0\ 1\ ...$
- $\{b'_i\} \to 1\ \underline{0}\ \underline{0}\ 1\ 0\ 1\ \underline{1}\ 0\ \underline{1}\ \underline{1}\ 1\ 0\ 1\ \underline{0}\ 1\ \underline{0}\ \underline{1}\ 0\ 1\ 1\ ...$
- $\{z_j\} \to 1\ 1\ 0\ 1\ 0\ 1\ 0\ 1\ 1\ 0\ 1\ 1\ ...$

The underlined bits $\underline{0}$ or $\underline{1}$ in $\{b'_i\}$ are discarded.

In brief, the sequence produced by an CCSG is an irregular double decimation of the sequence generated by SR_2 from the function X_t and the bits of SR_1. This construction allows one to generate a large family of different sequences by using the same LFSR initial states and characteristic polynomials but modifying the decimation function. Period, linear complexity and statistical properties of the generated sequences by CCSGs have been established in [15].

2.4. Cattel and Muzio Synthesis Algorithm. The Cattell and Muzio synthesis algorithm [5] presents a method of obtaining two CA (based on rules 90 and 150) corresponding to a given polynomial. Such an algorithm takes as input an irreducible polynomial $Q(x) \in GF(2)[x]$ defined over a finite field and computes two linear reversal CA whose output sequences have $Q(x)$ as characteristic polynomial. Such CA are written as binary strings with the previous codification: 0 = rule 90 and 1 = rule 150. The theoretical foundations of the algorithm can be found in [7]. The total number of operations required for this algorithm is listed in [5](Table II, page 334). It is shown that the number of operations grows linearly with the degree of the polynomial, so the method does not suffer from any sort of exponential blow-up. The method is efficient for all practical applications (e.g. in 1996 finding a pair of length 300 CA took 16 CPU seconds on a SPARC 10 workstation). For cryptographic applications, the degree of the irreducible (primitive) polynomial is $L_2 \approx 64$, so that the consuming time is negligible.

Finally, a list of One-Dimensional Linear Hybrid Cellular Automata of Degree Through 500 can be found in [6].

3. CA-Based Linear Models for the Shrinking Generator

In this section, an algorithm to determine the pair of CA corresponding to a given shrinking generator is presented. Such an algorithm is based on the following results:

LEMMA 3.1. *The characteristic polynomial of the shrunken sequence is of the form $P(x)^N$, where $P(x) \in GF(2)[x]$ is a L_2-degree primitive polynomial and N is an integer satisfying the inequality $2^{(L_1-2)} < N \leq 2^{(L_1-1)}$.*

PROOF. The shrunken sequence can be written as an interleaved sequence [12] made out of an unique PN-sequence starting at different points and repeated $2^{(L_1-1)}$ times. Such a sequence is obtained from $\{b_i\}$ taking digits separated a distance $2^{L_1} - 1$, that is the period of the sequence $\{a_i\}$. As $(2^{L_2} - 1, 2^{L_1} - 1) = 1$ due to the primality of L_2 and L_1, the result of the decimation of $\{b_i\}$ is a PN-sequence of primitive characteristic polynomial $P(x)$ of degree L_2. Moreover, the number of times that this PN-sequence is repeated coincides with the number of $1's$ in $\{a_i\}$ since each 1 of $\{a_i\}$ provides the shrunken sequence with $2^{L_2} - 1$ digits of $\{b_i\}$. Consequently, the characteristic polynomial of the shrunken sequence will be $P(x)^N$ with $N \leq 2^{(L_1-1)}$. The lower limit follows immediately from equation (2.4) that defines the linear recurrence relationship. $\square$

LEMMA 3.2. *Let $C_2(x) \in GF(2)[x]$ be the characteristic polynomial of SR_2 and let λ be a root of $C_2(x)$ in the extension field $GF(2^{L_2})$. Then, $P(x) \in GF(2)[x]$ is of the form*

$$(3.1) \qquad P(x) = (x + \lambda^E)(x + \lambda^{2E}) \ldots (x + \lambda^{2^{L_2-1}E})$$

being E an integer given by

$$(3.2) \qquad E = 2^0 + 2^1 + \ldots + 2^{L_1-1} \ .$$

PROOF. As the decimation of the sequence $\{b_i\}$ is realized taking one out of $2^{L_1} - 1$ digits, the obtained PN-sequence is nothing but the characteristic sequence associated to the *cyclotomic coset* $E = 2^{L_1} - 1$, see [11]. Hence, the roots of its characteristic polynomial will be $\lambda^E, \lambda^{2E}, \ldots, \lambda^{2^{L_2-1}E}$. According to the definition of cyclotomic coset, the value of E is given by equation (3.2). $\square$

Remark that $P(x)$ depends exclusively on the characteristic polynomial of the register SR_2 and on the length L_1 of the register SR_1. Based on the Cattell and Muzio synthesis algorithm [5], the following result is derived:

LEMMA 3.3. *Let $Q(x) \in GF(2)[x]$ be a polynomial defined over a finite field and let s_1 and s_2 two binary strings codifying the two linear CA obtained from the Cattell and Muzio algorithm. Then, the two CA in form of binary strings whose characteristic polynomial is $Q(x)^2$ are:*

$$S'_i = S_i * S^*_i \quad i = 1, 2$$

where S_i is the binary string s_i whose least significant bit has been complemented, S^*_i is the mirror image of S_i and the symbol $*$ denotes concatenation.

PROOF. The result is just a generalization of the Cattell and Muzio synthesis algorithm. The concatenation is due to the fact that rule 90 (150) at the end of the array in null automata is equivalent to two consecutive rules 150 (90) with identical sequences. The fact of that an automaton and its reversal version have the same characteristic polynomial completes the proof. $\square$

Proceeding in the same way a number of times, a multiplicative-polynomial cellular automaton 2.1 is obtained. In this way, the construction of a linear structure from the concatenation of a basic automaton is accomplished.

According to the previous results, an algorithm to linearize the shrinking generator is introduced:

Input: A shrinking generator characterized by two LFSRs, SR_1 and SR_2, with their corresponding lengths, L_1 and L_2, and the characteristic polynomial $C_2(x)$ of the register SR_2.

Step 1: From L_1 and $C_2(x)$, compute the polynomial $P(x)$ in $GF(2^{L_2})$ as
$$P(x) = (x + \lambda^E)(x + \lambda^{2E}) \ldots (x + \lambda^{2^{L_1-1}E})$$
with $E = 2^0 + 2^1 + \ldots + 2^{L_1-1}$.

Step 2: From $P(x)$, apply the Cattell and Muzio synthesis algorithm to determine two linear CA (with rules 90 and 150), notated s_i, whose characteristic polynomial is $P(x)$.

Step 3: For each s_i separately, proceed:

3.1: Complement its least significant bit. The resulting binary string is notated S_i.

3.2: Compute the mirror image of S_i, notated S_i^*, and concatenate both strings
$$S_i' = S_i * S_i^* \ .$$

3.3: Apply steps 3.1 and 3.2 to each S_i' recursively $L_1 - 1$ times.

Output: Two binary strings of length $L = L_2 \cdot 2^{L_1-1}$ codifying two CA corresponding to the given shrinking generator.

REMARK 3.4. In this algorithm the characteristic polynomial of the register SR_1 is not needed. Thus, all the shrinking generators with the same SR_2 but different registers SR_1 (all of them with the same length L_1) can be modelled by the same pair of one-dimensional linear CA.

REMARK 3.5. It can be noticed that the computation of both CA is proportional to L_1 concatenations. Consequently, the algorithm can be applied to shrinking generators in a range of practical application.

REMARK 3.6. In contrast to the nonlinearity of the shrinking generator, the CA-based models that generate the shrunken sequence are linear.

In order to clarify the previous steps a simple numerical example is presented.

Input: A shrinking generator characterized by two LFSRs SR_1 of length $L_1 = 3$ and SR_2 of length $L_2 = 5$ and characteristic polynomial $C_2(x) = 1 + x + x^2 + x^4 + x^5$.

Step 1: $P(x)$ is the characteristic polynomial of the cyclotomic *coset* $E = 7$. Thus,
$$P(x) = 1 + x^2 + x^5 \ .$$

Step 2: From $P(x)$ and applying the Cattell and Muzio synthesis algorithm, two reversal linear CA whose characteristic polynomial is $P(x)$ can be determined. Such CA are written in binary format as:

0 1 1 1 1
1 1 1 1 0

Step 3: Computation of the required pair of CA.

For the first automaton:

0 1 1 1 1
0 1 1 1 0 0 1 1 0
0 1 1 1 0 0 1 1 1 1 1 1 1 0 0 1 1 1 0

For the second automaton:
```
1 1 1 1 0
1 1 1 1 1 1 1 1 1
1 1 1 1 1 1 1 1 0 0 1 1 1 1 1 1 1 1 1
```
For each automaton, the procedure of concatenation has been carried out $L_1 - 1$ times.

Output: Two binary strings of length $L = L_2 \cdot 2^{(L_1-1)} = 20$ codifying the required pair of CA.

In this way, we have obtained a pair of linear CA able to generate the shrunken sequence corresponding to the given shrinking generator. In addition, for each one of the previous automata there is one state cycle where the shrunken sequence is generated at each one of the cells.

4. CA-Based Linear Models for the Clock-Controlled Shrinking Generators

In this section, an algorithm to determine the pair of one-dimensional linear CA corresponding to a given CCSG is presented. Such an algorithm is based on the following results:

LEMMA 4.1. *The characteristic polynomial of the output sequence of a CCSG is of the form $P'(x)^N$, where $P'(x) \in GF(2)[x]$ is a primitive L_2-degree polynomial and N is an integer satisfying the inequality $2^{(L_1-2)} < N \leq 2^{(L_1-1)}$.*

PROOF. The proof is analogous to that one developed in lemma 3.1. □

Remark that, according to the structure of the CCSGs, the polynomial $P'(x)$ depends on the characteristic polynomial of the register SR_2, the length L_1 of the register SR_1 and the decimation function X_t. Before, $P(x)$ was the characteristic polynomial of the *cyclotomic coset* E, where $E = 2^0 + 2^1 + \ldots + 2^{L_1-1}$ was a fixed separation distance between the digits drawn from the sequence $\{b_i\}$. Now, this distance D is variable as well as a function of X_t. The computation of D gives rise to the following result:

LEMMA 4.2. *Let $C_2(x) \in GF(2)[x]$ be the characteristic polynomial of SR_2 and let λ be a root of $C_2(x)$ in the extension field $GF(2^{L_2})$. Then, $P'(x) \in GF(2)[x]$ is the characteristic polynomial of cyclotomic coset D, where D is given by*

$$(4.1) \qquad D = 2^{L_1-w} \left(\sum_{i=1}^{2^w} i\right) - 1 = (1 + 2^w)\, 2^{L_1-1} - 1.$$

PROOF. The proof is analogous to that one developed in lemma 3.2. In fact, the distance D can be computed taking into account that the function X_t takes values in the interval $[1, 2, \ldots, 2^w]$ and the number of times that each one of these values appears in a period of the output sequence is given by 2^{L_1-w}. A simple computation, based on the sum of the terms of an arithmetic progression, completes the proof. □

From the previous results, it can be noticed that the algorithm that determines the pair of CA corresponding to a given CCSG is analogous to that one developed in section 3. Indeed, the expression of E in equation (3.2) must be replaced by the expression of D in equation (4.1).

In order to clarify the previous steps a simple numerical example is presented.

Input: A CCSG characterized by: Two LFSRs SR_1 of length $L_1 = 3$ and SR_2 of length $L_2 = 5$ and characteristic polynomial $C_2(x) = 1 + x + x^2 + x^4 + x^5$ plus the decimation function $X_t = 1 + 2^0 A_0(t) + 2^1 A_1(t) + 2^2 A_2(t)$ with $w = 3$.

Step 1: $P'(x)$ is the characteristic polynomial of the cyclotomic *coset* D. Now $D \equiv 4 \ mod \ 31$, that is we are dealing with the cyclotomic coset 1. Thus, the corresponding characteristic polynomial is:
$$P'(x) = 1 + x + x^2 + x^4 + x^5 .$$

Step 2: From $P'(x)$ and applying the Cattell and Muzio synthesis algorithm, two reversal linear CA whose characteristic polynomial is $P'(x)$ can be determined. Such CA are written in binary format as:

1 0 0 0 0
0 0 0 0 1

Step 3: Computation of the required pair of CA.
For the first automaton:

1 0 0 0 0
1 0 0 0 1 1 0 0 0 1
1 0 0 0 1 1 0 0 0 0 0 0 0 1 1 0 0 0 1

For the second automaton:

0 0 0 0 1
0 0 0 0 0 0 0 0 0
0 0 0 0 0 0 0 0 1 1 0 0 0 0 0 0 0 0

For each automaton, the procedure of concatenation has been carried out $L_1 - 1$ times.

Output: Two binary strings of length $L = 20$ codifying the required CA.

REMARK 4.3. From a point of view of the CA-based linear models, the shrinking generator or any one of the CCGS are entirely analogous. Thus, the fact of introduce an additional decimation function does neither increase the complexity of the generator nor improve its resistance against cryptanalytic attacks. Indeed, both kinds of generators can be linearized by the same class of CA-based models.

5. A Cryptanalytic Approach to this Class of Sequence Generators

Since CA-based linear models describing the behavior of CCSGs have been derived, a cryptanalytic attack that exploits the weaknesses of these models has been also developed. It consists in determining the initial states of both registers SR_1 and SR_2 from an amount of CCSG output sequence (the *intercepted sequence*). In this way, the rest of the output sequence can be reconstructed. For the sake of simplicity, the attack will be illustrated for the shrinking generator although the process can be extended to any CCSG. The proposed attack is divided into two different phases:

Phase 1: From bits of the intercepted sequence and using the CA-based linear models, additional bits of the shrunken sequence can be reconstructed.

Phase 2: Due to the intrinsic characteristics of this class of generators, a cryptanalytic attack can be mounted in order to determine the initial states of the LFSRs. The attack makes use of both intercepted bits as well as reconstructed bits.

Both phases will be considered separately.

5.1. Reconstruction of output sequence bits. Given r bits of the shrunken sequence $z_0, z_1, z_2, ..., z_{r-1}$, we can assume without loss of generality that this subsequence has been generated at the most left extreme cell of any of its corresponding CA. That is $x_1^t = z_0$, $x_1^{t+1} = z_1$, ..., $x_1^{t+r-1} = z_{r-1}$. From r bits of the shrunken sequence, it is always possible to reconstruct $r-1$ sub-sequences $\{x_i^t\}$ of lengths $r-i+1$ at the i-th cell of each automaton such as follows:

$$(5.1) \qquad x_i^t = \Phi_{i-1}(x_{i-2}^t, x_{i-1}^t, x_{i-1}^{t+1}) \quad (1 < i \leq r),$$

where Φ_{i-1} corresponds to either rule 90 or 150 depending on the value of R_{i-1}. From r intercepted bits, the application of equation (5.1) gives rise to a total of $(r+(r-1)+...+2+1)$ bits that constitute the first chained sub-triangle notated $\Delta 1$, see Table 2. Now, if any sub-sequence $\{x_i^t\}$ is placed at the most left extreme cell, then $r-2i+2$ bits are obtained at the i-th cell in the second chained sub-triangle notated $\Delta 2$. Repeating recursively n times the same procedure, $r - ni + n$ bits are obtained at the i-th cell in the n-th chained sub-triangle notated Δn. Table 2 shows the succession of 4 chained sub-triangles constructed from $r = 10$ bits of the shrunken sequence $\{z_i\} = \{0,0,1,1,1,0,1,0,1,1\}$ and first rules $R_1 = R_2 = 0$. In fact, the 10 initial bits generate 8 bits at the third cell in $\Delta 1$. These 8 bits are placed at the most left extreme cell producing 6 new bits at cell 3 in $\Delta 2$. With these 6 bits, we get 4 additional bits in $\Delta 3$. Finally, 2 new bits are obtained at cell 3 in the sub-triangle $\Delta 4$. Since rules 90 and 150 are additive, the generated sub-sequences will be sum of elements of the shrunken sequence. General expressions can be deduced for the elements of any sub-sequence in any chained sub-triangle. In fact, the i-th sub-sequence in the n-th chained sub-triangle includes the bits z_j corresponding to the exponents of $(P_{i-1}(x))^n$ where $P_{i-1}(x)$ is the characteristic polynomial of the sub-automaton $R_1 R_2 ... R_{i-1}$, see equation (2.2). More precisely, for the previous example the characteristic polynomial of the sub-automaton $R_1 R_2$ is $P_2(x) = x^2 + 1$. Then $(P_2(x))^2 = x^4 + 1$, $(P_2(x))^3 = x^6 + x^4 + x^2 + 1$, $(P_2(x))^4 = x^8 + 1$, ... Hence, x_3^t in the different sub-triangles will take the form:

$$x_3^t = z_0 + z_2 \quad in \quad \Delta 1$$
$$x_3^t = z_0 + z_4 \quad in \quad \Delta 2$$
$$x_3^t = z_0 + z_2 + z_4 + z_6 \quad in \quad \Delta 3$$
$$x_3^t = z_0 + z_8 \quad in \quad \Delta 4 \quad ...$$

For the successive bits $x_3^{t+1}, x_3^{t+2}, ...$ it suffices to add 1 to the previous subindexes. Table 3 shows the general expressions of the sub-sequence elements in $\Delta 1$ and $\Delta 2$ for the example under consideration.

On the other hand, Lemmas (3.1) and (3.2) show us that the shrunken sequence is the interleaving of $2^{(L_1-1)}$ different shifts of an unique *PN*-sequence of length $2^{L_2} - 1$ whose characteristic polynomial $P(x)$ is given by equation (3.1). Consequently, the elements of the shrunken sequence indexed z_{di}, with $i \in \{0, 1, ..., 2^{L_2} - 2\}$ and $d = 2^{(L_1-1)}$, belong to the same *PN*-sequence. Thus, if the element x_i^t of the i-th sub-sequence in the n-th chained sub-triangle takes the general form:

$$(5.2) \qquad x_i^t = z_{k_1} + z_{k_2} + ... + z_{k_j}$$

TABLE 2. Reconstruction of 4 chained sub-triangles from 10 bits of the shrunken sequence

$\Delta 1:$	R_1	R_2	R_3	...	$\Delta 2:$	R_1	R_2	R_3	...
	0	0	1	...		1	1	1	...
	0	1	1			1	0	0	
	1	1	0			0	1	0	
	1	1	1			1	0	1	
	1	0	0			0	0	0	
	0	1	0			0	0	1	
	1	0	0			0	1		
	0	1	1			1			
	1	1							
	1								

$\Delta 3:$	R_1	R_2	R_3	...	$\Delta 4:$	R_1	R_2	R_3	...
	1	0	1	...		1	1	1	...
	0	0	1			1	0	1	
	0	1	0			0	0		
	1	0	0			0			
	0	1							
	1								

with

(5.3) $$k_l \equiv 0 \ mod \ 2^{(L_1-1)} \quad (l=1,\ldots,j),$$

then x_i^t can be rewritten as

(5.4) $$x_i^t = z_{k_m},$$

with z_{k_m} satisfying equation (5.3). Therefore, $\{x_i^t\}$, the i-th sub-sequence in the n-th chained sub-triangle, is just a sub-sequence of the shrunken sequence shifted a distance δ from the r bits of the intercepted sequence. The value of δ depends on the extension field $GF(2^{L_2})$ generated by the roots of $P(x)$. In brief, the chained sub-triangles enable us to reconstruct additional bits of the shrunken sequence from bits of the intercepted sequence.

The number of reconstructed bits depends on the amount of intercepted bits. Indeed, if we know N_l bits in each one of the *PN*-sequence shifts, then the total number of reconstructed bits is given by:

(5.5) $$\sum_{l=1}^{2^{(L_1-1)}} \sum_{k=2}^{N_l} \binom{N_l}{k}$$

The required amount of intercepted sequence is 2^{L_1-1} that is exponential in the length of the shorter register SR_1. Remark that in this reconstruction process both reconstructed bits as well as their positions on the shrunken sequence are known with absolute certainty.

5.2. Reconstruction of LFSR Initial States. We denote by $IS_1 = (a_0, a_1, a_2, \ldots, a_{L_1-1})$ the initial state of SR_1 and by $IS_2 = (b_0, b_1, b_2, \ldots, b_{L_2-1})$ the initial

TABLE 3. General expressions for different sub-sequences in $\Delta 1$ and $\Delta 2$ with $R_1 = R_2 = 0$

$\Delta 1:$	R_1	R_2	R_3	$\ldots$	$\Delta 2:$	R_1	R_2	R_3	$\ldots$
	z_0	z_1	$z_0 + z_2$	$\ldots$		$z_0 + z_2$	$z_1 + z_3$	$z_0 + z_4$	$\ldots$
	z_1	z_2	$z_1 + z_3$			$z_1 + z_3$	$z_2 + z_4$	$z_1 + z_5$	
	z_2	z_3	$z_2 + z_4$			$z_2 + z_4$	$z_3 + z_5$	$z_2 + z_6$	
	z_3	z_4	$z_3 + z_5$			$z_3 + z_5$	$z_4 + z_6$	$z_3 + z_7$	
	z_4	z_5	$z_4 + z_6$			$z_4 + z_6$	$z_5 + z_7$	$z_4 + z_8$	
	z_5	z_6	$z_5 + z_7$			$z_5 + z_7$	$z_6 + z_8$	$z_5 + z_9$	
	z_6	z_7	$z_6 + z_8$			$z_6 + z_8$	$z_7 + z_9$		
	z_7	z_8	$z_7 + z_9$			$z_7 + z_9$			
	z_8	z_9							
	z_9								

state of SR_2. In order to avoid ambiguities on the initial states, it is assumed that $a_0 = 1$, thus the first element of the shrunken sequence is $z_0 = b_0$. In this way, the goal of this attack is to determine the sub-vectors $(a_1, a_2, \ldots, a_{L_1-1})$ as well as $(b_1, b_2, \ldots, b_{L_2-1})$.

According to equation (2.3), the period of the shrunken sequence is $T = (2^{L_2} - 1) 2^{(L_1-1)}$, so that such a sequence can be written as an $(2^{L_2}-1) \times (2^{(L_1-1)})$ matrix whose elements are the bits of the shrunken sequence. Its columns are denoted by $C_1, C_2, \ldots, C_{2^{(L_1-1)}}$, respectively. Each column of the matrix is the PN-sequence above referenced starting at different points. In addition, the first column C_1 corresponds to the decimation of the sequence $\{b_i\}$ from SR_2 by a factor $(2^{L_1} - 1)$ [11]. Thus, we can compute the position of the bits $b_1, b_2, \ldots, b_{L_2-1}$ on such a column. Indeed, the i-th bit, b_i, is at the $j_i - th$ position of C_1 where j_i is solution of the equation:

(5.6) $\quad j_i (2^{L_1} - 1) \equiv i \mod 2^{L_2} - 1 \quad (i = 1, \ldots, L_2 - 1).$

Moreover, the bits of IS_1 determine the initial bits of the subsequent columns C_i such as follows:

> **Hypothesis 1:** If the first bits of IS_1 are $(a_0 = 1, a_1 = 1)$, then C_2 will start at the $j_1 - th$ position of C_1 given by equation (5.6).
>
> **Hypothesis 2:** If the first bits of IS_1 are $(a_0 = 1, a_1 = 0, a_2 = 1)$, then C_2 will start at the $j_2 - th$ position of C_1 given by equation (5.6).
>
> $\vdots$
>
> **Hypothesis n:** If the first bits of IS_1 are $(a_0 = 1, a_1 = 0, \ldots, a_{n-1} = 0, a_n = 1)$, then C_2 will start at the $j_n - th$ position of C_1 given by equation (5.6).

We can formulate different hypothesis covering the first bits of IS_1 as well as each new hypothesis determines the initial bit of the following column. As we have intercepted and reconstructed bits in the columns C_i, we can check the previous hypothesis until getting a contradiction. In that case, all the IS_1 starting with the wrong configuration must be rejected. The search continues through the configurations of a_i free of contradiction by formulating new hypothesis. In brief, the attacker has not to traverse an entire search tree including all the initial states of SR_1, but the search is concentrated exclusively on the configurations not exhibiting contradiction with regard to the available bits. In this sense, the proposed attack reduces considerably the exhaustive search over the initial states of SR_1 as many contradictions occur at the first levels of the tree. On the other hand, the bits of the register SR_2 are easily determined as the starting bits of $C_2, C_3, C_4, \ldots$ in each one of the non-rejected branches. An illustrative example of Phases 1 and 2 is presented in the next subsection.

5.3. An Illustrative Example. Let us consider a shrinking generator with the following parameters: $L_1 = 4$, $L_2 = 5$, $C_1(x) = 1 + x^3 + x^4$ and $C_2(x) = 1 + x + x^3 + x^4 + x^5$. According to equation (3.1), we can compute the polynomial $P(x) = 1 + x + x^2 + x^4 + x^5$ while the two basic automata 1 0 0 0 0 and 0 0 0 0 1 are obtained from the algorithm of Cattell and Muzio. The corresponding CA of length $L = 40$ are computed via the algorithm developed in section 3. Indeed, they are $CA_1 = 0060110600$ and $CA_2 = 8C0300C031$ in hexadecimal notation. In addition, let α be a root of $P(x)$ that is $\alpha^5 = \alpha^4 + \alpha^2 + \alpha + 1$ as well as a generator element of the extension field $GF(2^{L_2})$. The period of the shrunken sequence is $T = (2^{L_2} - 1) \cdot 2^{(L_1-1)} = 248$ and the number of interleaved PN-sequences is $2^{(L_1-1)} = 8$. Finally, the intercepted sequence of length $r = 24$ is: $\{z_0, z_1, \ldots, z_{23}\} = \{1,0,1,0,0,0,0,1,1,0,0,1,1,1,0,0,1,1,0,1,0,0,1,1\}$. With the previous premises, we accomplish Phases 1 and 2.

Phase 1:

    For CA_1: The chained sub-triangles provide the following reconstructed bits. For $i = 3$, sub-automaton R_1R_2 and $P_2(x) = x^2 + 1$.

- In $\Delta 4$, $x_3^t = z_0 + z_8$, $x_3^{t+1} = z_1 + z_9$, $\ldots$, $x_3^{t+15} = z_{15} + z_{23}$. Considering z_0, z_8 as the first and second element of the PN-sequence and keeping in mind that in $GF(2^{L_2})$ the equality $1 + \alpha = \alpha^{19}$ holds, we get $x_3^t = z_{19 \cdot 8} = z_{152}$, $x_3^{t+1} = z_{153}$, $\ldots$, $x_3^{t+15} = z_{167}$. Thus, 16 new bits of the shrunken sequence have been reconstructed at positions $152, 153, \ldots, 167$.
- In $\Delta 8$, $x_3^t = z_0 + z_{16}$, $x_3^{t+1} = z_1 + z_{17}$, $\ldots$, $x_3^{t+7} = z_7 + z_{23}$. As $1 + \alpha^2 = \alpha^7$, we get $x_3^t = z_{7 \cdot 8} = z_{56}$, $x_3^{t+1} = z_{57}$, $\ldots$, $x_3^{t+7} = z_{63}$. Thus, 8 new bits of the shrunken sequence have been reconstructed at positions $56, 57, \ldots, 63$.

    For CA_2: The chained sub-triangles provide the following reconstructed bits. For $i = 3$, sub-automaton R_1R_2 and $P_2(x) = x^2 + x + 1$.

- In $\Delta 8$, $x_3^t = z_0 + z_8 + z_{16}$, $x_3^{t+1} = z_1 + z_9 + z_{17}$, $\ldots$, $x_3^{t+7} = z_7 + z_{15} + z_{23}$. As $1 + \alpha + \alpha^2 = \alpha^{23}$, we get $x_3^t = z_{23 \cdot 8} = z_{184}$, $x_3^{t+1} = z_{185}$, $\ldots$, $x_3^{t+7} = z_{191}$. Thus, 8 new bits of the shrunken sequence have been reconstructed at positions $184, 185, \ldots, 191$.

After Phase 1, the known bits of the shrunken sequence are depicted in Table 4. Rows 0,1,2 correspond to intercepted bits while rows 7, 19, 20 and 23 correspond to reconstructed bits. The symbol − represents the unknown bits. In brief, from 24 intercepted bits a total of 32 bits have been reconstructed.

Phase2: According to equation (5.6), the bits b_1, b_2, b_3, b_4 are placed at positions $29, 27, 25, 23$ of column C_1, respectively (see the first column of Table 4).

TABLE 4. The shrunken sequence produced by the shrinking generator described in subsection 5.3.

		C_1	C_2	C_3	C_4	C_5	C_6	C_7	C_8
	0	1	0	1	0	0	0	0	1
	1	1	0	0	1	1	1	0	0
	2	1	1	0	1	0	0	1	1
	3	–	–	–	–	–	–	–	–
	4	–	–	–	–	–	–	–	–
	5	–	–	–	–	–	–	–	–
	6	–	–	–	–	–	–	–	–
	7	0	1	1	1	0	0	1	0
	8	–	–	–	–	–	–	–	–
	9	–	–	–	–	–	–	–	–
	10	–	–	–	–	–	–	–	–
	11	–	–	–	–	–	–	–	–
	12	–	–	–	–	–	–	–	–
	13	–	–	–	–	–	–	–	–
	14	–	–	–	–	–	–	–	–
	15	–	–	–	–	–	–	–	–
	16	–	–	–	–	–	–	–	–
	17	–	–	–	–	–	–	–	–
	18	–	–	–	–	–	–	–	–
	19	0	0	1	1	1	1	0	1
	20	0	1	0	0	1	1	1	1
	21	–	–	–	–	–	–	–	–
	22	–	–	–	–	–	–	–	–
b_4	23	1	1	1	0	1	1	1	0
	24	–	–	–	–	–	–	–	–
b_3	25	–	–	–	–	–	–	–	–
	26	–	–	–	–	–	–	–	–
b_2	27	–	–	–	–	–	–	–	–
	28	–	–	–	–	–	–	–	–
b_1	29	–	–	–	–	–	–	–	–
	30	–	–	–	–	–	–	–	–

On the other hand, Table 5 shows the sequences corresponding to the following hypothesis.

Hypothesis 1: If the first bits of IS_1 are ($a_0 = 1, a_1 = 1$), then C_2 will start at the 29th position of C_1 given rise to the column H_1. In row 2, H_1 and C_2 have a common bit without contradiction. The union of both sequences allows us to construct C_2^1 the second column of the matrix for this hypothesis. A total of 13 bits are then known in C_2^1.

Hypothesis 2: If the first bits of IS_1 are ($a_0 = 1, a_1 = 0, a_2 = 1$), then C_2 will start at the 27th position of C_1 given rise to the column H_2. In row 23, H_2 and C_2 have a common bit with contradiction (starred bits). Thus, the initial states of SR_1 starting with bits 101 must be rejected.

Hypothesis 3: If the first bits of IS_1 are ($a_0 = 1, a_1 = 0, a_2 = 0, a_3 = 1$), then C_2 will start at the 25th position of C_1 given rise to the column H_3. In row 7, H_3 and C_2 have a common bit without contradiction. The union of both sequences allows us to construct C_2^3 the second column of the matrix for this hypothesis. A total of 13 bits are then known in C_2^3.

Hypothesis 4: If the first bits of IS_1 are ($a_0 = 1, a_1 = 0, a_2 = 0, a_3 = 0, a_4 = 1$), then C_2 will start at the 23th position of C_1 given rise to the column H_4. In row 0, H_2 and C_2 have a common bit with contradiction (starred bits). Thus, the initial state of SR_1 1000 must be rejected.

TABLE 5. Different hypothesis formulated on the bits of SR_1

	C_1	H_1	C_2	C_2^1	C_1	H_2	C_2	C_1	H_3	C_2	C_2^3	C_1	H_4	C_2
0	1	–	0	0	1	–	0	1	–	0	0	1	1*	0*
1	1	–	0	0	1	–	0	1	–	0	0	1	–	0
2	1	1	1	1	1	–	1	1	–	1	1	1	–	1
3	–	1	–	1	–	–	–	–	–	–	–	–	–	–
4	–	1	–	1	–	1	–	–	–	–	–	–	–	–
5	–	–	–	–	–	1	–	–	–	–	–	–	–	–
6	–	–	–	–	–	1	–	–	1	–	1	–	–	–
7	0	–	1	1	0	–	1	0	1	1	1	0	–	1
8	–	–	–	–	–	–	–	–	1	–	1	–	1	–
9	–	0	–	0	–	–	–	–	–	–	–	–	1	–
10	–	–	–	–	–	–	–	–	–	–	–	–	1	–
11	–	–	–	–	–	0	–	–	–	–	–	–	–	–
12	–	–	–	–	–	–	–	–	–	–	–	–	–	–
13	–	–	–	–	–	–	–	–	0	–	0	–	–	–
14	–	–	–	–	–	–	–	–	–	–	–	–	–	–
15	–	–	–	–	–	–	–	–	–	–	–	–	0	–
16	–	–	–	–	–	–	–	–	–	–	–	–	–	–
17	–	–	–	–	–	–	–	–	–	–	–	–	–	–
18	–	–	–	–	–	–	–	–	–	–	–	–	–	–
19	0	–	0	0	0	–	0	0	–	0	0	0	–	0
20	0	–	1	1	0	–	1	0	–	1	1	0	–	1
21	–	0	–	0	–	–	–	–	–	–	–	–	–	–
22	–	0	–	0	–	–	–	–	–	–	–	–	–	–
23	1	–	1	1	1	0*	1*	1	–	1	1	1	–	1
24	–	–	–	–	–	0	–	–	–	–	–	–	–	–
25	–	1	–	1	–	–	–	–	0	–	0	–	–	–
26	–	–	–	–	–	–	–	–	0	–	0	–	–	–
27	–	–	–	–	–	1	–	–	–	–	–	–	0	–
28	–	–	–	–	–	–	–	–	–	–	–	–	0	–
29	–	–	–	–	–	–	–	–	1	–	1	–	–	–
30	–	–	–	–	–	–	–	–	–	–	–	–	–	–
	Hypothesis 1				Hypothesis 2			Hypothesis 3				Hypothesis 4		

On the hypothesis free of contradiction, we can formulate other ones depicted in Table 6

Hypothesis 5: If the first bits of IS_1 are ($a_0 = 1, a_1 = 1, a_2 = 1$), then C_3 will start at the 27th position of C_1 given rise to the column H_5. In row 23, H_5 and C_3 have a common bit with contradiction (starred bits). Thus, the initial states of SR_1 starting with bits 111 must be rejected.

Hypothesis 6: If the first bits of IS_1 are ($a_0 = 1, a_1 = 1, a_2 = 0, a_3 = 0, a_4 = 1$), then C_3 will start at the 23th position of C_1 given rise to the column H_6. Bits 24 and 25 of C_1 have been deduced from C_2^1 in Hypothesis 1. In row 2, H_6 and C_6 have a common bit with contradiction (starred bits). Thus, the initial state of SR_1 1100 must be rejected.

From Hypothesis 5 and 6, Hypothesis 1 must be rejected. Remark that the configuration ($a_0 = 1, a_1 = 0, a_2 = 0, a_3 = 1$) in Hypothesis 3 is the only one free

TABLE 6. Different hypothesis formulated on the bits of SR_1

	C_1	H_5	C_3	C_1	H_6	C_3	C_1	C_2^3
0	1	–	1	1	1	1	1	0
1	1	–	0	1	0	0	1	0
2	1	–	0	1	1*	0*	1	1
3	–	–	–	–	–	–	–	–
4	–	1	–	–	0	–	–	–
5	–	1	–	–	0	–	–	–
6	–	1	–	–	0	–	–	1
7	0	–	1	0	–	1	0	1
8	–	–	–	–	1	–	–	1
9	–	–	–	–	1	–	–	–
10	–	–	–	–	1	–	–	–
11	–	0	–	–	–	–	–	–
12	–	–	–	–	–	–	–	–
13	–	–	–	–	–	–	0	0
14	–	–	–	–	–	–	1	–
15	–	–	–	–	0	–	–	–
16	–	–	–	–	–	–	–	–
17	–	–	–	–	–	–	1	–
18	–	–	–	–	–	–	–	–
19	0	–	1	0	–	1	0	0
20	0	–	0	0	–	0	0	1
21	–	–	–	–	–	–	–	–
22	–	–	–	–	–	–	–	–
23	1	0*	1*	1	–	1	1	1
24	–	0	–	0	–	–	–	–
25	–	–	–	1	–	–	0	0
26	–	–	–	–	–	–	0	0
27	–	1	–	–	0	–	1	–
28	–	–	–	–	0	–	–	–
29	–	–	–	–	–	–	–	1
30	–	–	–	–	–	–	–	–
	Hypothesis 5			Hypothesis 6			Solution	

of contradiction. See the search tree in figure 1. Thus, it corresponds to the actual initial state of SR_1. The successive bits of SR_1, that is the PN-sequence $\{1, 0, 0, 1, 0, 0, 0, 1, \ldots\}$, are checked by the successive columns $C_4, C_5, \ldots, C_8$ of the shrunken sequence. Concerning the initial state of SR_2, in Table 6 (column Solution) we can see that bits b_4, b_3, b_2 can be obtained from the known bits of C_1 in rows 23, 25 and 27 respectively. In fact, $b_4 = 1, b_3 = 0, b_2 = 1$. The bit b_1 in row 29 satisfies the equality

$$(5.7) \qquad b_1 = z_{29 \cdot 8} = z_{1 \cdot 8} + z_{2 \cdot 8} + z_{4 \cdot 8},$$

as $\alpha + \alpha^2 + \alpha^4 = \alpha^{29}$ in the extension field $GF(2^{L_2})$. We know that $z_8 = 1, z_{16} = 1$ while z_{32} can be easily deduced from the equality $z_{14 \cdot 8} = z_{1 \cdot 8} + z_{4 \cdot 8}$ as $1 + \alpha^4 = \alpha^{14}$. Thus, $z_{32} = 1 + 1 = 0$ and substituting in b_1 we get $b_1 = 1 + 1 + 0 = 0$.

The final issues of Phases 1 and 2 are the initial states of both LFSRs $IS_1 = (a_0, a_1, \ldots, a_3) = (1, 0, 0, 1)$ and $IS_2 = (b_0, b_1, \ldots, b_4) = (1, 0, 1, 0, 1)$. From the knowledge of both initial states the whole shrunken sequence can be reconstructed.

5.4. Computational Features of the Attack. The computational complexity of the previous cryptanalytic attack can be considered in two different phases: off-line and on-line complexity.

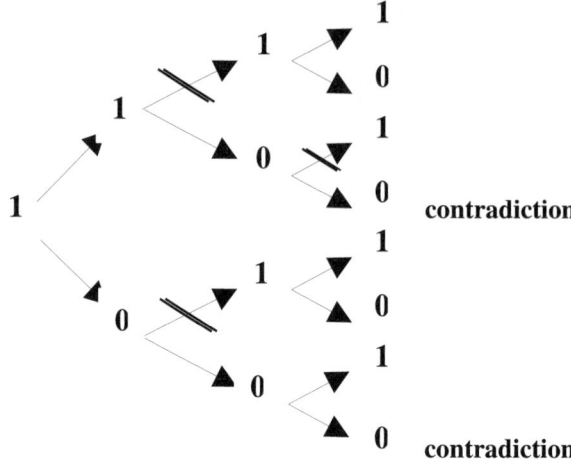

FIGURE 1. Search tree for the initial sates of SR_1

Off-line computational complexity: This phase is to be executed before intercepting sequence. It includes:
- Computation of the characteristic polynomials $P_i(x)$ of the sub-automata $R_1 R_2 \ldots R_i$ $(1 < i \leq l)$ by means of equation (2.2) where l is related to the amount of intercepted sequence $(l \cdot 2^{L_1-1} \sim r)$. This computation is necessary in order to obtain general expressions for the elements of the chained sub-triangles in the reconstruction procedure.
- Computation of the positions of the bits b_i $(i = 1, 2, \ldots, L_2 - 1)$ on C_1 the first column of the shrunken sequence matrix by means of equation (5.6). This computation is necessary in order to determine the bits of the initial state of SR_2.
- Computation of different elements of the extension field $GF(2^{L_2})$ such as $1+\alpha, 1+\alpha^2, \ldots, 1+\alpha^{N_l}$ and linear combinations of them by means of the Zech log table method [1] for arithmetic over $GF(2^m)$. This computation is necessary in order to determine the distance between the intercepted sequence and the portions of reconstructed shrunken sequence.

On-line computational complexity: This phase is to be executed after intercepting sequence. According to the previous subsections, the computational method consists in the comparison of series of bits coming from formulated hypothesis and from intercepted/reconstructed bits. The comparison is realized by means of bitwise logical operations so the computational complexity is rather low. Occasionally, the computation of the any element of $GF(2^{L_2})$ must be realized in order to determine additional elements of the PN-sequences. The most consuming time of this cryptanalytic attack is the search over the 2^{L_1-1} possible initial states of SR_1 (supposed $a_0 = 1$). Due to contradictions found in the first levels of the search tree, the exhaustive search can be dramatically improved. On average, we can say that in the worst case the search can be reduced to the half, so that the computational complexity of this attack is $O(2^{L_1-2})$. In addition, several considerations must be kept in mind:

(1) The improved exhaustive search is carried out over the state space of the shorter register SR_1.
(2) Every checking of hypothesis is realized only over the $1's$ of the configuration under consideration, then the procedure speeds for configurations with a low number of $1's$.

Finally, comparing the proposed attack with those ones found in the literature we get that all of them are exponential in the lengths of the registers. In particular, the complexity of the divide-and-conquer attack proposed in [**22**] is $O(2^{L_1})$. The probabilistic correlation attack described in [**13**] has a computational complexity of $O(L_2^2 \cdot 2^{L_2})$. Also the probabilistic correlation attack introduced in [**14**] is exponential in L_2. In this work a deterministic attack has been proposed that improves the complexity of the previous cryptanalytic approaches.

6. Conclusions

A wide family of LFSR- based sequence generators, the so- called Clock Controlled Shrinking Generators, has been analyzed and identified with a subset of linear cellular automata. In this way, sequence generators conceived and designed as complex nonlinear models can be written in terms of simple linear models. An easy algorithm to compute the pair of one- dimensional linear hybrid cellular automata that generate the CCSG output sequences has been derived. In addition, a cryptanalytic attack that reconstructs the output sequence of such generators has been proposed too. The procedure is based on the linearity of these CA-based models as well as on the characteristics of this class of generators. The cryptanalytic approach is deterministic and improves an exhaustive search over the states of the shorter register. Computing the initial state of the longer register is a direct consequence of the previous step. From the obtained results, we can create linear cellular automata- based models to analyze/cryptanalyze the class of clock- controlled generators.

References

[1] F. Assis and C. Pedreira, *An Architecture for Computing Zech's Logarithms in GF(2m)*, IEEE Transactions on Computers **49** (5) (2000), 519- 524.
[2] F. Bao, *Crytanalysis of a New Cellular Automata Cryptosystem*, 8th Australasian Conference on Information Security and Privacy- - ACISP 2003. Lecture Notes in Computer Science, Springer Verlag **2727** (2003), 416- 427.
[3] S. Blackburn, S. Merphy and K. Paterson, *Comments on 'Theory and Applications of Cellular Automata in Cryptography'*, IEEE Transactions on Computers **46** (1997), 637- 638.
[4] K. Cattell and J. Muzio, *Analysis of One- Dimensional Linear Hybrid Cellular Automata over GF(q)*, IEEE Transactions on Computers **45** (7) (1996), 782- 792.
[5] K. Cattell and J. Muzio, *Synthesis of One- Dimensional Linear Hybrid Cellular Automata*, IEEE Transactions on Computer- Aided Design of Integrated Circuits and Systems **15** (3) (1996), 325- 335.
[6] K. Cattell and Z. Shujian, *Minimal Cost One- Dimensional Linear Hybrid Cellular Automata of Degree Through 500*. J. of Electronic Testing: Theory and Applications **6** (1995), 255- 258.
[7] K. Cattell and J. Muzio, *A Linear Cellular Automata Algorithm: Theory*, Dept. of Computer Science. University of Victoria, Canada, Tech. Rep. DCS- 161- IR, 1991.

[8] D. Coppersmith, H. Krawczyk and Y. Mansour, *The Shrinking Generator,* Advances in Cryptology- - CRYPTO'93. Lecture Notes in Computer Science, Springer Verlag, **773** (1994), 22- 39.

[9] S. Cho, C. Un- Sook and H. Yoon- Hee, *Computing Phase Shifts of Maximum- Length 90/150 Cellular Automata Sequences,* Proc. of ACRI 2004. Lecture Notes on Computer Science, Springer- Verlag, **3305** (2004), 31- 39.

[10] A.K. Das, A. Ganguly, A. Dasgupta, S. Bhawmik and P.P. Chaudhuri, *Efficient Characterisation of Cellular Automata,* IEE Proc., Part E. **1** (1990), 81- 87.

[11] S. Golomb, *Shift- Register Sequences (revised edition),* Aegean Press (1982).

[12] G. Gong, *Theory and Applications of q- ary interleaved sequences,* IEEE Transactions on Information Theory **41** (1995), 400- 411.

[13] J. Golic, L. O'Connors, *A Cryptanalysis of Clock-Controlled Shift Registers with Multiple Steps,* Cryptography: Policy and Algorithms **41** (1995), 174- 185.

[14] T. Johansson, *Complexity Correlation Attacks on Two Clock-Controlled Generators* , Proc. of Asiacrypt'98. Lecture Notes in Computer Science, Springer Verlag **1426** (1998), 342- 356.

[15] A. Kanso, *Clock- Controlled Shrinking Generator of Feedback Shift Registers,* 8th Australasian Conference on Information Security and Privacy- - ACISP 2003. Lecture Notes in Computer Science, Springer Verlag **2727** (2003), 443- 451.

[16] E.L. Key, *An Analysis of the Structure and Complexity of Nonlinear Binary Sequence Generators,* IEEE Transactions on Information Theory **22** (6) (1976), 732- 736.

[17] O. Martin, A.M. Odlyzko and S. Wolfram, *Algebraic Properties of Cellular Automata,* Commun. Math. Phys. **93** (1984), 219- 258.

[18] A.J. Menezes, P. van Oorschot and S.A. Vanstone, *Handbook of Applied Cryptography,* CRC Press, New York, 1997.

[19] S. Nandi, B.K. Kar and P.P. Chaudhuri, *Theory and Applications of Cellular Automata in Cryptography,* IEEE Transactions on Computers **43** (1994), 1346- 1357.

[20] R.A. Rueppel, *Stream Ciphers,* in Gustavus J. Simmons (Ed), Contemporary Cryptology, The Science of Information. IEEE Press (1992), 65- 134.

[21] M. Serra, T. Slater, J. Muzio and D.M.Miller *The Analysis of One- dimensional Linear Cellular Automata and Their Aliasing Properties,* IEEE Transactions on Computer- Aided Design of Integrated Circuits and Systems **9** (7) (1990), 767- 778.

[22] L. Simpson *et al.,* Clock- A probabilistic Correlation Attack on the Shrinking Generator , Proc. of Australasian Conference on Information Security and Privacy- - ACISP 1998. Lecture Notes in Computer Science, Springer Verlag **1438** (1998), 147- 158.

[23] H.S. Stone, *Discrete mathematical Structures and Their Applications,* Chicago, IL. Science Research (1973).

[24] X. Sun, E. Kontopidi, M. Serra and J. Muzio, *The Concatenation and Partitioning of Linear Finite State Machines,* Int. J. Electronics. **78** (1995), 809- 839.

[25] S. Wolfram, *Random Sequence generation by Cellular Automata. Advances in Applied Mathematics,* **7** (123) (1986).

[26] S. Wolfram, *Cryptography with Cellular Automata,* Advances in Cryptology- - CRYPTO'85. Lecture Notes in Computer Science, Springer Verlag **218** (1994), 22- 39.

[27] S. Zhang, *Quantitative Analysis for Linear Hybrid CA and LFSR as BIST Generators for Sequential Faults,* J. Electronic Testing, **7** (3) (1995), 209- 221.

INSTITUTO DE FÍSICA APLICADA, C.S.I.C., SERRANO 144, 28006 MADRID, SPAIN
E-mail address: amparo@iec.csic.es

Linear and Nonlinear Sequences and Applications to Stream Ciphers

Tor Helleseth

ABSTRACT. A short introduction to the fundamental theory of linear and nonlinear feedback shift registers is given as well as a presentation of some basic applications to the design and analysis of stream ciphers.

1. Introduction

Linear feedback shift registers (LFSRs) are major components in modern communication systems. They are inexpensive, easy to implement and their mathematical properties are fairly well understood. Their applications include constructions of pseudo random sequences which are frequently used in radar systems, synchronization of data, Global Positioning Systems (GPS), coding theory and Code Division Multiple-Access (CDMA) communication systems. One of the main applications of LFSRs is within cryptography, in particular in the construction of stream ciphers. Pseudo random sequences can be constructed using LFSRs whose properties can be described by mathematical methods from finite Galois fields. Therefore the study of LFSRs represents an area where theory and applications meet.

The main idea behind using linear shift registers is that they are useful in constructing sequences with good pseudo random distribution and predictable periodic properties. However, linear shift registers are not sufficiently complex and do not usually provide enough security by themselves. Therefore, to construct a secure stream cipher, the LFSRs need to be combined in a controlled and nonlinear way to increase the overall complexity and security of the system.

The purpose of this paper is to present an overview of the basic theory of linear and nonlinear shift registers and to focus on some basic applications to the design and analysis of stream ciphers in cryptography.

In Section 2 we give an overview of basic results on LFSRs. Important aspects are their periodic as well as their randomness properties. The main pseudo random sequences found in most applications and generated by an LFSR are the maximal length linear shift register sequences (called m-sequences). These are extremely

---

1991 *Mathematics Subject Classification.* Primary 94A55; Secondary 94A60, 94B05.

Key words and phrases. linear shift registers, nonlinear shift registers, stream ciphers, cryptography.

This research was supported in part by the Norwegian Research Council.

FIGURE 1. Shift register for $s_{t+3} = s_{t+1} + s_t \pmod 2$

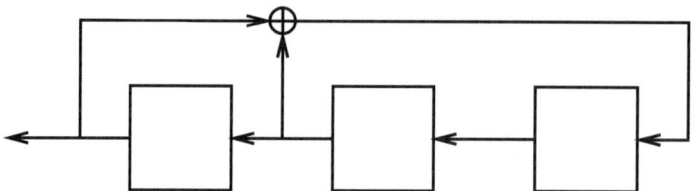

popular in stream cipher systems due to their long period and pseudo random properties and they are essential components in many stream ciphers. In Section 3 we describe properties of m-sequences. In Section 4 we focus on nonlinear shift registers and on how to combine linear shift registers in a nonlinear way. Finally, in Section 5 we present simple examples of design and analysis of stream ciphers.

For more comprehensive information on the theory of linear shift register sequences the reader is referred to [S], [R] and [GG]. For nonlinear shift registers the main references are [G] and [BP].

2. Linear feedback shift registers

A simple and efficient way to generate sequences is using linear recursions. For example the recursion

$$s_{t+3} = s_{t+1} + s_t \pmod 2$$

with initial conditions $(s_0, s_1, s_2) = (001)$ generates the periodic sequence

$$0010111 \; 0010111 \; 0010111 \; 0010111 \; ...$$

of period $\epsilon = 7$. Different initial states give different sequences that in general can be cyclic shifts of each other. The recursion above generate sequences forming two cycles (0010111) or (0).

Binary sequences can easily be generated in hardware using shift registers. One example is provided in Figure 1. The register contains three "flip-flops" each containing 0 or 1. The register is controlled by an external clock (not shown in the figure) that at any time shifts each bit one step to the left and replaces the rightmost bit with the sum (mod 2) of the two leftmost bits. The shift register in Figure 1 implements the recursion $s_{t+3} = s_{t+1} + s_t \pmod 2$ that with initial state $(s_0, s_1, s_2) = (001)$ leads to the periodic sequence 0010111... above. We sometimes denote the periodic sequence 0010111... by (0010111). Table 1 shows the content of the shift register at any time. The three "flip-flops" are denoted from left to right by $S0$, $S1$ and $S2$ respectively. Since the maximal number of states in this register is 8 and the zero state is always followed by the zero state, it follows that the maximal period in this case is $\epsilon = 7$. This is therefore an example of an m-sequence.

A linear recursion of degree n is given by

$$\sum_{i=0}^{n} c_i \, s_{t+i} = 0$$

TABLE 1. Content of the shift register from Figure 1 generating m-sequence

t	S0	S1	S2
0	0	0	1
1	0	1	0
2	1	0	1
3	0	1	1
4	1	1	1
5	1	1	0
6	1	0	0
7	0	0	1
.	.	.	.

where the coefficients $c_i \in GF(2)$ for $0 < i < n$ and $c_0 = c_n = 1$. The *characteristic polynomial* of the recursion is defined by

$$f(x) = \sum_{i=0}^{n} c_i x^i.$$

The initial state and the given recursion uniquely determine the generated sequence. A linear shift register with characteristic polynomial $f(x)$ of degree n therefore generates 2^n different sequences corresponding to the 2^n different initial states, and these 2^n sequences form a vector space $\Omega(f)$ over $GF(2)$. Different sequences in $\Omega(f)$ can be cyclic shifts of each other.

EXAMPLE 2.1. Take $f(x) = x^3 + x + 1$, then $\Omega(f)$ consists of the zero sequence (0) and all cyclic shifts of the periodic sequence (0010111). In this case $\Omega(f)$ consist of two cycles, the all zero cycle (0) and the cycle of maximal length (0010111).

EXAMPLE 2.2. Take $f(x) = x^3 + x^2 + x + 1$, then $\Omega(f)$ consists of (0), (1), (01) and (1100) and all their cyclic shifts. In this case $\Omega(f)$ consists of four cycles.

We next describe some basic results needed when finding information about the period of the sequences generated by $f(x)$. Given a sequence $s_0, s_1, s_2, \ldots$, we define the generating function

$$G(x) = \sum_{i=0}^{\infty} s_i x^i.$$

Let $f^*(x) = x^n f(1/x)$ denote the reciprocal polynomial of $f(x)$.

THEOREM 2.3. *Let (s_t) be a sequence in $\Omega(f)$. Then*

$$G(x) f^*(x) = \phi^*(x)$$

where

$$\phi(x) = s_0 x^{n-1} + (s_1 + c_{n-1} s_0) x^{n-2} + \cdots + (s_{n-1} + c_{n-1} s_{n-2} + \cdots + c_1 s_0).$$

PROOF. The main idea is to calculate $G(x) f^*(x)$ and to collect the coefficients of the terms x^k of this product. In particular, the coefficient of x^{n+t}, for $t \geq 0$ is

$$\sum_{i=0}^{n} c_i s_{t+i} = 0.$$

We observe that due to the recursion all coefficients for x^k disappear for $k \geq n$ and we are left with a product being a polynomial $\phi^*(x)$, of degree $< n$. Hence, we obtain
$$G(x)f^*(x) = \phi^*(x)$$
where
$$\phi(x) = s_0 x^{n-1} + (s_1 + c_{n-1}s_0)x^{n-2} + \cdots + (s_{n-1} + c_{n-1}s_{n-2} + \cdots + c_1 s_0)$$
and $\phi^*(x)$ is the reciprocal polynomial of $\phi(x)$, where we consider $\phi(x)$ to have (formal) degree $n-1$. □

REMARK 2.4. Note that from the definitions of $f(x)$ and $\phi(x)$ there is a one-to-one correspondence between the 2^n sequences (s_t) in $\Omega(f)$ and the 2^n polynomials $\phi(x)$ of degree $< n$.

COROLLARY 2.5. *The sequences in $\Omega(f)$ can be represented by,*
$$\Omega(f) = \left\{ \frac{\phi^*(x)}{f^*(x)} \mid \deg(\phi^*(x)) < \deg(f^*(x)) = n \right\}.$$

Another useful consequence of Theorem 2.3 is the following result.

COROLLARY 2.6. *We have $\Omega(g) \subset \Omega(f)$ if and only if $g(x)$ divides $f(x)$.*

PROOF. If $\Omega(g) \subset \Omega(f)$, then in particular the sequence $\frac{1}{g^*(x)}$ in $\Omega(g)$ also belongs to $\Omega(f)$. Therefore, $\frac{1}{g^*(x)} = \frac{h^*(x)}{f^*(x)}$ for some $h^*(x)$ of smaller degree than $f^*(x)$. This implies that $f(x) = g(x)h(x)$.

In the case when $g(x)$ divides $f(x)$, then for some $h(x)$ we have $f(x) = g(x)h(x)$. Any sequence in $\Omega(g)$ can be written $\frac{p^*(x)}{g^*(x)}$ where $\deg(p^*(x)) < \deg(g^*(x))$. However, since $\frac{p^*(x)}{g^*(x)} = \frac{p^*(x)h^*(x)}{g^*(x)h^*(x)} = \frac{b^*(x)}{f^*(x)}$, and $\deg(b^*(x)) < \deg(f^*(x))$, the sequence also belongs to $\Omega(f)$. □

EXAMPLE 2.7. The sequence (0010111) of period 7 is generated by $f(x) = x^3 + x + 1$. The generating function of the sequence is
$$G(x) = x^2 + x^4 + x^5 + x^6 + x^9 + x^{11} + x^{12} + x^{13} + x^{16} + \cdots.$$
In this case we find $\phi(x) = 1$ and its (formal) reciprocal to be $\phi^*(x) = x^2$. Hence,
$$G(x) = \frac{x^2}{x^3 + x^2 + 1} = x^2 + x^4 + x^5 + x^6 + x^9 + x^{11} + x^{12} + x^{13} + x^{16} + \cdots.$$

In the next theorem we obtain a relation that also involves the period ϵ of any sequence (s_t) in $\Omega(f)$.

THEOREM 2.8. *Let $(s_t) \in \Omega(f)$ be a periodic sequence of period ϵ. Then*
$$(x^\epsilon - 1)\phi(x) = \sigma(x)f(x)$$
where $\sigma(x) = s_0 x^{\epsilon-1} + s_1 x^{\epsilon-2} + \cdots + s_{\epsilon-1}$.

PROOF. Let (s_t) be a periodic sequence of period ϵ. Then the generating function can be written as,
$$\begin{aligned} G(x) &= (s_0 + s_1 x + s_2 x^2 + \cdots + s_{\epsilon-1} x^{\epsilon-1})(1 + x^\epsilon + x^{2\epsilon} + x^{3\epsilon} + \cdots) \\ &= (s_0 + s_1 x + s_2 x^2 + \cdots + s_{\epsilon-1} x^{\epsilon-1})/(1 - x^\epsilon) \\ &= \frac{\sigma^*(x)}{1 - x^\epsilon}. \end{aligned}$$

Since $(s_t) \in \Omega(f)$ we can combine this relation with the result in Theorem 2.3 and obtain the result. □

The result in Theorem 2.8 is the key to studying the periodic properties of LFSRs. To study the periods of the sequences in $\Omega(f)$ it is very useful to define the period of the polynomial $f(x)$.

DEFINITION 2.9. Let $f(x)$ be a polynomial such that x does not divide $f(x)$. The period of a polynomial $f(x)$ is defined as the smallest positive integer e such that $f(x) \mid x^e - 1$. We use the notation $e = per(f)$.

Note that the period exists for any polynomial $f(x)$ not divisible by x. This is due to the fact that x^i for $i = 0, 1, 2, ..$ can not all be distinct (mod $f(x)$). Hence, $x^i = x^j$ (mod $f(x)$) for some nonzero distinct integers i and j and thus (if we assume $i > j$) we obtain $f(x) \mid x^{i-j} - 1$.

It turns out that the period of the sequences generated by $\Omega(f)$ is heavily related to the period of the polynomial $f(x)$. It is also useful to observe that it is easy to show that if $f(x) | x^E - 1$ for some positive integer E then $e | E$.

THEOREM 2.10. Let (s_t) be a sequence in $\Omega(f)$.
 (i) The period $\epsilon = per(s_t)$ of the sequence (s_t) divides the period $e = per(f)$ of the polynomial $f(x)$.
 (ii) There is at least one sequence $(u_t) \in \Omega(f)$ with period $per(u_t) = per(f)$.

PROOF. (i) From the definition of e it follows that $f(x)F(x) = x^e - 1$ for some polynomial $F(x)$. Theorem 2.3 gives

$$G(x) = \frac{\phi^*(x)}{f^*(x)}$$

$$= \frac{\phi^*(x)F^*(x)}{f^*(x)F^*(x)}$$

$$= \frac{\phi^*(x)F^*(x)}{1 - x^e}$$

which since the degree of $\phi^*(x)F^*(x)$ is less than the degree of $1 - x^e$ implies that the coefficients of $G(x)$ repeat with period e. Hence, $(s_t) \in \Omega(f)$ repeats with period e and therefore $\epsilon \leq e$, which by a straightforward argument further leads to the conclusion that ϵ divides e.

(ii) From Theorem 2.8 it follows that

$$(x^\epsilon - 1)\phi(x) = \sigma(x)f(x).$$

Select $\phi(x) = 1$ then $f(x) | x^\epsilon - 1$ Hence, by definition of the period e of $f(x)$ it follows that $\epsilon \geq e$ and therefore by (i) the sequence in $\Omega(f)$ with $\phi(x) = 1$ has period e. □

Since all sequences in $\Omega(f)$ repeat with period $e = per(f)$, it follows from Theorem 2.8 that we can use $\sigma(x)$ to represent $\Omega(f)$, and therefore

$$\Omega(f) = \left\{ \frac{x^e - 1}{f(x)} \phi(x) \mid \deg(\phi(x)) < n \right\}.$$

Therefore $\Omega(f)$ is a principal ideal in the polynomial ring $GF(2)[x]$ (mod $x^e - 1$), leading to the following useful results.

COROLLARY 2.11. *Given the polynomials $g(x)$ and $h(x)$. Then*
  (i) $\Omega(g) \cap \Omega(h) = \Omega(\gcd(g,h))$,
  (ii) $\Omega(g) + \Omega(h) = \Omega(\operatorname{lcm}(g,h))$.

We can now describe the cycle structure of $\Omega(f)$ when $f(x)$ is an irreducible polynomial over $GF(2)$.

THEOREM 2.12. *Let (s_t) be a nonzero sequence in $\Omega(f)$ where $f(x)$ is irreducible. Then $per(s_t) = per(f) = e$.*

PROOF. From Theorem 2.8 we obtain $(x^\epsilon - 1)\phi(x) = \sigma(x)f(x)$ where $per(s_t) = \epsilon$. Since $f(x)$ is irreducible and $\deg(\phi(x)) < \deg(f(x))$ we get $\gcd(\phi(x), f(x)) = 1$, and therefore $f(x) | x^\epsilon - 1$, leading to $per(s_t) = \epsilon \geq e = per(f)$. Hence, from (i) in Theorem 2.10 we get $\epsilon = e$. □

REMARK 2.13. It follows from the proof above that the period of a sequence (s_t) equals the period of the polynomial $f(x)$ of smallest degree such that $(s_t) \in \Omega(f)$.

In the following we will find the cycle structure of $\Omega(f)$ for any polynomial $f(x)$. Let $f(x) = \prod_{i=1}^{r} f_i(x)^{k_i}$, where $f_i(x)$ is irreducible for all i. To determine the cycle structure of $\Omega(f)$ it is sufficient to solve the following problems.

- Determine the cycle structure of $\Omega(f_i^{k_i})$ from the cycle structure of $\Omega(f_i)$.
- Determine the cycle structure of $\Omega(gh)$ given the cycle structures of $\Omega(g)$ and $\Omega(h)$ when $\gcd(g(x), h(x)) = 1$.

We start by considering the cycle structure of $\Omega(f^k)$ for an irreducible polynomial $f(x)$ of period e.

THEOREM 2.14. *Let $f(x)$ be an irreducible polynomial of degree n and period e. Determine κ such that $2^\kappa < k \leq 2^{\kappa+1}$. Then $\Omega(f^k)$ contains the following number of sequences with the following periods,*

Number	1	$2^n - 1$	$2^{2n} - 2^n$	$2^{4n} - 2^{2n}$	...	$2^{2^\kappa n} - 2^{2^{\kappa-1} n}$	$2^{kn} - 2^{2^\kappa n}$
Period	1	e	$2e$	$4e$	...	$2^\kappa e$	$2^{\kappa+1} e$

PROOF. For $k = 1$ the result follows from the cycle structure of $\Omega(f)$. For $k = 2$ we need to consider the new sequences in $\Omega(f^2) \setminus \Omega(f)$. The number of such sequences is $2^{2n} - 2^n$. Since $f(x)$ is irreducible it follows from Remark 2.13 that the period of each of these new sequences equals the period of $f(x)^2$.

Note that an irreducible polynomial $f(x)$ has simple zeros. Let E be the period of $f(x)^2$. Since $f(x)$ divides $x^e - 1$, we observe that $f(x)^2$ divides $(x^e - 1)^2 = x^{2e} - 1$ and therefore that E divides $2e$. Furthermore, since $f(x) | f(x)^2 | x^E - 1$ it follows that e divides E. Therefore, we obtain $e | E | 2e$. Since $f(x)^2$ has multiple zeros we have $E > e$ and therefore $E = 2e$.

Similarly for $k = 3$ and $k = 4$ we can show that all sequences in $\Omega(f^4) \setminus \Omega(f^2)$ have period $4e$. Continuing in a similar way we find the period of the sequences in $\Omega(f^{2^i}) \setminus \Omega(f^{2^{i-1}})$ to be $2^i e$ for all positive integers i, which gives the result. □

EXAMPLE 2.15. Let $f(x) = x^2 + x + 1$, i.e. $n = 2$, $e = 3$. Let $[d(\lambda)]$ denote that there are d cycles of period λ in $\Omega(f)$. Then, by Theorem 2.14, the cycle structure of $\Omega(f^2)$ consists of 1 cycle of period 1, one cycle of period 3 and 2 cycles of period 6, denoted $[1(1)+1(3)+2(6)]$. In fact, the cycles are as follows $\Omega(f^2) = \{(0), (011), (000101), (001111)\}$.

THEOREM 2.16. Let $\gcd(g, h) = 1$, then $\Omega(gh) = \Omega(g) \oplus \Omega(h)$, i.e. any sequence in $\Omega(gh)$ can be uniquely written as a sum of a sequence in $\Omega(g)$ and one in $\Omega(h)$.

PROOF. From Corollary 2.11 it follows since $\gcd(g, h) = 1$ that $\Omega(g) + \Omega(h) = \Omega(gh)$. The uniqueness of the representation follows since $|\Omega(g)||\Omega(h)| = |\Omega(gh)|$. □

THEOREM 2.17. Let $\gcd(g, h) = 1$. Let $(u_t) \in \Omega(g)$ and $(v_t) \in \Omega(h)$. Then
$$per((u_t) + (v_t)) = \mathrm{lcm}(per(u_t), per(v_t))$$

PROOF. Let τ be the smallest integer such that
$$(u_{t+\tau}) + (v_{t+\tau}) = (u_t) + (v_t).$$
Hence,
$$(u_{t+\tau}) + (u_t) = (v_{t+\tau}) + (v_t) \in \Omega(g) \cap \Omega(h) = \{(0)\}.$$
Therefore, $per(u_t)|\tau$ and $per(v_t)|\tau$, which since the period of $(u_t) + (v_t)$ is at most $\mathrm{lcm}(per(u_t), per(v_t))$, implies that $\tau = \mathrm{lcm}(per(u_t), per(v_t))$. □

The full cycle structure of $\Omega(gh)$ can now be determined.

THEOREM 2.18. Let $\gcd(g, h) = 1$ and let $\Omega(g)$ contain d_1 cycles of length λ_1, denoted $[d_1(\lambda_1)]$. Let $\Omega(h)$ contain d_2 cycles of length λ_2, denoted $[d_2(\lambda_2)]$. Combine by adding in all possible ways the corresponding sequences. This leads to
$$d_1 \lambda_1 d_2 \lambda_2$$
sequences all of period
$$\mathrm{lcm}\{\lambda_1, \lambda_2\}.$$
The number of cycles obtained in this way is
$$d_1 d_2 \gcd(\lambda_1, \lambda_2).$$

Formally the cycle structure obtained from combining the d_1 cycles of length λ_1 and the d_2 cycles of length λ_2 can be written
$$[d_1(\lambda_1)][d_2(\lambda_2)] = [d(\lambda)]$$
where
$$d = d_1 d_2 \gcd(\lambda_1, \lambda_2) \text{ and } \lambda = \mathrm{lcm}\{\lambda_1, \lambda_2\}.$$

REMARK 2.19. Note that both $\Omega(g)$ and $\Omega(h)$ may contain many cycles. Then we use Theorem 2.18 repeatedly to combine sequences from all cycles in $\Omega(g)$ with sequences from all the cycles in $\Omega(h)$.

EXAMPLE 2.20. Let $f(x) = (x^2 + x + 1)(x + 1)^2$, and define $g(x) = x^2 + x + 1$ and $h(x) = (x + 1)^2$. Then the cycle structure of $\Omega(g)$ is $[1(1) + 1(3)]$ and the cycle structure of $\Omega(h)$ is $[2(1) + 1(2)]$. The cycle structure of $\Omega(f)$ is therefore obtained by combining the two cycle structures. Theorem 2.18 leads to the cycle structure
$$[2(1) + 1(2) + 2(3) + 1(6)].$$
In fact, $\Omega(f)$ contains the cycles (000111), (001), (011), (01), (1), (0).

Based on repeated use of Theorem 2.14 and Theorem 2.18 we are now able to find the complete cycle structure of $\Omega(f)$ from the factorization of $f(x)$ and the period of all its irreducible factors. We first find all the cycle structure of the powers of the irreducible components. Thereafter we combine all sequences coming from all cycles from relatively prime polynomials.

DEFINITION 2.21. The *minimal polynomial* of a periodic sequence (s_t) is the polynomial of smallest degree such that $(s_t) \in \Omega(f)$.

If the complete sequence is known one easily finds the minimal polynomial of the periodic sequence (s_t) of period ϵ. From Theorem 2.8 we have

$$(x^\epsilon - 1)\phi(x) = \sigma(x)f(x).$$

The minimal polynomial $f(x)$ of (s_t) must obey $\gcd(\phi(x), f(x)) = 1$. Dividing both sides by $\gcd(x^\epsilon - 1, \sigma(x))$ gives

$$f(x) = \frac{x^\epsilon - 1}{\gcd(x^\epsilon - 1, \sigma(x))}.$$

We can determine the minimal polynomial $f(x) = x^n + c_{n-1}x^{n-1} + ... + c_0$ of a sequence (s_t) from $2n$ successive bits $s_0, s_1, \ldots, s_{2n-1}$. This follows since the linear recursion gives a system of n equations in n unknowns. This system can be solved since the coefficient matrix turns out to have rank n when the minimal polynomial has degree n.

There is an efficient algorithm due to Berlekamp-Massey that finds the degree of the smallest recursion that generates a sequence (not necessarily periodic) from $2n$ successive bit in complexity $O(n^2)$. The linear complexity of a sequence is the smallest degree of the recursion that generates the sequence. Because of the Berlekamp-Massey algorithm a keystream needs a very high linear complexity to be secure. Therefore it is important to find simple methods to construct sequences with large linear complexity. Such constructions require nonlinear constructions such as nonlinear shift registers to be studied in Section 4.

In order to construct linear sequences with good pseudo random properties and long period, m-sequences discussed in the next section are frequently used as main components.

3. M-sequences

An n-bit linear shift register takes on at most 2^n different states. Since the zero state is always followed by the zero state all sequences generated by the shift register have period at most $2^n - 1$. A *maximal length sequence* (m-sequence) is a periodic sequence of maximal period $2^n - 1$ generated by a linear shift register of degree n. Let $f(x)$ be an irreducible polynomial of degree n and period $e = 2^n - 1$. Such polynomials are called primitive polynomials and there are $\frac{\phi(2^n-1)}{n}$ such polynomials of degree n where ϕ denotes Euler's ϕ function. The corresponding shift register generates an m-sequence when the initial state is different from the all zero state. Any m-sequence has a primitive polynomial as its characteristic polynomial.

Binary m-sequences are perhaps the best known and most important sequences, and are frequently used in many communication systems. Table 2 shows some examples of short m-sequences and corresponding characteristic polynomials. Important properties for a binary m-sequence (s_t) of period $2^n - 1$ are:

TABLE 2. Characteristic polynomials and m-sequences

Degree	$f(x)$	m-sequence	Period
2	$x^2 + x + 1$	011	3
3	$x^3 + x + 1$	0010111	7
3	$x^3 + x^2 + 1$	0011101	7
4	$x^4 + x + 1$	000100110101111	15
4	$x^4 + x^3 + 1$	000111101011001	15

THEOREM 3.1. *Let (s_t) be an m-sequence in $\Omega(f)$.*

(i) *The m-sequence (s_t) is "balanced", i.e. during a period of the m-sequence there are 2^{n-1} ones and $2^{n-1} - 1$ zeros.*

(ii) *When t runs through $0, 1, \ldots, 2^n - 2$, the n-tuple*

$$(s_t, s_{t+1}, \cdots, s_{t+n-1})$$

runs through all elements of $GF(2)^n$ exactly once, except for the n-tuple $(0, 0, \ldots, 0)$ which does not occur.

(iii) *For any value of τ, $0 < \tau < 2^n - 1$, there is a δ, depending on τ, such that*

$$(s_{t+\tau}) + (s_t) = (s_{t+\delta})$$

for all t.

PROOF. From the definition of an m-sequence it follows that all possible $2^n - 1$ nonzero states occur in an m-sequence and thus (i) and (ii) follow. (iii) Since $\Omega(f)$ is a vector space and $0 < \tau < 2^n - 1$, it follows that the sequence $(s_t) + (s_{t+\tau})$ is a nonzero sequence in $\Omega(f)$ and thus a shift of (s_t). □

Given a sequence (s_t) of period ϵ. The *autocorrelation* of (s_t) at shift τ is defined by

$$\theta_s(\tau) = \sum_{t=0}^{\epsilon-1} (-1)^{s_{t+\tau} - s_t}.$$

An important property of an m-sequence is its two-level autocorrelation function.

LEMMA 3.2. *The autocorrelation of an m-sequence (s_t) of period $\epsilon = 2^n - 1$ is given by:*

$$\theta_s(\tau) = \begin{cases} -1 & \text{for } \tau \not\equiv 0 \pmod{2^n - 1}, \\ 2^n - 1 & \text{for } \tau \equiv 0 \pmod{2^n - 1}. \end{cases}$$

PROOF. Define $u_t = s_{t+\tau} - s_t$ and note that (u_t) obeys the same linear recursion as (s_t). This implies that (u_t) is an m-sequence when $\tau \not\equiv 0 \pmod{2^n - 1}$ and the balance property of the m-sequence gives

$$\theta_s(\tau) = \sum_{t=0}^{\epsilon-1} (-1)^{s_{t+\tau} - s_t} = \sum_{t=0}^{\epsilon-1} (-1)^{u_t} = -1.$$

□

Golomb's randomness postulates express properties one expects to find in random sequences. These postulates are inspired by the randomness properties of m-sequences which obey all these properties. Let a *run* denote a set of consecutive 0's or consecutive 1's. A run of 0's must be preceded by a 1 and followed by a 1 and vice verse for a run of 1's. A *block* is a run of 1's and a *gap* is a run of 0's. Then the three postulates are:

- **R1.** The number of zeros and number of ones differ by at most one during a period of the sequence.
- **R2.** Half of the runs in a full cycle have length 1, 1/4 of all runs have length 2, 1/8 have length 3 etc, as long as the number of runs exceeds one. Moreover, for each of these lengths there are equally many gaps and blocks.
- **R3.** The out-of-phase autocorrelation of the sequence always has the same value.

4. Nonlinear shift registers

Linear shift registers are important building blocks in stream ciphers since using LFSRs one can control the period and the randomness of the generated sequences. The Berlekamp-Massey algorithm implies the need for sequences with very high linear complexity. One therefore needs to introduce nonlinearity into the shift registers to increase the complexity of the sequences generated by a stream cipher. For this reasons nonlinear shift registers offer an important option to significantly increase the complexity of the sequences (or the *keystreams*) generated by the cipher.

The challenges and most difficult problems are that no general theory exists for sequences generated by nonlinear shift registers and that it is in general very difficult to determine analytically their period and randomness properties. Often linear and nonlinear shift registers are combined in a controlled manner to maintain the period and randomness properties provided by the linear shift registers and to use the nonlinearity to increase the complexity of a stream cipher.

A nonlinear shift register uses a nonlinear feedback function in n-variables. There are altogether 2^{2^n} Boolean functions in n variables, since any Boolean function is uniquely defined by a *truth table* giving the value of $f(x_1, x_2, \ldots, x_n)$ for all 2^n possible input arguments.

Let $x = (x_1, x_2, \ldots, x_n)$ and $S = \{1, 2, \ldots, n\}$. For any subset $I = \{i_1, i_2, \ldots, i_r\}$ of S, let $x_I = x_{i_1} x_{i_2} \cdots x_{i_r}$ where we use the convention $x_\emptyset = 1$. Any Boolean function can be represented uniquely in its *algebraic normal form* by

$$f(x) = \sum_{I \subset S} a_I x_I.$$

EXAMPLE 4.1. The function $f(x_1, x_2, x_3) = 1 + x_1 + x_2 + x_2 x_3$ is an example of a nonlinear Boolean function. Table 3 shows the truth table of this function, i.e. a list of all possible values of $f(x_1, x_2, x_3)$ for all possible binary input triples (x_1, x_2, x_3).

Given the truth table it is easy to find the algebraic normal form of the corresponding nonlinear function. Suppose we know the truth table of a function as for example given by Table 3. We can write the corresponding Boolean function as a sum of nonlinear terms. If the truth table has a 1 for the input argument $(b_1, b_2, \ldots, b_n)$ we include the term $\prod_{i=1}^n (x_i + b_i + 1)$ which is a Boolean function

TABLE 3. Truth table of $f(x_1, x_2, x_3) = 1 + x_1 + x_2 + x_2x_3$

x_1	x_2	x_3	$f(x_1, x_2, x_3)$
0	0	0	1
0	0	1	1
0	1	0	0
0	1	1	1
1	0	0	0
1	0	1	0
1	1	0	1
1	1	1	0

taking the value 1 if and only if the argument is $(b_1, b_2, \ldots, b_n)$. For Table 3 we therefore need to add four terms to find the algebraic form of f as follows,

$$\begin{aligned} f(x_1, x_2, x_3) &= (x_1+1)(x_2+1)(x_3+1) + (x_1+1)(x_2+1)x_3 \\ &\quad + (x_1+1)x_2x_3 + x_1x_2(x_3+1) \\ &= 1 + x_1 + x_2 + x_2x_3. \end{aligned}$$

There exists a more efficient algorithm similar to the fast Fourier transform to find the algebraic normal form in complexity $O(n2^n)$.

One method to construct complex cryptographic transformations in a simple manner is by using a *multiplexer*, a table with 2^n entries representing the truth table of a Boolean function. If the table contains 2^n entries $y_1, y_2, \cdots, y_8$ (where we use $n = 3$), the transformation is represented by the Boolean function

$$F = y_1(x_1+1)(x_2+1)(x_3+1) + y_2(x_1+1)(x_2+1)x_3 + \cdots + y_8 x_1 x_2 x_3.$$

From the initial state $(s_0, s_1, \ldots, s_{n-1})$ and a nonlinear Boolean function in n variables $f(x_1, x_2, \ldots, x_n)$ one can generate the sequence

$$s_{t+n} = f(s_t, s_{t+1}, \ldots, s_{t+n-1}) \text{ for } t = 0, 1, 2, \ldots.$$

This can be implemented using an n-stage nonlinear shift register.

EXAMPLE 4.2. Using the Boolean function $f(x_1, x_2, x_3) = 1 + x_1 + x_2 + x_2 x_3$, the periodic sequence generated by the nonlinear recursion

$$s_{t+3} = 1 + s_t + s_{t+1} + s_{t+1}s_{t+2}$$

starting from $(s_0, s_1, s_2) = (001)$ is the sequence of period 8 given by $(s_t) = (00111010)$. In particular, all consecutive triples occur in a period of this sequence. Therefore, the sequence is as long as it can possibly be for a recursion of degree 3. Such a sequence is an example of a de Bruijn sequence.

A binary *de Bruijn sequence* of order n is a sequence of period 2^n which contains each binary n-tuple exactly once during its period. An example of a binary de Bruijn sequence of period $2^4 = 16$ is $(s_t) = (0000111101100101)$, generated by $s_{t+4} = f(s_t, s_{t+1}, s_{t+2}, s_{t+3})$, using the initial state (0000) and the Boolean function

$$f(x_1, x_2, x_3, x_4) = 1 + x_1 + x_2 + x_2 x_3 x_4.$$

All binary 4-tuples occur exactly once during a period of this sequence. In general, binary de Bruijn sequences are balanced, containing the same number of 0's and 1's, and they satisfy many randomness criteria, although they are generated using deterministic methods. They have been used as a source of pseudo random numbers and occur frequently in sequence generators of stream ciphers.

The binary de Bruijn graph B_n of order n is a directed graph with 2^n nodes. Each node is labeled with a unique binary n-tuple and has an edge from node $S = (s_0, s_1, \ldots, s_{n-1})$ to node $T = (t_0, t_1, \ldots, t_{n-1})$ if and only if $(s_1, s_2, \ldots, s_{n-1}) = (t_0, t_1, \ldots, t_{n-2})$. The successive n-tuples in a de Bruijn sequence therefore form a Hamiltonian cycle in the de Bruijn graph. There are in total $2^{2^{n-1}-n}$ de Bruijn sequences of period 2^n. This is far larger than the number $\phi(2^n - 1)/n$ of m-sequences of period $2^n - 1$.

EXAMPLE 4.3. Consider the Boolean function $f(x_1, x_2, x_3) = 1 + x_1 + x_2 + x_3 + x_1 x_2 + x_1 x_3 + x_2 x_3$. This function contains a *branch point* in the sense that using the function f to generate a sequence

$$s_{t+3} = 1 + s_t + s_{t+1} + s_{t+2} + s_t s_{t+1} + s_t s_{t+2} + s_{t+1} s_{t+2}$$

one observes that (010) is the successor of both (101) and (001). Such a function f is said to be singular.

Any Boolean function f such that the mapping

(4.1) $\qquad (x_1, x_2, \ldots, x_n) \to (x_2, x_3, \ldots, x_n, f(x_1, x_2, \ldots, x_n))$

is a permutation of the set of binary n-tuples is called a nonsingular Boolean function. A straightforward observation from the definition of a nonsingular function is the following result.

THEOREM 4.4. *A Boolean function $f(x_1, x_2, \ldots, x_n)$ is nonsingular if and only if $f = x_1 + g(x_2, x_3, , x_n)$ for some Boolean function g in $n - 1$ variables.*

The truth table of a Boolean function g is a list of the values of $g(x_2, x_3, \ldots, x_n)$ for all binary $(n-1)$-tuples. The weight of the truth table of g is the number of ones in this list. The number of nonsingular Boolean functions in n variables is $2^{2^{n-1}}$. For a nonsingular function f the lower half of the truth table of f is the complement of its upper half. Any nonsingular f decomposes the de Bruijn graph B_n into disjoint cycles under the mapping (4.1). One interesting observation proved by Mykkeltveit [M] is that the maximal number of cycles that B_n is decomposed into occurs in the case $f = x_1$, i.e. $g = 0$. The number of cycles is then known to be

$$Z(n) = \frac{1}{n} \sum_{d|n} \phi(d) 2^{n/d}.$$

It is useful to observe that $Z(n)$ is an even integer for any positive integer $n \neq 2$. This observation can be used to derive some necessary conditions for constructions of de Bruijn sequences.

There are many ways to construct de Bruijn sequences. One way is to start with a nonsingular Boolean function with a certain cycle decomposition of the de Bruijn graph. Then by repeated changes of the truth table one can join the cycles one by one until a de Bruijn sequence remains. To join two cycles (or split a cycle into two cycles) one needs to change the truth table of g in one suitable position, leading to two changes of the truth table of f. In particular, a single joining (or splitting) of two cycles changes both the parity of the number of cycles as well as the parity of the weight of the truth table of g. Any nonsingular Boolean function with truth table of weight w can be obtained by changing the truth table of the

Boolean function corresponding to $g = 0$ in w positions. Since the Boolean function of weight $w = 0$ decomposes B_n into an even number ($=Z(n)$) of cycles it follows that the number of cycles obtained from any Boolean function $f = x_1 + g$ has the same parity as the weight of the truth table of g.

It follows therefore for a de Bruijn sequence that the truth table of its g has odd weight. Further, all n variables have to be present in the Boolean function for a de Bruijn sequence in order for the truth table of its g to have odd weight.

There is an easy way to construct a de Bruijn sequence from an m-sequence. One can change the longest run of zeros in the m-sequence by appending an extra 0. The result is a de Bruijn sequence.

EXAMPLE 4.5. The sequence (0000100110101111) is a de Bruijn sequence obtained from an m-sequence of period 15, with characteristic polynomial $f(x) = x^4 + x + 1$, by appending an extra 0 in the longest runs of zeros. This de Bruijn sequence is therefore "almost linear". However, its linear complexity is as large as possible for a de Bruijn sequence of this period. This is in fact true for any de Bruijn sequence of period 2^n constructed in this way from an m-sequence of period $2^n - 1$. This is an illustration that linear complexity in itself is no guarantee for security.

The linear complexity of a de Bruijn sequence is defined as the length of the shortest linear shift register that can be used to generate the sequence. The linear complexity L of a binary de Bruijn sequence of period 2^n, $n \geq 3$, satisfies the double inequality,
$$2^{n-1} + n \leq L \leq 2^n - 1.$$
There exist de Bruijn sequences that meet the upper and lower bounds with equality.

Alternative methods to generate sequences with large linear complexity is to combine linear sequences in a nonlinear way. One classical way to describe $\Omega(f)$ is from the zeros of its characteristic polynomial $f(x)$. Let $\alpha_i, i = 1, 2, \ldots, n$ be the zeros of $f(x)$, where we for simplicity assume the zeros are distinct. Then any sequence $(s_t) \in \Omega(f)$ can be written as

$$s_t = \sum_{i=1}^{n} a_i \alpha_i^t$$

for some a_i in some extension field of $GF(2)$. There may be conditions on the constants a_i in order for (s_t) to be a binary sequence. The linear complexity of (s_t) equals the number of nonzero a_i's occurring in this representation.

A natural question is to see what happens with the linear complexity after multiplying two sequences generated by linear shift registers of degree m and n respectively.

Let $(u_t) \in \Omega(f)$ and $(v_t) \in \Omega(g)$ where $deg(f) = n$ and $deg(g) = m$ and we assume both polynomials have simple zeros. Let $u_t = \sum_{i=1}^{n} a_i \alpha_i^t$, where α_i, $i = 1, 2, \ldots, n$ are the zeros of $f(x)$ and $v_t = \sum_{j=1}^{m} b_j \beta_j^t$, where β_j, $j = 1, 2, \ldots, m$ are the zeros of $g(x)$.

THEOREM 4.6. *The sequence* $(w_t) = (u_t v_t)$ *can be written*

$$w_t = \sum_{i=1}^{n} \sum_{j=1}^{m} a_i b_j (\alpha_i \beta_j)^t$$

and belongs to $\Omega(P)$ where $P(x)$ is the binary polynomial that has all products $\alpha_i \beta_j$ for $i = 1, 2, \ldots, n$ and $j = 1, 2, \ldots, m$ as zeros.

It follows from this theorem that the multiplication of two sequences roughly multiplies the linear complexities. One can prove that this is exactly the case when both polynomials are irreducible of relatively prime degrees. In general, the exact determination of the linear complexity of the product sequence needs a closer study. One has to determine the number of different elements $\alpha_i \beta_j$ such that $(\alpha_i \beta_j)^t$ occur with a nonzero coefficient. However, the disadvantage with this construction of multiplying two sequences is that the product sequence is highly unbalanced, so one needs to regain balance by other means.

It is rather easy to control the period of the product of two sequences with relatively prime periods.

LEMMA 4.7. *Let* $\gcd(per(u_t), per(v_t)) = 1$ *then* $per(u_t v_t) = per(u_t) \cdot per(v_t)$.

PROOF. If $per(u_t v_t) \neq per(u_t) \cdot per(v_t)$ then we can assume without loss of generality that $per(u_t v_t) \mid k \cdot per(u_t)$ where $k \mid per(v_t)$ and that $u_0 \neq 0$. Decimating $(u_t v_t)$ by $e = per(u_t)$ gives

$$(u_0 v_0), (u_0 v_e), (u_0 v_{2e}), \cdots$$

of period $k < per(v_t)$. Since, $\gcd(e, per(v_t)) = 1$ this is a contradiction. Note that a decimation relatively prime to the period can not reduce the period, since the inverse decimation then would increase the period, which clearly is impossible. □

It is often useful to use a Boolean function to combine output from different positions in a sequence (s_t). The linear complexity can frequently be lower bounded as in the following two results. The idea behind the proofs is to write (s_t) in terms of the zeros in the characteristic polynomial and to show that the product of two or more sequences from adjacent taps has at least the given number of zeros of its characteristic polynomial occurring with nonzero coefficients.

LEMMA 4.8. *Let* (s_t) *be an m-sequence of period* $2^n - 1$. *Let* $1 \leq k \leq n$ *and let* $\gcd(2^n - 1, \tau) = 1$. *Let* (u_t) *be the sequence defined by* $u_t = s_t s_{t+\tau} \cdots s_{t+(k-1)\tau}$. *Then the linear complexity of* (u_t) *is at least* $\binom{n}{k}$. *Further, let*

$$z_t = \sum_{i=0}^{N-1} c_i s_{t+i} s_{t+i+\tau} \cdots s_{t+i+(k-1)\tau}.$$

Then the linear complexity of (z_t) *is at least* $\binom{n}{k} - (N-1)$ *when at least one* c_i *is nonzero.*

Another popular construction is to combine the output from n different LFSRs that are generating m-sequences and to use a Boolean function in n variables to generate a nonlinear output sequence. Let x_i denote the output bit from the i-th register LFSRi at time t. The linear complexity of this construction is as follows.

THEOREM 4.9. *Let LFSRi generate an m-sequence of period* $2^{L_i} - 1$, $L_i \geq 2$ *for* $i = 1, 2, \ldots, n$. *Let* $\gcd(L_i, L_j) = 1$ *for all* $i \neq j$. *Let* x_i *be the output from LFSRi and let* $z_t = f(x_1, x_2, \cdots, x_n)$ *be the output sequence. Then the linear complexity of* (z_t) *is* $f(L_1, L_2, \cdots, L_n)$, *calculated over the integers.*

5. Applications to stream ciphers

Linear feedback shift registers have numerous applications in coding theory, communication systems and in cryptography. In this section we will focus on their cryptographic applications to stream ciphers.

The one-time pad is a provable secure symmetric key cryptosystem. The plaintext is usually transformed into a bitstream (p_t) and a random binary key (k_t) is added (mod 2) to provide the cipher text (c_t) where $c_t = p_t + k_t$ (mod 2). The receiver possesses an identical copy of the key (k_t). When the recipient receives the cipher text (c_t) he adds the key (k_t) and recovers the plaintext. The one-time pad has been proved to be secure provided the following conditions are met: (1) the key is random, (2) the key is as long as the plaintext and (3) the key is only used once. There are practical problems with this system since it requires a perfect random generator to generate the key (k_t) and that the length of the key is as long as the plaintext. In most applications one uses a shorter secret key to initialize a system of linear and nonlinear shift registers that are used to generate a long pseudo random key. This long pseudo random key plays a similar role as the (k_t) in a one-time-pad system, except that it is generated in a deterministic manner and is therefore not truly random.

From the properties of the one-time-pad it is important that the generated sequences have long period, high nonlinear complexity and good randomness properties.

The Advanced Encryption Standard (AES) is a block cipher which is fast and efficient. Block ciphers are frequently used in a stream cipher mode such as the counter mode. There is a recent interest in studying stream ciphers. One motivation is that a direct construction of a stream cipher can improve performance to obtain higher speed in software, less complexity in hardware and lower power consumption compared with what is possible by using a block cipher in a stream cipher mode. The security of stream ciphers has been less studied in the open literature so recent efforts are underway to construct stream ciphers with security similar to block cipher in the sense that the fastest attack is an exhaustive key search.

Many known constructions and designs of stream ciphers apply linear feedback shift register and m-sequences, in particular, as building blocks to provide long period and good randomness properties. Further, it is important to provide additional nonlinearity into the design of the stream cipher to avoid attacks based on the Berlekamp-Massey algorithm as well as attacks based on linear approximations. Some frequently used basic designs involve nonlinear filter generators (Figure 2), nonlinear combiners (Figure 3) or clock controlled generators (Figure 4). Usually each involved register generates an m-sequence while these basic constructions provide a greater nonlinearity and still retain long periods and good randomness properties.

A *nonlinear filter generator* uses an LFSR that generates an m-sequence (s_t) of period $2^n - 1$ in combination with a Boolean function f in k variables, that needs to possess some good cryptographic properties. The output bit is computed by selecting k, $k \leq n$, fixed positions from the LFSR and computing

$$z_t = f(s_{t+\tau_1}, s_{t+\tau_2}, \ldots, s_{t+\tau_k})$$

FIGURE 2. Nonlinear filter generator

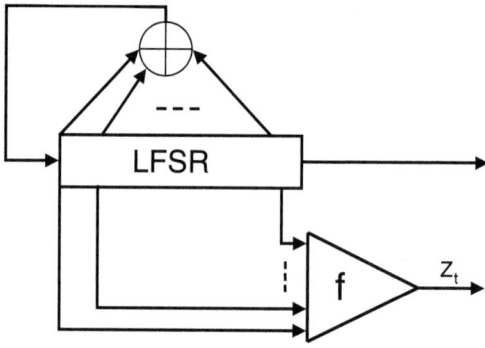

FIGURE 3. Nonlinear combination generator

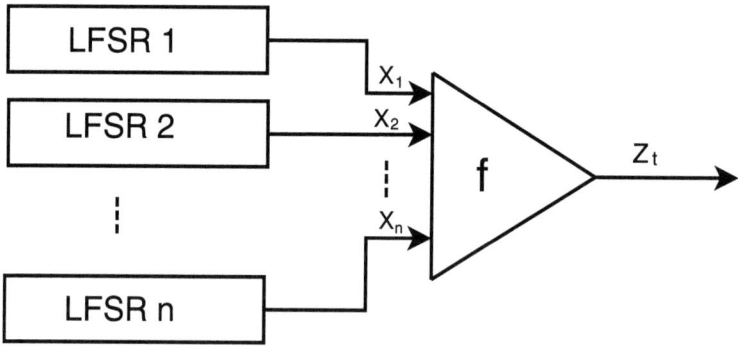

for some fixed positions τ_i, $i = 1, 2, \ldots, k$, where $0 \leq \tau_1 < \tau_2 < \cdots < \tau_k < n$. We will therefore sometimes write the relation as

$$z_t = f(s_t, s_{t+1}, \ldots, s_{t+n-1})$$

to indicate that it depends on the register state at time t.

An illustration of the nonlinear filter generator is shown in Figure 2. Observe that every bit s_t is a linear combination of $s_0, s_1, \ldots, s_{n-1}$. Therefore each known z_t gives an equation in the n variables $s_0, s_1, \ldots, s_{n-1}$.

The *nonlinear combination generator* combines the output of n linear shift registers using a Boolean function f in n variables. Each shift register generates an m-sequence. At each time unit the contribution x_i from the i-th shift register is combined by a Boolean function f to provide an output bit z_t at each time unit given by $z_t = f(x_1, x_2, \ldots, x_n)$. An illustration of the nonlinear combination generator is shown in Figure 3.

The *clock controlled generator* uses one shift register to clock another one. An illustration of a clock controlled generator is shown in Figure 4, where the output of the upper register is converted to an integer c_t that is used to select the next output bit from the lower register. This can be done in many different ways (for example by discarding the next c_t bits of the lower register). Perhaps one of the

FIGURE 4. A clock controlled generator

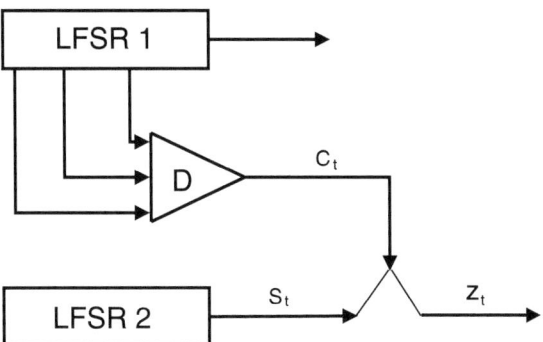

most popular variants is the *shrinking generator*, where a bit in one register decides whether a bit in another register should be discarded or not and thus *shrinks* the output of this register that after shrinking is considered to be the pseudo random keystream.

The standard assumption when attacking a stream cipher is a known plaintext attack. In this case, by adding the known plaintext and the known cipher text, the corresponding part of the keystream is therefore known. The aim of the attacker is to determine more of the keystream bits or, even better, to recover the secret key. Other types of attacks are distinguishing attacks where one wants to build a distinguisher that can distinguish the keystream from a truly random stream of bits. Further attacks include prediction of the next symbol, power analysis or timing attacks.

Basic attacks on stream ciphers include *correlation attacks* and *algebraic attacks*. The correlation attack is a divide and conquer attack. The cipher text is viewed as a very noisy version of the plaintext. Coding techniques are used to restore the key from the keystream. Algebraic attacks, on the other hand, consider the cipher as a multivariate system of equations and mathematical methods for solving equations in several variables are used to find the key.

We illustrate the principles of these two types of attacks with some simple examples. More sophisticated variations of these attacks exist, but due to space limitations we only consider the basic ideas.

The m-sequences generated by an LFSR can be considered as codewords in a code C with generator matrix G, i.e, C is the row space of G. For later illustrations we consider the code with generator matrix G that generates $\Omega(g)$ for $g(x) = x^4 + x^3 + 1$ given by

$$G = \begin{bmatrix} 1 & 0 & 0 & 0 & 1 & 1 & 1 & 1 & 0 & 1 & 0 & 1 & 1 & 0 & 0 \\ 0 & 1 & 0 & 0 & 0 & 1 & 1 & 1 & 1 & 0 & 1 & 0 & 1 & 1 & 0 \\ 0 & 0 & 1 & 0 & 0 & 0 & 1 & 1 & 1 & 1 & 0 & 1 & 0 & 1 & 1 \\ 0 & 0 & 0 & 1 & 1 & 1 & 1 & 0 & 1 & 0 & 1 & 1 & 0 & 0 & 1 \end{bmatrix}.$$

This is a code of rate $R = 4/15$ since 15 bits are used to represent the four information bits s_0, s_1, s_2 and s_3 that are encoded into the codeword $(s_0, s_1, \ldots, s_{14})$ of length 15 via the linear recursion $s_{t+4} = s_{t+3} + s_t$ or equivalently by

$$(s_0, s_1, \ldots, s_{14}) = (s_0, s_1, s_2, s_3)G.$$

In general for an m-sequence of period $2^n - 1$ this code is called the simplex code.

If the initial state is (s_0, s_1, s_2, s_3) then one observes that column number t of G describes s_t in terms of its initial state. For example the last column implies that $s_{14} = s_2 + s_3$. The decoding problem is for any vector of length $2^n - 1$ to find the closest codeword (i.e., the codeword that differ in fewest coordinates from the received vector). Typically we only know only N bits where $N < 2^n - 1$. This corresponds to considering the code with generator matrix consisting of the first N columns of G.

5.1. Algebraic attacks. Consider the recursion $s_{t+4} + s_{t+3} + s_t = 0$ with characteristic polynomial $g(x) = x^4 + x^3 + 1$ of period 15. We illustrate the attack on the nonlinear filter function given by

$$f(x_1, x_2, x_3) = x_1 x_2 + x_2 x_3 + x_3.$$

We let the fixed tap positions be such that at time t we have

$$x_1 = s_t,\ x_2 = s_{t+1},\ x_3 = s_{t+3}.$$

Then the output at time t is given by

$$z_t = f(s_t, s_{t+1}, s_{t+3}) = s_t s_{t+1} + s_{t+1} s_{t+3} + s_{t+3}.$$

For example for $t = 3$ we get

$$\begin{aligned} z_3 &= f(s_3, s_4, s_6) \\ &= f(s_3, s_0 + s_3, s_0 + s_1 + s_2 + s_3) \\ &= s_0 s_1 + s_0 s_2 + s_0 s_3 + s_1 s_3 + s_2 s_3 + s_1 + s_2 + s_3. \end{aligned}$$

Calculating the expressions for z_t for $t = 0, 1, 2, \cdots$ we obtain a set of equations relating (z_t) and (s_t). Note that due to the linear recursion any s_t can be represented as a linear combination of the bits in the initial state. This leads to a set of equations for z_t in terms of s_0, s_1, s_2 and s_3 for $t = 0, 1, 2, \ldots, 14$, beginning by

$$\begin{aligned} z_0 &= s_0 s_1 + s_1 s_3 + s_3 \\ z_1 &= s_0 s_2 + s_1 s_2 + s_2 s_3 + s_0 + s_3 \\ z_2 &= s_0 s_3 + s_1 s_3 + s_2 s_3 + s_0 + s_1 \\ z_3 &= s_0 s_1 + s_0 s_2 + s_0 s_3 + s_1 s_3 + s_2 s_3 + s_1 + s_2 + s_3 \\ z_4 &= s_0 s_1 + s_0 s_2 + s_0 s_3 + s_1 s_2 + s_2 s_3 + s_0 + s_2 + s_3 \\ z_5 &= s_0 s_1 + s_0 s_3 + s_1 s_2 + s_2 s_3 + s_0 + s_1 + s_3 \\ &\cdots \end{aligned}$$

Replacing each linear and quadratic term by a new variable is called linearization. This gives a linear system with $\binom{4}{2} + \binom{4}{1} = 10$ unknowns,

$$\begin{aligned} z_0 &= a_4 + a_5 + a_3 \\ z_1 &= a_6 + a_8 + a_9 + a_0 + a_3 \\ z_2 &= a_7 + a_5 + a_9 + a_0 + a_1 \\ z_3 &= a_4 + a_6 + a_7 + a_5 + a_9 + a_1 + a_2 + a_3 \\ z_4 &= a_4 + a_6 + a_7 + a_8 + a_9 + a_0 + a_2 + a_3 \\ z_5 &= a_4 + a_7 + a_8 + a_9 + a_0 + a_1 + a_3 \\ &\cdots \end{aligned}$$

To solve this linear system one needs a sufficient number of keybits to ensure that one has at least 10 linear independent equations. In this case we find the initial state of the register and recover the keystream.

A more complicated but real stream cipher is the LILI cipher. This cipher uses the Boolean filter function $f_{LILI}(x_1, x_2, ..., x_{10})$ of degree 6 and containing 46 terms. The m-sequence is generated by $g(x) = x^{89} + x^{83} + x^{80} + ... + 1$. To perform the attack above the number of unknowns after linearization is

$$\binom{89}{6} + \binom{89}{5} + \cdots + \binom{89}{1} \approx 2^{29.2}.$$

The number of calculations needed for solving this system by Gaussian elimination is therefore approximately $(2^{29.2})^3 \approx 2^{88}$.

To decrease the complexity of the algebraic attack an elegant trick is to multiply $f_{LILI}(x_1, x_2, \ldots, x_{10})$ by $x_8 x_{10}$. Then it turns out that

$$f_{LILI}(x_1, x_2, \ldots, x_{10}) \cdot x_8 x_{10} = x_8 x_{10} \cdot (x_2 x_9 + x_3 x_7 + x_4 x_7 + x_5 x_9 + x_1 + x_4 + x_5 + x_6)$$

of degree 4 and 8 terms. The number of unknowns after linearization now becomes

$$\binom{89}{4} + \binom{89}{3} + \binom{89}{2} + \binom{89}{1} \approx 2^{21}.$$

The number of calculations needed in this case is reduced to approximately $(2^{21})^3 \approx 2^{63}$.

Let A denote the linear transformation taking the n-bit state of the linear register to the next state. In general, the filter generator provides the following set of equations

$$\begin{aligned} z_0 &= f(s_0, s_1, ..., s_{n-1}) \\ z_1 &= f(A(s_0, s_1, ..., s_{n-1})) \\ &\ldots \\ z_t &= f(A^t(s_0, s_1, ..., s_{n-1})) \\ &\ldots \end{aligned}$$

This leads to a system of equations in n variables $s_0, s_1, \ldots, s_{n-1}$ of degree d_1 where d_1 is the degree of the Boolean function f. We can solve the system by linearization. The number of unknowns is

$$S_1 = \sum_{i=1}^{d_1} \binom{n}{i} \approx n^{d_1}/d_1!.$$

Hence, we need at least this number of keystream bits and the complexity to solve the system by linearization is approximately S_1^3.

In algebraic attacks on the filter generator the annihilator of the Boolean functions f and $1 + f$ play an important role. The annihilator of the Boolean function f is defined by

$$An(f) = \{g \mid g(x_1, \ldots, x_n) f(x_1, \ldots, x_n) = 0 \text{ for all } (x_1, \ldots, x_n) \in GF(2)^n\}.$$

Let $\mathbf{x_t} = A^t(s_0, \ldots, s_{n-1})$, then for any $g \in An(f)$ we have $g(\mathbf{x_t}) f(\mathbf{x_t}) = 0$. Therefore, $g(\mathbf{x_t}) = 0$ for all t with $z_t = 1 = f(\mathbf{x_t})$. For any $g \in An(1 + f)$ then $g(\mathbf{x_t})(1 + f(\mathbf{x_t})) = 0$, i.e, $g(\mathbf{x_t}) = 0$ for all t with $z_t = 0 = f(\mathbf{x_t})$.

Let

$$d = \min\{\deg(g) \mid g \in An(f) \cup An(1+f), g \neq 0\}.$$

The number d is called the algebraic immunity, $AI(f)$, of f. In this way we obtain a system of equations in n variables of degree $d = AI(f)$. Consider N bits in the keystream. Let N_1 be the number of linearly independent equations obtained when $z_t = 1$ such that

$$g(A^t(s_0, ..., s_{n-1})) = 0, g \in An(f), deg(g) = d$$

and let N_0 be the number of linearly independent equations obtained when $z_t = 0$ such that

$$g(A^t(s_0, ..., s_{n-1})) = 0, g \in An(1+f), deg(g) = d.$$

From a keystream of length N we expect about $(N_0 + N_1)N/2$ linear independent equations. The required number of keystream bits needed to get enough linearly independent equations is at least $S \approx n^d/d!$, which implies that N must be at least $2n^d/(d!(N_0 + N_1))$. The complexity of solving the system is approximately $S^3 \approx (n^d/d!)^3$.

To make the filter function resistant to these algebraic attacks it is therefore necessary to select the Boolean function f such that $d = AI(f)$ is large. It is known that $AI(f) \leq (n+1)/2$.

For further information on algebraic attacks on stream ciphers the reader is referred to [**CM**].

5.2. Correlation attacks. In this section we consider correlation attacks on nonlinear combination generators. We first illustrate the basic correlation attack using the Geffe generator shown in Figure 5. This is a simple nonlinear combination generator that combines three shift registers where LFSRi generates an m-sequence of period $2^{L_i} - 1$, for $i = 1, 2, 3$, where $\gcd(L_i, L_j) = 1$ for $i \neq j$. The key is the initial state of the registers. If x_1, x_2, x_3 are the output bits from the three shift registers at a given time t then the output bit z_t at this time is

$$z_t = f(x_1, x_2, x_3) = x_1 x_2 + x_2 x_3 + x_3.$$

Even though this construction is known to give an output sequence of maximal period $\epsilon = (2^{L_1} - 1)(2^{L_2} - 1)(2^{L_3} - 1)$ and good linear complexity $L = L_1 L_2 + L_2 L_3 + L_3$, the generator can still easily be attacked.

The idea behind the basic correlation attack is that the choice of the Boolean function implies that there is a correlation $3/4$ between the keystream bit z_t and the output x_1 from the LFSR1, i.e.

$$P(z_t = x_1) = 3/4 \neq 1/2.$$

This follows directly from the definition of f since $x_2 = 1$ implies that $z_t = x_1$ and $x_2 = 0$ implies that $f = x_3$, which equals x_1 with probability $1/2$. The correlation attack guesses the initial content of LFSR1 and compares the resulting output of LFSR1 from this guess with the observed keystream. If the guess is wrong we expect a correlation of $1/2$ while if the guess is correct we expect a correlation of $3/4$. Therefore in this case we select the guess which leads to the output of LFSR1 which is closest to the observed keystream. In a similar way we can find the initial state of LFSR3 since

$$P(z_t = x_3) = 3/4 \neq 1/2,$$

and finally we can determine the initial state of LFSR2 by complete search. This is an example of a divide and conquer attack.

FIGURE 5. Geffe generator

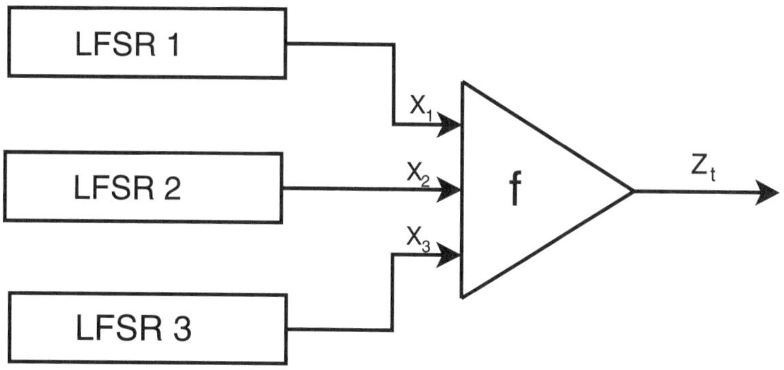

In general the complexity of the attack to guess a component LFSR is $O(2^L N)$ where N is the number of keystream bits needed and L is the length of the component shift register. The number of bits needed depends on the correlation. The closer it is to $1/2$ the more bits are required for the attack and this number can be estimated using methods from coding theory.

In correlation attacks we consider all 2^L sequences that can be generated by a component LFSR as codewords in a linear code, the simplex code, consisting of the m-sequence and all its cyclic shifts and the zero sequence. Since we consider N bits in the keystream the (shortened) code has rate $R = L/N$. The error probability p of the corresponding binary channel (BSC) depends on the Boolean combiner function. The error-probability p is the probability that the keystream bit is different from the corresponding bit in the component LFSR. For the attack to be successful one needs that $p \neq 1/2$.

The keystream is considered to be a noisy version of a sequence from the component LFSR. Reconstructing the initial state is exactly the problem of decoding the code on the binary symmetric channel (BSC) on a very noisy communication channel with a probability of error being p which is close to $1/2$. Decoding techniques from coding theory can be applied to recover the initial state.

Let $C(p) = 1 + p \log_2 p + (1-p) log_2(1-p)$ be the capacity of the binary symmetric channel with error probability p. A famous result by Shannon shows that it is possible to communicate reliable over a communication channel using a code of rate R less than the capacity, i.e., $R < C(p)$. This implies that in order to reconstruct the component LFSR one needs $R = L/N < C(p)$, i.e., $N > L/C(p)$. To have a probability of success close to 1 one normally needs twice as many bits which implies that $N \geq 2L/C(p)$.

For example, for the reconstructing of LFSR1 in the Geffe generator above we have $p = P(z_t \neq x_1) = 1/4$ and thus $C(p) = 0.19$. In the case $L = 40$ we need $N \geq 424$ bits. Thus reconstructing this register has complexity $O(2^{40} \cdot 424)$ which is approximately $O(2^{49})$. To avoid correlation attacks it is therefore important to select the Boolean function carefully.

EXAMPLE 5.1. Consider the simple example where a component LFSR generates the recursion $s_{t+4} + s_{t+3} + s_t = 0$ with characteristic polynomial $g(x) = x^4 + x^3 + 1$ of period 15. The correlation attack counts the number of equations that holds

$$z_0 \approx s_0 = s_0$$
$$z_1 \approx s_1 = s_1$$
$$z_2 \approx s_2 = s_2$$
$$z_3 \approx s_3 = s_3$$
$$z_4 \approx s_4 = s_0 + s_3$$
$$z_5 \approx s_5 = s_0 + s_1 + s_3$$
$$z_6 \approx s_6 = s_0 + s_1 + s_2 + s_3$$
$$z_7 \approx s_7 = s_0 + s_1 + s_2$$
$$z_8 \approx s_8 = s_1 + s_2 + s_3$$
$$z_9 \approx s_9 = s_0 + s_2$$
$$\cdots$$

where $\approx$ means that relations hold with a probability being the correlation between the component LFSR and the keystream. Since the correlation is 3/4 (or error-probability $p = 1/4$), the optimal attack selects the guess which gives the sequence (s_t) "codeword" being closest to the "received word" (z_t).

In general for the basic correlation attack above we need to guess a full component shift register of length L generating an m-sequence of period $2^L - 1$. To improve on this we can use fast correlation attacks. The main idea is to construct relations involving only $s_0, s_1, \cdots, s_{B-1}$, $B < L$, and only guess these bits. One selects linear combinations only involving these bits. For a given w we search for indexes $i_1, i_2, ..., i_w$ such that

$$s_{i_1} + s_{i_2} + \cdots + s_{i_w} = c_0 s_0 + c_1 s_1 + \cdots + c_{B-1} s_{B-1}$$

where usually w is small, say 2, 3 or 4. In this way we get an estimate of $c_0 s_0 + c_1 s_1 + \ldots + c_{B-1} s_{B-1}$, by replacing the left hand side with the observed keystream bits, i.e.,

$$z_{i_1} + z_{i_2} + \cdots + z_{i_w} \approx c_0 s_0 + c_1 s_1 + \cdots + c_{B-1} s_{B-1}.$$

However, the estimates are less reliable since we use w unreliable bits in the estimates. This is compensated for by the fact that we can in general construct significantly more equations. This can be done efficiently by using the generator matrix of the simplex code corresponding to the component shift register and find many relations of w columns that added together lead to a relation between the B required bits (i.e. find w columns such that the last $L - B$ bits in their sum are all 0). The more relations we find the more reliable our estimates will be. This leads to a set of equations of the form,

$$y_0 = z_{0,0} + z_{0,1} + \cdots + z_{0,w-1} \approx c_{0,0} s_0 + \cdots + c_{0,B-1} s_{B-1}$$
$$y_1 = z_{1,0} + z_{1,1} + \cdots + z_{1,w-1} \approx c_{1,0} s_0 + \cdots + c_{1,B-1} s_{B-1}$$
$$\cdots$$

This gives a code of rate $R = B/m$ where m equals the number of equations. We may consider the bits $y_0, y_1, \ldots, y_{m-1}$ as an estimate of the linear relation of the information bits $s_0, s_1, \ldots, s_{B-1}$ given at the right hand side. We know an estimate of each bit y_t as a linear combination of w bits from the keystream (z_t).

Since each "received bit" y_t is a sum of w bits each with a probability p of being incorrect, the so-called "Piling-up-lemma" implies that the bit error probability of the channel after adding w unreliable bits is
$$p_w = 1/2 - 2^{w-1}(1/2 - p)^w$$
where
$$p_w = P(a_1 + \cdots + a_w \neq b_1 + \cdots + b_w)$$
and where $P(a_i \neq b_i) = p$. The channel gets worse with increasing w. The attack is as follows (i) guess bits $s_0, s_1, ..., s_{B-1}$, (ii) select the guess that satisfies the most number of equations. The complexity and the number of keystream bits needed for the attack is determined by coding theory.

The number of keystream bits needed for a fast correlation attack is determined by the number of equations m required which by coding theory arguments must obey $R = B/m < C(p_w)$. To have a very high probability for the attack to be successful we need about twice as many equations, i.e., $m \geq 2B/C(p_w)$. The expected number of equations m that can be found is approximately $\binom{N}{w}/2^{L-B}$, where N is the number of keystream bits. This follows since there are $\binom{N}{w}$ ways to sum w of the first N columns of the generator matrix of the simplex code and a fraction $1/2^{L-B}$ of these are expected to be 0 in the last $L - B$ coordinates.

The run time complexity of the fast correlation attack is approximately $O(2^B m)$ since 2^B is the number of guesses of $s_0, \cdots, s_{B-1}$ and m is the number of equations $\binom{L}{w}/2^{L-B} \geq 2B/C(p_w)$. This is better than the complexity needed in the general correlation attack, even though more bits are needed in the attack due to a worse channel since $|p_w - 1/2| < |p - 1/2|$.

EXAMPLE 5.2. Let $w = 2, B = 2$ and observe that $s_1 = s_4 + s_5, s_0 + s_1 = s_6 + s_{14}, s_0 = s_5 + s_{10}$. Substituting the keystream on the right hand side we get several estimates of linear combinations of s_0 and s_1 using a sum of two keystream bits,

$$\begin{aligned} z_4 + z_5 &\approx s_1 \\ z_6 + z_{14} &\approx s_0 + s_1 \\ z_5 + z_{10} &\approx s_0 \\ &\cdots \end{aligned}$$

We guess s_0, s_1 and observe that if the guess is correct then the probability that each equation holds is $p^2 + (1-p)^2$. If the guess is wrong the the probability that each equation holds is $1/2$.

Note that because of the cyclic structure, these equations hold for all t

$$\begin{aligned} z_{t+4} + z_{t+5} &\approx s_{t+1} \\ z_{t+6} + z_{t+14} &\approx s_t + s_{t+1} \\ z_{t+5} + z_{t+10} &\approx s_t \\ &\cdots \end{aligned}$$

A simple but useful observation is that if the equation
$$z_{i_0} + z_{i_1} + \ldots + z_{i_{w-1}} \approx s_{i_0} + s_{i_1} + \ldots + s_{i_{w-1}} = c_0 s_0 + c_1 s_1 + \ldots + c_{B-1} s_{B-1}$$
holds for $t = 0$, then it holds for any $t \geq 0$ that
$$z_{t+i_0} + z_{t+i_1} + \ldots + z_{t+i_{w-1}} \approx s_{t+i_0} + \ldots + s_{t+i_{w-1}} = c_0 s_t + \ldots + c_{B-1} s_{t+B-1}.$$

This gives more reliability in finding the initial state $s_0, s_1, .., s_{B-1}$. The metric for the best guess is obtained by counting the number of equations that hold for $t = 0, 1, \ldots, T$ for the equations involving $(s_t, s_{t+1}, ..., s_{t+B-1})$ for $t = 0, 1, \ldots, T$. As the metric we use the number of equations that hold. The best guess (when $p_w < 1/2$) maximizes as many equations as possible to hold. This problem was observed in [J] to be equivalent to a convolutional code of rate $R = 1/m$ where m is the number of equations. The celebrated Viterbi decoder with 2^B states is an efficient method for finding the best guess (for small B).

5.3. Clock controlled generator. In the following we only consider the simple clock controlled generator in Figure 4. The two shift registers LFSR1 and LFSR2 generate m-sequences of period $2^{n_1} - 1$ and $2^{n_2} - 1$ respectively. One easy way to attack this generator is to guess the initial content of the upper register LFSR1 with complexity $O(2^{n_1})$. From the observed output keystream one can write a set of linear equations in the n_2 unknown bits in the initial state of LFSR2. This system can be solved by Gaussian elimination with a complexity $O(n_2^3)$. Hence the overall complexity is $O(2^{n_1} n_2^3)$. In [**MO**] the complexity of this attack is reduced to $O(2^{n_1})$, by running through the guesses of the initial state of LFSR1 in the order where a state is succeeded by the next state obtained by shifting the register.

6. Conclusions

This paper has given a basic introduction to the theory of linear and nonlinear shift registers as well as some examples presenting general common principles for the construction and analysis of stream ciphers.

7. Acknowledgement

The author thanks Håvard Molland and Alexander Kholosha for numerous interesting discussions about stream ciphers and the referee for many useful comments.

References

[BP] H. Beker and F. Piper, *Ciphers systems: the Protection of Communications*, Northwood Books, London, 1982.

[CM] N.T. Courtois and W. Meier, Algebraic attacks on stream ciphers with linear feedback, *Advances in Cryptology - EURORYPT 2003*, Lecture Notes in Computer Science, vol. 2656, Springer-Verlag, 2003, 345-359.

[GG] S.W. Golomb and G. Gong *Signal Design*, Cambridge University Press, New York, 2005.

[G] S.W. Golomb, *Shift Register Sequences*, Holden-Day series in information systems. Holden-Day, Inc., San Francisco, 1967. Revised ed., Laguna Hills: Aegean Park, 1982.

[J] T. Johansson and F. Jönsson, Improved fast correlation attacks on stream ciphers via convolutional codes, *Advances in Cryptology - CRYPTO 1999*, Lecture Notes in Computer Science, vol. 1592, Springer-Verlag, 1999, 347-362.

[MO] H. Molland, Improved linear consistency attack on irregularly clocked keystream generators, in *Fast Software Encryption, FSE 2004*, Lecture Notes in Computer Science, vol. 3017, Springer-Verlag, 2004, 109-126.

[M] J. Mykkeltveit, A proof of Golomb's conjecture for the de Bruijn graph, J. Combinatorial Theory, Ser B, 13, 1972, 40-45.

[R] R.A. Rueppel, *Analysis and Design of Stream Ciphers*, Communications and Control Engineering Series, Springer-Verlag, Berlin, 1986.

[S] E.S. Selmer, *Linear Recurrence Relations over Finite Fields*, Lecture Notes, University of Bergen, Norway, 1966.

The Selmer Center, Department of Informatics, Høyteknologisenteret, University of Bergen, PB 7800, N-5020, Bergen, NORWAY

Current address: The Selmer Center, Department of Informatics, Høyteknologisenteret, University of Bergen, PB 7800, N-5020, Bergen, NORWAY

E-mail address: `Tor.Helleseth@ii.uib.no`

An Introduction to Pairing-Based Cryptography

Alfred Menezes

ABSTRACT. Bilinear pairings have been used to design ingenious protocols for such tasks as one-round three-party key agreement, identity-based encryption, and aggregate signatures. Suitable bilinear pairings can be constructed from the Tate pairing for specially chosen elliptic curves. This article gives an introduction to the protocols, Tate pairing computation, and curve selection.

1. Introduction

The discrete logarithm problem (DLP) has been extensively studied since the discovery of public-key cryptography in 1975. Recall that the DLP in an additively-written group $G = \langle P \rangle$ of order n is the problem, given P and Q, of finding the integer $x \in [0, n-1]$ such that $Q = xP$. The DLP is believed to be intractable for certain (carefully chosen) groups including the multiplicative group of a finite field, and the group of points on an elliptic curve defined over a finite field. The closely related Diffie-Hellman problem (DHP) is the problem, given P, aP and bP, of finding abP. It is easy to see that the DHP reduces in polynomial time to the DLP. It is generally assumed, and has been proven in some cases (e.g., see [10, 38]), that the DLP reduces in polynomial time to the DHP.

The assumed intractability of the DHP is the basis for the security of the Diffie-Hellman key agreement protocol [20] illustrated in Figure 1. The objective of this protocol is to allow Alice and Bob to establish a shared secret by communicating over a channel that is being monitored by an eavesdropper Eve. The group pa-

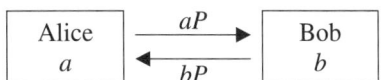

FIGURE 1. Two-party one-round key agreement protocol.

rameters n and P are public knowledge. Alice randomly selects a secret integer $a \in [1, n-1]$ and sends aP to Bob. Similarly, Bob randomly selects a secret integer $b \in [1, n-1]$ and sends bP to Alice. Both Alice and Bob can use their secret integers

---

1991 *Mathematics Subject Classification.* Primary 94A60.

Key words and phrases. Public-key cryptography, elliptic curves, Tate pairing.

to calculate the shared secret $K = abP$. The eavesdropper is faced with the task of computing K given P, aP and bP, which is precisely an instance of the DHP.

The Diffie-Hellman protocol can be viewed as a one-round protocol because the two exchanged messages are independent of each other. The protocol can easily be extended to three parties, as illustrated by the two-round protocol depicted in Figure 2; the secret shared by Alice, Bob and Chris is $K = abcP$. The protocol is

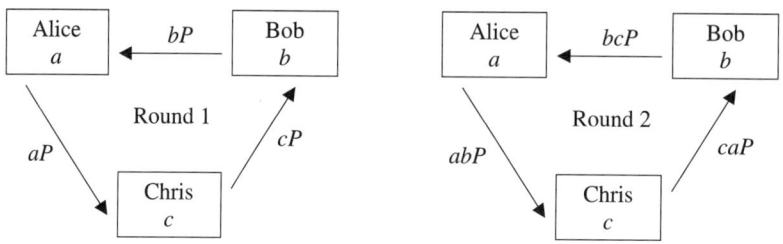

FIGURE 2. Three-party two-round key agreement protocol.

secure against eavesdroppers if the problem of computing $K = abcP$ given P, aP, bP, cP, abP, bcP and caP is intractable. This problem is presumably no easier than the DHP.

A natural question to ask is whether there exists a three-party one-round key agreement protocol that is secure against eavesdroppers. This question remained open until 2000 when Joux [32] devised a surprisingly simple protocol that used bilinear pairings. Joux's paper was of great interest to cryptographers, who started investigating further applications of pairings. The next two important applications of pairings were the identity-based encryption scheme of Boneh and Franklin [14] and the short signature scheme of Boneh, Lynn and Shacham [16]. Since then, there has been a flurry of activity in the design and analysis of cryptographic protocols using pairings. Pairings have been accepted as an indispensable tool for the protocol designer. There has also been a tremendous amount of work on the realization and efficient implementation of bilinear pairings using the Tate pairing on elliptic curves, hyperelliptic curves, and more general kinds of abelian varieties.

The purpose of this paper is to provide an introduction to pairing-based cryptography. We will present some of the important developments in protocol design, Tate pairing computation, and elliptic curve selection. Our treatment will be neither exhaustive nor complete, but nonetheless we hope that it will be sufficiently detailed so that the reader will appreciate the crucial ideas. More in-depth studies of these topics can be found in the expository articles by Galbraith [25] and Paterson [45], and in the extensive research literature.

The remainder of this paper is organized as follows. Bilinear pairings are introduced in §2. In §3 we present Joux's key agreement protocol, the Boneh-Lynn-Shacham short signature scheme, and the Boneh-Franklin identity-based encryption scheme. Relevant properties of elliptic curves are reviewed in §4, and then in §5 we describe how the Tate pairing on elliptic curves can be used to construct bilinear pairings. In §6, we present methods for generating suitable elliptic curves. §7 makes some concluding remarks.

2. Bilinear pairings

Let n be a prime number. Let $G_1 = \langle P \rangle$ be an additively-written group of order n with identity ∞, and let G_T be a multiplicatively-written group of order n with identity 1.

DEFINITION 2.1. A *bilinear pairing* on (G_1, G_T) is a map
$$\hat{e} : G_1 \times G_1 \to G_T$$
that satisfies the following conditions:
 (1) (*bilinearity*) For all $R, S, T \in G_1$, $\hat{e}(R + S, T) = \hat{e}(R, T)\hat{e}(S, T)$ and $\hat{e}(R, S + T) = \hat{e}(R, S)\hat{e}(R, T)$.
 (2) (*non-degeneracy*) $\hat{e}(P, P) \neq 1$.
 (3) (*computability*) $\hat{e}$ can be efficiently computed.

The following properties of bilinear pairings can be easily verified. Property (5) is another way of defining non-degeneracy. For all $S, T \in G_1$:
 (1) $\hat{e}(S, \infty) = 1$ and $\hat{e}(\infty, S) = 1$.
 (2) $\hat{e}(S, -T) = \hat{e}(-S, T) = \hat{e}(S, T)^{-1}$.
 (3) $\hat{e}(aS, bT) = \hat{e}(S, T)^{ab}$ for all $a, b \in \mathbb{Z}$.
 (4) $\hat{e}(S, T) = \hat{e}(T, S)$.
 (5) If $\hat{e}(S, R) = 1$ for all $R \in G_1$, then $S = \infty$.

One consequence of the bilinearity property is that the DLP in G_1 can be efficiently reduced to the DLP in G_T. For, if (P, Q) is an instance of the DLP in G_1 where $Q = xP$, then $\hat{e}(P, Q) = \hat{e}(P, xP) = \hat{e}(P, P)^x$. Thus $\log_P Q = \log_g h$, where $g = \hat{e}(P, P)$ and $h = \hat{e}(P, Q)$ are elements of G_T.

The security of many pairing-based protocols is dependent on the intractability of the following problem.

DEFINITION 2.2. Let $\hat{e}$ be a bilinear pairing on (G_1, G_T). The *bilinear Diffie-Hellman problem (BDHP)* is the following: Given P, aP, bP, cP, compute $\hat{e}(P, P)^{abc}$.

Hardness of the BDHP implies the hardness of the DHP in both G_1 and G_T. First, if the DHP in G_1 can be efficiently solved, then one could solve an instance of the BDHP by computing abP and then $\hat{e}(abP, cP) = \hat{e}(P, P)^{abc}$. Also, if the DHP in G_T can be efficiently solved, then the BDHP instance could be solved by computing $g = \hat{e}(P, P)$, $g^{ab} = \hat{e}(aP, bP)$, $g^c = \hat{e}(P, cP)$ and then g^{abc}. Nothing else is known about the intractability of the BDHP, and the problem is generally assumed to be just as hard as the DHP in G_1 and G_T.

We note that the decisional Diffie-Hellman problem (DDHP) in G_1 can be efficiently solved. The DDHP is to decide whether a given quadruple (P, aP, bP, cP) of elements in G_1 is a valid Diffie-Hellman quadruple, i.e., whether $cP = abP$. This can be accomplished by computing $\gamma_1 = \hat{e}(P, cP) = \hat{e}(P, P)^c$ and $\gamma_2 = \hat{e}(aP, bP) = \hat{e}(P, P)^{ab}$; then $cP = abP$ if and only if $\gamma_1 = \gamma_2$.

3. Protocols

This section presents three fundamental pairing-based protocols. There are many other examples of innovative applications of pairings including short group signature schemes [**12**] and mechanisms for allowing selective searches on encrypted data [**13**].

3.1. Three-party one-round key agreement.

Joux's key agreement protocol [**32**], as modified by Verheul [**53**], uses a bilinear pairing on (G_1, G_T) for which the BDHP is intractable. As depicted in Figure 3, Alice randomly selects a secret integer $a \in [1, n-1]$ and broadcasts the point aP to the other two parties. Similarly (and simultaneously), Bob and Chris broadcast the points bP and cP. After receiving bP and cP, Alice (and also Bob and Chris) can compute the shared

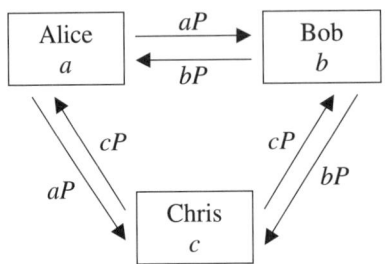

FIGURE 3. Three-party one-round key agreement protocol.

secret $K = \hat{e}(bP, cP)^a = \hat{e}(P, P)^{abc}$. An eavesdropper who wishes to compute K is faced with the task of solving an instance of the BDHP.

Joux's protocol can be generalized to an l-party one-round protocol by using an efficiently computable multilinear map $\hat{e}_n : G_1^{l-1} \to G_T$ for which the following analogue of the BDHP is intractable: given P, $a_1 P, a_2 P, \ldots, a_l P$, compute $\hat{e}_n(P, P, \ldots, P)^{a_1 a_2 \cdots a_l}$. The existence of such multilinear maps for any $l > 3$ remains an open question. In fact Boneh and Silverberg [**17**] have given some evidence that, unlike the case $l = 3$, it may not be possible to construct multilinear maps with $l > 3$ from natural maps that arise in algebraic geometry.

Joux's protocol is not interesting from a practical point of view because it is only resistant to passive attacks and needs at least one additional round of communications in order to resist active attacks. Nonetheless, it serves as an elegant example of the potential of pairings in protocol design.

3.2. Short signatures.

Most discrete logarithm signature schemes such as the DSA [**22**] are variants of the ElGamal signature scheme [**21**]. In such schemes, signatures are generally comprised of a pair of integers modulo n, where n is the order of the underlying group $G_1 = \langle P \rangle$. Boneh, Lynn and Shacham (BLS) [**16**] proposed the first signature scheme in which signatures are comprised of a single group element (and where the group element can be represented using roughly the same number of bits as an integer modulo n).

The BLS short signature scheme utilizes a bilinear pairing $\hat{e}$ on (G_1, G_T) for which the DHP in G_1 is intractable. It also uses a cryptographic hash function $H : \{0,1\}^* \to G_1 \setminus \{\infty\}$. Alice's private key is a randomly selected integer $a \in [1, n-1]$, while her public key is the group element $A = aP$. Alice's signature on a message $m \in \{0,1\}^*$ is the single group element $S = aM$, where $M = H(m)$. Any party possessing Alice's public key can verify the signature by computing $M = H(m)$ and checking that (P, A, M, S) is a valid Diffie-Hellman quadruple. This is precisely an instance of the DDHP in G_1 (see §2) which the verifier can solve by checking that $\hat{e}(P, S) = \hat{e}(A, M)$.

An attacker who wishes to forge Alice's signature on a message m needs to compute $S = aM$ given P, A and $M = H(m)$. This is an instance of the DHP in G_1, which presumably is intractable.

The BLS signature scheme is very simple and has many interesting features. For example, signatures can be aggregated [15]. Suppose that for each i, $1 \le i \le t$, (m_i, S_i) is a signed message generated by party i with key pair (A_i, a_i). Suppose also that the messages are pairwise distinct. Then the aggregate signature is defined to be $S = \sum_{i=1}^{t} S_i$. A verifier who possesses the public keys A_i, the messages m_i and S, checks that $\hat{e}(P, S) = \prod_{i=1}^{t} \hat{e}(A_i, M_i)$, where $M_i = H(m_i)$, and thereby obtains the assurance that each m_i was signed by party i. The BLS signature scheme has also been used to design protocols for threshold, multisignature and blind signatures [11].

3.3. Identity-based encryption. When using public-key encryption to send a message securely to Alice, Bob encrypts the message using Alice's public key. Alice then uses her corresponding private key to decrypt. Bob should be certain that he possesses an authentic copy of Alice's public key because otherwise an attacker could induce Bob to use the attacker's public key, and would thereafter be able to decrypt Bob's messages that were intended only for Alice.

Large-scale deployments of public-key cryptography generally employ the services of a certifying authority (CA) who is responsible for generating *certificates* for public keys. Such a certificate for Alice would consist of Alice's identifying information and her public key, together with the CA's signature on this data. Any party who possesses an authentic copy of the CA's public key can verify the signature contained in the certificate, and thereby be assured of the authenticity of Alice's public key.

Although the notion of a certificate is very simple, there are many practical difficulties with managing certificates. For example, Bob may not know how to obtain Alice's certificate. Also, Bob should have the assurance that Alice's public key is still valid, i.e., her certificate has not been revoked by the CA on account of Alice having left her place of employment, or because her private key has somehow been compromised.

In 1984, Shamir [51] introduced the notion of identity-based cryptography to alleviate many of the problems inherent with managing certificates. Shamir proposed that Alice's public key consist of her identifying information ID_A (such as Alice's email address). A trusted third party (TTP) would use its private key to generate Alice's private key from ID_A and securely transmit it to Alice. Any other party Bob could encrypt messages for Alice using only ID_A and the TTP's public key. Notice that, unlike the case with traditional certificate-based encryption schemes, Bob can encrypt a message for Alice even before Alice has generated a key pair. In fact, Bob could include in ID_A any set of conditions that should be met before the TTP issues the private key. Such conditions could include a credit rating, employment status, or a minimum age requirement. In this way the TTP acts as a policy enforcer. The key revocation problem inherent with traditional certificates can be circumvented by including a date in ID_A; the TTP would only give Alice the corresponding private key if it has not been revoked by that date.

In 2001, Boneh and Franklin [14] proposed the first practical identity-based encryption scheme. Their scheme employs a bilinear pairing $\hat{e}$ on (G_1, G_T) for which the BDHP is intractable. It also uses two cryptographic hash functions

$H_1 : \{0,1\}^* \to G_1 \setminus \{\infty\}$ and $H_2 : G_T \to \{0,1\}^l$, where l is the bitlength of the plaintext. The TTP's private key is a randomly selected integer $t \in [1, n-1]$, and its public key is $T = tP$. It is assumed that all parties are able to obtain an authentic copy of T. When Alice requests her private key d_A, the TTP creates Alice's identity string ID_A, computes $d_A = tH_1(\text{ID}_A)$, and securely delivers d_A to Alice. Notice that d_A can be considered as the TTP's BLS signature on the message ID_A.

To encrypt a message $m \in \{0,1\}^l$ for Alice using the basic Boneh-Franklin scheme, Bob computes $Q_A = H_1(\text{ID}_A)$, selects a random integer $r \in [1, n-1]$, and computes $R = rP$ and $c = m \oplus H_2(\hat{e}(Q_A, T)^r)$. Bob then transmits the ciphertext (R, c) to Alice. To decrypt, Alice uses her private key d_A to compute $m = c \oplus H_2(\hat{e}(d_A, R))$. Decryption works because

$$\hat{e}(d_A, R) = \hat{e}(tQ_A, rP) = \hat{e}(Q_A, tP)^r = \hat{e}(Q_A, T)^r.$$

An eavesdropper who wishes to recover m from (R, c) must compute $\hat{e}(Q_A, T)^r$ given (P, Q_A, T, R); this is precisely an instance of the BDHP.

While secure against eavesdroppers, the basic encryption scheme is not resistant to chosen-ciphertext attacks where the attacker, who is trying to learn some information about the plaintext that corresponds to a target ciphertext, is able to obtain the decryption of any ciphertext of its choice (except for the target ciphertext). Given a target ciphertext (R, c), the attacker can simply flip the first bit of c to get c', and thereafter obtain the decryption m' of the modified ciphertext (R, c'). She then flips the first bit of m' to recover m.

Resistance to chosen-ciphertext attacks can be achieved by modifying the basic scheme as follows. In addition to H_1 and H_2, two hash function $H_3 : \{0,1\}^* \to [1, n-1]$ and $H_4 : \{0,1\}^l \to \{0,1\}^l$ are employed. To encrypt m, Bob randomly selects a bitstring $\sigma \in \{0,1\}^l$ and computes $g = \hat{e}(Q_A, T)$, $r = H_3(\sigma, m)$, $R = rP$, $c_1 = \sigma \oplus H_2(g^r)$, and $c_2 = m \oplus H_4(\sigma)$. The ciphertext is (R, c_1, c_2). To decrypt, Alice computes $g^r = \hat{e}(d_A, R)$, $\sigma = c_1 \oplus H_2(g^r)$, $m = c_2 \oplus H_4(\sigma)$, and $r = H_3(\sigma, m)$. Alice accepts the plaintext m provided that $R = rP$. Note that the attack described in the previous paragraph fails because of the integrity check on R.

As mentioned above, identity-based encryption schemes have several advantages over traditional certificate-based systems. However, there are some drawbacks such as the necessity of a secure channel for the transmission of private keys and the need for a TTP who has the ability to generate all private keys. A detailed comparison of the relative benefits and drawbacks of identity-based and certificate-based systems can be found in [**46**].

4. Elliptic curves

An elliptic curve E over a field K is defined by a non-singular Weierstrass equation

(4.1) $$y^2 + a_1 xy + a_3 y = x^3 + a_2 x^2 + a_4 x + a_6,$$

where $a_1, a_2, a_3, a_4, a_6 \in K$. The set $E(K)$ of K-rational points consists of the point at infinity ∞ and the points $(x, y) \in K \times K$ that satisfy (4.1). Suppose now that K is the finite field $\mathbb{F}_q$ of order q and characteristic p. Hasse's theorem gives tight bounds for the cardinality of $E(K)$:

$$(\sqrt{q} - 1)^2 \leq \#E(K) \leq (\sqrt{q} + 1)^2.$$

Hence we can write $\#E(K) = q + 1 - t$ where $|t| \leq 2\sqrt{q}$. If $p \mid t$ then E is said to be *supersingular*; otherwise E is *ordinary*. If $|t| \leq 2\sqrt{q}$ and $p \nmid t$, then there exists an elliptic curve E over $\mathbb{F}_q$ with $\#E(\mathbb{F}_q) = q + 1 - t$. In fact, if q is prime then for each t, $|t| < 2\sqrt{q}$, there exists an elliptic curve E defined over $\mathbb{F}_q$ with $\#E(\mathbb{F}_q) = q + 1 - t$.

If $p > 3$, then a linear change of variables transforms equation (4.1) into the simpler form
$$y^2 = x^3 + ax + b$$
where $a, b \in K$ and $4a^3 + 27b^2 \neq 0$. The following are two other simplified equations that will be considered later. If E is supersingular and $p = 3$, then (4.1) simplifies to
$$y^2 = x^3 + ax + b$$
where $a, b \in K$ and $b \neq 0$. If E is supersingular and $p = 2$, then (4.1) simplifies to
$$y^2 + cy = x^3 + ax + b$$
where $a, b, c \in K$ and $c \neq 0$.

The chord-and-tangent rule for adding two points in $E(K)$ endows $E(K)$ with the structure of an abelian group. The point at infinity ∞ serves as the identity element. The negative of a point $P = (x_1, y_1)$ is $-P = (x_1, y_2)$ where y_1, y_2 are the two roots of the defining equation for E with $x = x_1$. If $P, Q \in E(K) \setminus \{\infty\}$ with $P \neq \pm Q$, then $P + Q$ is defined to be R where $-R$ is the third point of intersection of the line through P and Q with the curve. The group law is depicted in Figure 4 for the elliptic curve $y^2 = x^3 - x$ over the real numbers.

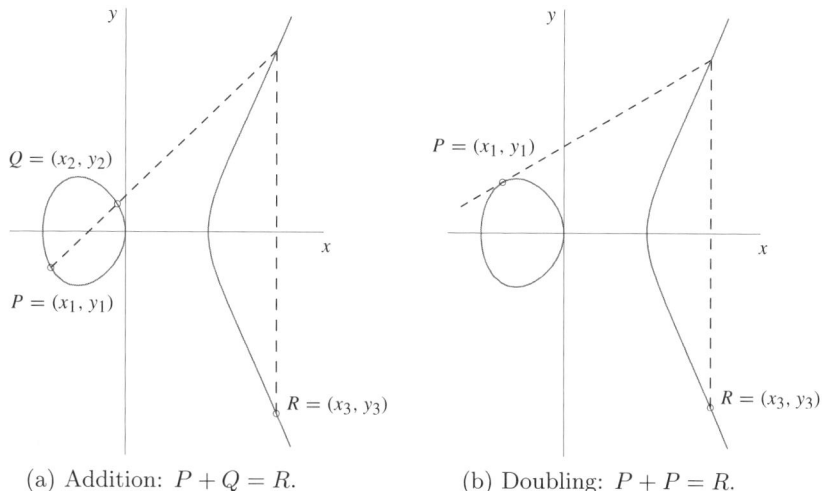

(a) Addition: $P + Q = R$. (b) Doubling: $P + P = R$.

FIGURE 4. Geometric addition and doubling of elliptic curve points.

The rank of $E(K)$ is at most two. More precisely, we have $E(K) \cong \mathbb{Z}_{n_1} \oplus \mathbb{Z}_{n_2}$ where $n_2 \mid n_1$ and $n_2 \mid q - 1$.

Now, let $P \in E(K)$ be a point of prime order n, and suppose that $\gcd(n, q) = 1$. The elliptic curve discrete logarithm problem (ECDLP) in $\langle P \rangle$ is the following: given P and $Q \in \langle P \rangle$, find the integer l such that $Q = lP$. The best generic algorithm known for solving the ECDLP is Pollard's rho method [47] which has an expected running time of $O(\sqrt{n})$. If $n \approx q$, as should be the case if one wishes to maximize resistance to Pollard's rho method for a fixed field $\mathbb{F}_q$, then the running time is fully exponential in $\log q$. However, there may be other discrete log solvers that are faster for certain families of elliptic curves. In particular, it was shown in the early 1990s [24, 39] that the Weil and Tate pairings can be used to transfer the ECDLP instance to an instance of the discrete logarithm problem in an extension field $\mathbb{F}_{q^k}$, where the embedding degree k is defined as follows.

DEFINITION 4.1. Let E be an elliptic curve defined over $\mathbb{F}_q$, and let $P \in E(\mathbb{F}_q)$ be a point of prime order n. Suppose that $\gcd(n, q) = 1$. Then the *embedding degree* of $\langle P \rangle$ is the smallest positive integer k such that $n \mid q^k - 1$.

If the embedding degree k is small, then there is the possibility that the known subexponential-time index-calculus algorithms (e.g., [1, 18, 29]) for solving the DLP in $\mathbb{F}_{q^k}$ are faster than Pollard's rho method for solving the ECDLP in $\langle P \rangle$. This is indeed the case for all supersingular curves since $k \in \{1, 2, 3, 4, 6\}$ for these curves. However, one can expect that $k \approx n$ for most elliptic curves (and this was proven to be the case for elliptic curves of prime order over prime fields [5]), and thus for most elliptic curves the ECDLP is not vulnerable to the Weil and Tate pairing attacks.

Following the discovery of these attacks in the early 1990s, the consensus was that elliptic curves with low embedding degrees should not be used in discrete log protocols. In fact many standards for elliptic curve cryptography such as ANSI X9.62 [3] explicitly forbid the use of such curves. However, low-embedding degree elliptic curves are now very much back in vogue since they are crucial for the efficient realization of the pairing-based protocols that were presented in §3. In §5 we define the Tate pairing for elliptic curves and show how it can be used to design bilinear pairings that meet the requirements of §2. Techniques for finding suitable elliptic curves of low embedding degree are presented in §6.

5. Tate pairing

Let E be an elliptic curve defined over $K = \mathbb{F}_q$ by a Weierstrass equation $r(x, y) = 0$, and let $\overline{K}$ denote the algebraic closure of K. We will denote $E(\overline{K})$ by E.

A divisor on E is a formal sum of points $D = \sum_{P \in E} n_P(P)$, where the n_P are integers only a finite number of which are nonzero. The support of D is the set of points $P \in E$ for which $n_P \neq 0$. The divisor D is called a zero divisor if $\sum_{P \in E} n_P = 0$. D is said to be defined over K if $D^\sigma = \sum_P n_P(P^\sigma) = D$ for all automorphisms σ of $\overline{K}$ over K, where $P^\sigma = (\sigma(x), \sigma(y))$ if $P = (x, y)$, and $\infty^\sigma = \infty$. The set of all divisors that are defined over K is denoted by $\text{Div}_K(E)$.

The function field of E over K is the field of fractions $K(E)$ of $K[x, y]/(r(x, y))$. The divisor of a function $f \in K(E)$ is $\text{div}(f) = \sum_{P \in E} m_P(P)$, where m_P is the multiplicity of P as a root of f. Note that $\text{div}(f)$ determines f up to multiplication by a nonzero field element. The divisors of functions are called principal divisors. The following result characterizes principal divisors.

THEOREM 5.1. *A divisor* $D = \sum_{P \in E} n_P(P)$ *is principal if and only if*

$$\sum_{P \in E} n_P = 0 \quad \text{and} \quad \sum_{P \in E} n_P P = \infty.$$

Two divisors $D_1, D_2 \in \text{Div}_K(E)$ are said to be equivalent, written $D_1 \sim D_2$, if $D_1 = D_2 + \text{div}(f)$ for some $f \in K(E)$. Let $f \in K(E)$ and $D = \sum n_P(P) \in \text{Div}_K(E)$ be such that $\text{div}(f)$ and D have disjoint support. Then $f(D)$ is defined to be $\prod_{P \in E} f(P)^{n_P}$; note that $f(D)$ is a nonzero element of K.

5.1. Tate pairing definition. Suppose that $\#E(\mathbb{F}_q) = hn$ where n is a prime such that $\gcd(n, q) = 1$. Let k be the smallest positive integer such that $n \mid q^k - 1$. The set of all points $P \in E(\overline{K})$ satisfying $nP = \infty$ is denoted by $E[n]$; it is known that $E[n] \cong \mathbb{Z}_n \oplus \mathbb{Z}_n$. By μ_n we denote the order-n subgroup of $\mathbb{F}_{q^k}^*$.

We make some further assumptions that will simplify our description of the Tate pairing. We first assume that $n \nmid q - 1$, and so $k > 1$. A result of Balasubramanian and Koblitz [5] tells us that $E[n] \subseteq E(\mathbb{F}_{q^k})$, and hence $n^2 \mid \#E(\mathbb{F}_{q^k})$. We further assume that $\gcd(n, h) = 1$ and that $n \nmid \#E(\mathbb{F}_{q^k})/n^2$.

The (modified) Tate pairing is a map
$$e : E[n] \times E[n] \to \mu_n$$
defined as follows. Let $P, Q \in E[n]$. Let f_P be a function with $\text{div}(f_P) = n(P) - n(\infty)$, i.e., f_P has a zero of order n at P, a pole of order n at ∞, and no other zeros and poles. (The existence of f_P is guaranteed by Theorem 5.1.) Let $R \in E[n]$ such that $R \notin \{\infty, P, -Q, P - Q\}$, and let $D_Q = (Q + R) - (R)$. Note that the choice of R ensures that D_Q and $\text{div}(f_P)$ have disjoint support. Then

$$(5.1) \qquad e(P, Q) = f_P(D_Q)^{(q^k-1)/n} = \left(\frac{f_P(Q+R)}{f_P(R)}\right)^{(q^k-1)/n}.$$

The Tate pairing is well defined, i.e., the value $e(P, Q)$ does not depend on the choice of function f_P and point R. Moreover, it is bilinear and non-degenerate.

5.2. Miller's algorithm. We next describe Miller's algorithm [40] for computing the Tate pairing. The crucial ingredient of the algorithm is a procedure for determining, given $P \in E[n]$, a function f_P with divisor $n(P) - n(\infty)$.

For each $i \geq 1$, let f_i be a function whose divisor is
$$\text{div}(f_i) = i(P) - (iP) - (i-1)(\infty).$$
Note that $f_1 = 1$ and $f_n = f_P$. The following result enables the efficient computation of f_n.

LEMMA 5.2. *Let $P \in E[n]$, and let i and j be positive integers. Let l be the line through iP and jP, and let v be the vertical line through $iP + jP$. Then*

$$(5.2) \qquad f_{i+j} = f_i f_j \frac{l}{v}.$$

PROOF. The divisors of the lines l and v encode the definition of the group law for E (cf. Figure 4). We have

$$\begin{aligned}
\text{div}(f_i f_j \frac{l}{v}) &= \text{div}(f_i) + \text{div}(f_j) + \text{div}(l) - \text{div}(v) \\
&= \{i(P) - (iP) - (i-1)(\infty)\} + \{j(P) - (jP) - (j-1)(\infty)\} \\
&\quad + \{(iP) + (jP) + (-(i+j)P) - 3(\infty)\} \\
&\quad - \{((i+j)P) + (-(i+j)P) - 2(\infty)\} \\
&= (i+j)(P) - ((i+j)P) - (i+j-1)(\infty) \\
&= \text{div}(f_{i+j}).
\end{aligned}$$

Let $n = (n_t, \ldots, n_1, n_0)_2$ be the binary representation of n. The function f_P can be efficiently computed by a left-to-right double-and-add method. Suppose that after the leftmost $t - u$ bits of n have been examined, one has computed f_m where $m = (n_t, n_{t-1}, \ldots, n_{u+1})_2$. One then computes f_{2m} using (5.2) with $i = j = m$. Furthermore, if $n_u = 1$, then one computes f_{2m+1} using (5.2) with $i = 2m$ and $j = 1$. After $t + 1$ iterations, f_P will have been computed.

When evaluating the Tate pairing (5.1), one only needs the values of f_P at the points $Q + R$ and R. Thus, only the values of the intermediate functions f_i at these points are computed. Miller's algorithm for computing $e(P, Q)$ where $P, Q \in E[n]$ is the following.

(1) Let the binary representation of n be $n = (n_t, \ldots, n_1, n_0)_2$.
(2) Select a point $R \in E[n] \setminus \{\infty, P, -Q, P - Q\}$.
(3) Set $f \leftarrow 1, T \leftarrow P$.
(4) For i from t down to 0 do:
   (a) Let l be the tangent line through T, and let v be the vertical line through $2T$.
   (b) $T \leftarrow 2T$.
   (c) $f \leftarrow f^2 \cdot \frac{l(Q+R)}{v(Q+R)} \cdot \frac{v(R)}{l(R)}$.
   (d) If $n_i = 1$ then
      (i) Let l be the line through T and P, and let v be the vertical line through $T + P$.
      (ii) $T \leftarrow T + P$.
      (iii) $f \leftarrow f \cdot \frac{l(Q+R)}{v(Q+R)} \cdot \frac{v(R)}{l(R)}$.
(5) Return($f^{(q^k-1)/n}$).

Miller's algorithm may fail if one of the intermediate lines l or v has a zero at $Q + R$ or R. However, this is not a concern in pairing-based protocols because one generally has $P \in E(\mathbb{F}_q)$ and $Q \notin E(\mathbb{F}_q)$. In this case, the zeros of l and v are all in $\langle P \rangle \subseteq E(\mathbb{F}_q)$ and hence selecting $R \in E[n] \setminus E(\mathbb{F}_q)$ ensures that l and v do not have zeros at $Q + R$ or R.

Miller's algorithm has $O(\log n)$ iterations, each requiring a constant number of arithmetic operations in $\mathbb{F}_{q^k}$. Several improvements have been proposed that significantly reduce the operation count (e.g., see [**7, 26, 8**]), as a result of which pairing-based protocols can now be implemented to meet the performance demands of most applications.

5.3. Bilinear pairings from the Tate pairing. Although the Tate pairing is bilinear, non-degenerate and efficiently computable, it does not satisfy Definition 2.1 since $E[n]$ is not a (cyclic) group of order n. This deficiency can be remedied in two ways.

If E is supersingular and $k > 1$, then one selects a point $P \in E(\mathbb{F}_q)$ of order n and an endomorphism $\Psi : E \to E$ for which $\Psi(P) \notin \langle P \rangle$. Then $\hat{e} : \langle P \rangle \times \langle P \rangle \to \mu_n$ defined by $\hat{e}(Q, R) = e(Q, \Psi(R))$ satisfies $\hat{e}(P, P) \neq 1$ [**25**, Lemma IX.14]. Thus $\hat{e}$ is a bilinear pairing on $(\langle P \rangle, \mu_n)$ in the sense of Definition 2.1. Ψ is called a distortion map.

If E is ordinary and $k > 1$, then no such distortion map exists [**53**]. Instead one selects order-n points $P \in E(\mathbb{F}_q)$ and $Q \notin E(\mathbb{F}_q)$ and defines $\hat{e} : \langle P \rangle \times \langle Q \rangle \to \mu_n$

by $\hat{e}(R,S) = e(R,S)$. This restriction of the Tate pairing is a non-degenerate asymmetric bilinear pairing $\hat{e} : G_1 \times G_2 \to G_T$, where $G_1 = \langle P \rangle$, $G_2 = \langle Q \rangle$, $G_T = \mu_n$ are cyclic groups of order n. The protocols described in §3 can be modified to use these kinds of pairings instead of the symmetric pairings of Definition 2.1.

6. Curve selection

This section describes some of the known methods for generating elliptic curves that are suitable for implementing pairing-based protocols. Recall that E is an elliptic curve defined over $\mathbb{F}_q$, n is a prime divisor of $\#E(\mathbb{F}_q)$ such that $\gcd(n,q) = 1$, and k is the smallest positive integer such $n \mid q^k - 1$. The parameters q, n and k should satisfy the following conditions:

(1) n should be sufficiently large so that Pollard's rho method for computing discrete logarithms in an order-n subgroup of $E(\mathbb{F}_q)$ is infeasible.
(2) k should be sufficiently large so that the index-calculus methods for solving the DLP in $\mathbb{F}_{q^k}$ are infeasible.
(3) k should be small enough so that arithmetic in $\mathbb{F}_{q^k}$ can be efficiently performed.

For example, if an 80-bit security level is desired then one should select $n \approx 2^{160}$ and $q^k \approx 2^{1024}$. For an 128-bit security level, one should select $n \approx 2^{256}$ and $q^k \approx 2^{3072}$. Some other conditions may be imposed on the elliptic curve parameters in order to accelerate the computation of the Tate pairing, e.g., one might require that n have low Hamming weight so that most of the doubling operations (step 4(d)) in Miller's algorithm are eliminated.

As mentioned earlier, one can expect that $k \approx n$ for a randomly selected elliptic curve. Thus one cannot expect to generate suitable elliptic curves by random selection. Two classes of supersingular elliptic curves that are suitable for pairing applications are described in §6.1. In §6.2 we present three methods for generating suitable ordinary curves.

6.1. Supersingular curves.
Recall that the embedding degree k for a supersingular elliptic curve E satisfies $k \in \{1,2,3,4,6\}$. If E is defined over a prime field $\mathbb{F}_q$ with $q > 3$, then $k = 1$ or $k = 2$. All supersingular elliptic curves with $k = 4$ are defined over characteristic two finite fields, while those with $k = 6$ are defined over characteristic three finite fields. The $k = 4$ and $k = 6$ supersingular curves are studied in this section. The next result is useful for determining group orders.

THEOREM 6.1 ([52, §V.2]). *Let E be an elliptic curve defined over $\mathbb{F}_q$, and let $t = q + 1 - \#E(\mathbb{F}_q)$. Let α, β be the complex roots of $T^2 - tT + q \in \mathbb{Z}[T]$. Then $\#E(\mathbb{F}_{q^m}) = q^m + 1 - \alpha^m - \beta^m$ for all $m \geq 1$.*

6.1.1. *Supersingular curves with $k = 4$.* Consider the supersingular elliptic curve
$$E_1 : y^2 + y = x^3 + x + 1$$

defined over $\mathbb{F}_2$. One can check that $\#E_1(\mathbb{F}_2) = 1$. Let $q = 2^m$ and $i = \sqrt{-1}$. Using Theorem 6.1 one can deduce that

$$\#E_1(\mathbb{F}_{2^m}) = 2^m + 1 - (1+i)^m - (1-i)^m \text{ for all } m \geq 1$$

$$= \begin{cases} q + 1 - 2\sqrt{q}, & \text{if } m \equiv 0 \pmod{8}, \\ q + 1 - \sqrt{2q}, & \text{if } m \equiv \pm 1 \pmod{8}, \\ q + 1, & \text{if } m \equiv \pm 2 \pmod{8}, \\ q + 1 + \sqrt{2q}, & \text{if } m \equiv \pm 3 \pmod{8}, \\ q + 1 + 2\sqrt{q}, & \text{if } m \equiv 4 \pmod{8}. \end{cases}$$

Suppose now that m is odd, and let n be a prime divisor of $\#E_1(\mathbb{F}_q) = q+1\pm\sqrt{2q}$. Since

$$q^2 + 1 = (q + 1 - \sqrt{2q})(q + 1 + \sqrt{2q}),$$

we have $n \mid q^2 + 1$ and hence $n \mid q^4 - 1$. Furthermore, since $n \mid q^2 + 1$ and n is odd, we have $n \nmid q^2 - 1$ and hence $n \nmid q - 1$. Also, $n \nmid q^2 + q + 1$ and thus $n \nmid (q^3 - 1) = (q-1)(q^2 + q + 1)$. It follows that the embedding degree of any prime-order subgroup of $E_1(\mathbb{F}_q)$ is $k = 4$.

The map $\Psi : E_1 \to E_1$ defined by

$$\Psi : (x, y) \mapsto (x + s^2, y + sx + t),$$

where $s, t \in \mathbb{F}_{2^{4m}}$, $s^4 = s$, and $t^2 + t = s^6 + s^2$, is a distortion map. Hence, if $P \in E_1(\mathbb{F}_{2^m})$ is a point of order n, then the map $\hat{e} : \langle P \rangle \times \langle P \rangle \to \mu_n$ defined by $\hat{e}(Q, R) = e(Q, \Psi(R))$ is a bilinear pairing that is suitable for implementing the protocols described in §3. Some values of m for which $\#E_1(\mathbb{F}_{2^m})$ is prime are $m = 239, 283, 367$ and 457.

Similarly, one can show that the supersingular elliptic curve

$$E_2 : y^2 + y = x^3 + x$$

defined over $\mathbb{F}_2$ has the property that any prime-order subgroup of $E_2(\mathbb{F}_{2^m})$ with m odd has embedding degree $k = 4$, and the distortion map Ψ can be used to define a bilinear pairing as above.

6.1.2. *Supersingular curves with $k = 6$*. Consider the supersingular elliptic curve

$$E_3 : y^2 = x^3 - x - 1$$

defined over $\mathbb{F}_3$. One can verify using Theorem 6.1 that if $m \equiv \pm 1 \pmod{6}$, then $\#E_3(\mathbb{F}_{3^m}) = 3^m + 1 \pm 3^{(m+1)/2}$. Furthermore, the embedding degree of any prime-order subgroup of $E_3(\mathbb{F}_{3^m})$ is $k = 6$. The map $\Omega : E_3 \to E_3$ defined by

$$\Omega : (x, y) \mapsto (-x + r, iy),$$

where $r, i \in \mathbb{F}_{3^{6m}}$, $i^2 = -1$, and $r^3 - r = -1$, is a distortion map. Some values of m for which $\#E_3(\mathbb{F}_{3^m})$ is prime are $m = 163, 193, 239, 317$ and 353.

Similarly, one can show that the supersingular elliptic curve

$$E_4 : y^2 = x^3 - x + 1$$

defined over $\mathbb{F}_3$ has the property that any prime-order subgroup of $E_4(\mathbb{F}_{3^m})$ with $m \equiv \pm 1 \pmod{6}$ has embedding degree $k = 6$, and Ω (with $r^3 - r = 1$) is a distortion map.

6.2. Ordinary curves. We begin by establishing a condition that the embedding degree must satisfy. Recall that if k is a positive integer and $\omega = e^{2\pi i/k} \in \mathbb{C}$, the kth cyclotomic polynomial is

$$\Phi_k(X) = \prod_{\substack{1 \leq i \leq k \\ \gcd(i,k)=1}} (X - \omega^i) \in \mathbb{Z}[X].$$

The first six cyclotomic polynomials are $\Phi_1(X) = X - 1$, $\Phi_2(X) = X + 1$, $\Phi_3(X) = X^2 + X + 1$, $\Phi_4(X) = X^2 + 1$, $\Phi_5(X) = X^4 + X^3 + X^2 + X + 1$, and $\Phi_6(X) = X^2 - X + 1$. The factorization of $X^k - 1$ into irreducible polynomials over $\mathbb{Z}$ is

$$X^k - 1 = \prod_{d \mid k} \Phi_d(X).$$

LEMMA 6.2. *Let n and q be primes such that $n \mid \Phi_k(q)$ and $n \nmid k$. Then $n \nmid q^d - 1$ for each $1 \leq d \leq k - 1$.*

PROOF. Let $f(X) = X^k - 1$, and let $\mathbb{F}$ be the field of integers modulo n. Since $n \nmid k$, we have $\gcd(f(X), f'(X)) = 1$ in $\mathbb{F}[X]$, and hence $f(X)$ does not have any repeated roots in $\mathbb{F}$. Thus, since q is a root of $\Phi_k(X)$ over $\mathbb{F}$, $\Phi_d(q) \not\equiv 0 \pmod{n}$ for each proper divisor d of k, from which it follows that $n \nmid q^d - 1$ for each proper divisor d of k. Finally, if $d \in [1, k-1]$ is not a divisor of k, then $n \nmid q^d - 1$ because otherwise $n \mid q^e - 1$ where $e = \gcd(d, k)$ is a proper divisor of k. □

6.2.1. *Complex multiplication method.* All known techniques for generating ordinary elliptic curves with low embedding degree use the complex multiplication (CM) method.

Let q be a prime, and let t be a nonzero integer satisfying $|t| < 2\sqrt{q}$. The CM norm equation is

$$(6.1) \qquad t^2 - 4q = -DV^2,$$

where the *discriminant* D is positive and squarefree if t is odd, and $D = 4d$ with d positive and squarefree if t is even. The *complex multiplication method* [4, 43] is an algorithm for finding an elliptic curve E over $\mathbb{F}_q$ with $\#E(\mathbb{F}_q) = N = q + 1 - t$. (More precisely, the elliptic curve E has complex multiplication by an order in the imaginary quadratic number field $\mathbb{Q}(\sqrt{-D})$.) The running time of the CM method is exponential in $\log q$; however it is efficient in practice if D is relatively small (e.g., $D < 10^9$).

If $D = 3$ and N is prime, then the CM method is especially simple. Since $D = 3$, the equation for E takes the form $E_b : y^2 = x^3 + b$. All isomorphic curves are also of this form, and there are precisely 6 isomorphism classes of such curves. Thus E can be very quickly generated by selecting arbitrary $b \in \mathbb{F}_q$ until $E_b(\mathbb{F}_q)$ has a point $P \neq \infty$ that satisfies $NP = \infty$.

6.2.2. *MNT curves.* Miyaji, Nakabayashi and Takano (MNT) [41] were the first to describe a procedure for generating ordinary elliptic curves of low embedding degree. Their method is based on the following result.

THEOREM 6.3 ([41]). *Let $q > 64$ be a prime number. Let E be an ordinary elliptic curve defined over $\mathbb{F}_q$ such that $n = \#E(\mathbb{F}_q)$ is prime, and let $t = q + 1 - n$. Suppose that the embedding degree of $E(\mathbb{F}_q)$ is k.*

(i) *$k = 3$ if and only if $q = 12l^2 - 1$ and $t = -1 \pm 6l$ for some $l \in \mathbb{Z}$.*
(ii) *$k = 4$ if and only if $q = l^2 + l + 1$ and $t \in \{-l, l+1\}$ for some $l \in \mathbb{Z}$.*

(iii) $k = 6$ if and only if $q = 4l^2 + 1$ and $t = 1 \pm 2l$ for some $l \in \mathbb{Z}$.

PROOF. We prove (iii) and leave the proofs of (i) and (ii) as exercises for the reader.

Suppose first that $q = 4l^2 + 1$ and $t = 1 \pm 2l$ for some integer l. Then $n = q + 1 - t = 4l^2 \mp 2l + 1$, and
$$\Phi_6(q) = q^2 - q + 1 = 16l^4 + 4l^2 + 1 = (4l^2 + 2l + 1)(4l^2 - 2l + 1).$$
Thus $n \mid \Phi_6(q)$. Since $q > 64$, it follows from Hasse's theorem that $n > 6$. Hence by Lemma 6.2 we have $k = 6$.

Suppose now that $k = 6$. Let $\Phi_6(q) = q^2 - q + 1 = \lambda n$ where $\lambda \in \mathbb{Z}$. Then
$$q^2 - q + 1 = (q + 1)^2 - t^2 + t^2 - 3q = \lambda(q + 1 - t)$$
and so

(6.2) $$(q + 1 - t)(q + 1 + t - \lambda) = 3q - t^2.$$

Dividing both sides by q yields
$$\left(1 + \frac{1}{q} - \frac{t}{q}\right)(q + 1 + t - \lambda) = 3 - \frac{t^2}{q}.$$

Let $L = 1 + \frac{1}{q} - \frac{t}{q}$. The inequality $|t| < 2\sqrt{q}$ implies that $-1 < 3 - \frac{t^2}{q} < 3$. Hence

(6.3) $$-1 < L(q + 1 + t - \lambda) < 3.$$

Now $L = (q + 1 - t)/q$ and so by Hasse's theorem we have
$$\frac{(\sqrt{q} - 1)^2}{q} < L < \frac{(\sqrt{q} + 1)^2}{q}.$$

Since $q > 64$, we have $\frac{49}{64} < L < \frac{81}{64}$ and it follows from (6.3) that $q + 1 + t - \lambda \in \{-1, 0, 1, 2, 3\}$. If $q + 1 + t - \lambda = 0$, then (6.2) simplifies to $t^2 = 3q$; this is impossible since $q > 3$ is prime. If $q + 1 + t - \lambda \in \{-1, 1, 3\}$, then reducing (6.2) modulo 2 gives $t^2 + t + 1 \equiv 0 \pmod{2}$, which again is impossible. Therefore it must be the case that $q + 1 + t - \lambda = 2$, and (6.2) simplifies to $t^2 - 2t - q + 2 = 0$. The result now follows by solving for t and noting that q is odd. □

We now show how Theorem 6.3 can be used to generate ordinary elliptic curves with embedding degree $k = 6$. (The cases $k = 3$ and $k = 4$ are similar.)

The first algorithm suggested by Theorem 6.3 is to choose integers l of the appropriate size until both $q = 4l^2 + 1$ and $n = q + 1 - t = 4l^2 \mp 2l + 1$ are prime. One then writes $t^2 - 4q = -DV^2$, and uses the CM method to construct the desired elliptic curve. Unfortunately this algorithm will in general not be efficient because one expects that V is small and thus $D \approx q$. (Recall that the CM method is only efficient if D is small.) What is needed is a technique for selecting suitable t and q so that D is guaranteed to be small.

Miyaji, Nakabayashi and Takano [41] observed that the norm equation (6.1) with $t = 1 \pm 2l$ and $q = 4l^2 + 1$ can be written as
$$(6l \pm 1)^2 + 8 = 3DV^2.$$

Letting $U = 6l \pm 1$ yields a quadratic Diophantine equation

(6.4) $$U^2 - 3DV^2 = -8.$$

Suppose that this equation has at least one integer solution. (This implies that -8 should be a quadratic residue modulo 3 and modulo D.) A solution (U, V) to an equation of the form $U^2 - 3DV^2 = c$ is associated with the real number $U + V\sqrt{3D}$. Suppose also that $3 \nmid D$. One first uses continued fractions to find the smallest integer solution (X, Y) with $X > 0$ and $Y > 0$ to the related Pell equation $X^2 - 3DY^2 = 1$; for example see [44, §7.8]. Then any solution (U_0, V_0) of (6.4) yields an infinite class of solutions $\{(U_j, V_j)\}$, $j \in \mathbb{Z}$, where

$$U_j + V_j\sqrt{3D} = (U_0 + V_0\sqrt{3D})(X + Y\sqrt{3D})^j.$$

The so-called fundamental solutions (U_0, V_0) can be used to describe all solutions to equation (6.4); these fundamental solutions can be found using the techniques described in [37, 42].

The MNT curve generation strategy is to repeatedly select small discriminants D and search for a solution (U, V) to (6.4) for which $U \equiv \pm 1 \pmod{6}$ (in which case $l = (U \mp 1)/6$) and $q = 4l^2 + 1$ and $n = 4l^2 \mp 2l + 1$ are primes of the desired size. Then an elliptic curve E with $k = 6$ can be efficiently constructed with the CM method. Luca and Shparlinski [36] (see also [33]) showed that MNT curves are very rare. Nonetheless, it appears that the MNT curve generation method can be successful in practice.

6.2.3. *BN curves.* In 2005, Barreto and Naehrig (BN) [9] discovered the following elegant method for constructing elliptic curves E of prime order n over prime fields $\mathbb{F}_q$ with embedding degree $k = 12$.

Let $t = q + 1 - n$, so $q \equiv t - 1 \pmod{n}$. Since $k = 12$, we have $n \mid \Phi_{12}(q)$, and hence $\Phi_{12}(t - 1) \equiv 0 \pmod{n}$; here $\Phi_{12}(X) = X^4 - X^2 + 1$. Barreto and Naehrig observed that if $t(z) = 6z^2 + 1$, then

$$\Phi_{12}(t(z) - 1) = (36z^4 + 36z^3 + 18z^2 + 6z + 1)(36z^4 - 36z^3 + 18z^2 - 6z + 1).$$

Setting $n(z) = 36z^4 + 36z^3 + 18z^2 + 6z + 1$, we have

$$q(z) = n(z) + t(z) - 1 = 36z^4 + 36z^3 + 24z^2 + 6z + 1$$

and the CM norm equation (6.1) becomes

(6.5) $$t(z)^2 - 4q(z) = -3(1 + 4z + 6z^2)^2.$$

Note that the square-free part of (6.5) is $D = 3$.

A BN curve can be constructed by selecting integers z of the appropriate size until both $q(z)$ and $n(z)$ are prime. Then the CM method with $D = 3$ (see §6.2.1) can be used to generate the desired elliptic curve.

EXAMPLE 6.4. $q(7) = 100003$ and $n(7) = 99709$ are both prime. The elliptic curve $E : y^2 = x^3 + 37$ satisfies $\#E(\mathbb{F}_q) = n$, and $P = (1, 11498)$ is a point of order n. One can check that $n \mid \Phi_{12}(q)$, and so the embedding degree of $E(\mathbb{F}_q)$ is $k = 12$.

6.2.4. *Cocks-Pinch method.* Cocks and Pinch (see §IX.15.2 of [25]) described a method for generating elliptic curves for any embedding degree. In their method, which is based on the following lemma, one first selects an embedding degree k, point order n, and discriminant D (subject to some mild conditions), and subsequently determines a prime q such that the existence of an elliptic curve over $\mathbb{F}_q$ having the chosen values for k, n and D is guaranteed. The desired elliptic curves can then be constructed using the CM method.

LEMMA 6.5. *Let k be a positive integer, and $n \equiv 1 \pmod{k}$ a prime. Let $D > 0$ be a squarefree integer such that $D \equiv 3 \pmod 4$ and $-D$ is a square modulo n. Let g be a primitive kth root of unity modulo n, and let $a = 2^{-1}g \bmod n$ and $t = 2a + 1$. Let $V_0 = \pm(t-2)/\sqrt{-D} \bmod n$, and let $j \geq 0$ be an integer such that $q = (t^2 + D(V_0 + jn)^2)/4$ is prime. (To ensure that q is an integer, j should be even if V_0 is odd, and odd otherwise.) Then there exists an elliptic curve E defined over $\mathbb{F}_q$ satisfying:*

(i) *$n \mid \#E(\mathbb{F}_q)$;*
(ii) *the norm equation is $t^2 - 4q = -D(V_0 + jn)^2$; and*
(iii) *the order-n subgroup of $E(\mathbb{F}_q)$ has embedding degree k.*

PROOF. Let $N = q + 1 - t$. We first note that an elliptic curve E defined over $\mathbb{F}_q$ with $\#E(\mathbb{F}_q) = N$ exists by Hasse's theorem since

$$q \geq \frac{t^2 + DV_0^2}{4} \geq \frac{t^2}{4}.$$

Now, $n \mid \#E(\mathbb{F}_q)$ since

$$\begin{aligned}
4N &= 4(q + 1 - t) = t^2 + D(V_0 + jn)^2 + 4 - 4t \\
&\equiv t^2 + D\frac{(t-2)^2}{-D} + 4 - 4t \equiv 0 \pmod{n}.
\end{aligned}$$

Statement (ii) about the norm equation is immediate. Finally, $t - 1 = 2a \equiv g \pmod n$, whence $\Phi_k(t-1) \equiv 0 \pmod n$. Since $q \equiv t - 1 \pmod n$, it follows that $\Phi_k(q) \equiv 0 \pmod n$ and therefore the embedding degree of the order-n subgroup of $E(\mathbb{F}_q)$ is k. □

By trying different values for n, D and g, one can expect to quickly find an elliptic curve with the desired embedding degree. Note that n can be selected to have low Hamming weight, which accelerates Tate pairing computations. Note also that since $V_0 \approx n$, one expects the bitlength of q to be at least twice that of n.

EXAMPLE 6.6. We select $n = 100003$, $k = 21$, $D = 3$ and $g = 96699$. Then $t = 196703$ and $V_0 = (t-2)/\sqrt{-D} \bmod n = 88367$. For $j = 2$,

$$q = (t^2 + D(V_0 + jn)^2)/4 = 72042257899$$

is prime. The elliptic curve $E : y^2 = x^3 + 6$ has order

$$N = q + 1 - t = 72042061197 = 3 \cdot 439 \cdot 547 \cdot 100003.$$

One can check that $P = (46359640528, 5962208999) \in E(\mathbb{F}_q)$ has order n. Finally, $n \mid \Phi_{21}(q)$, and so the embedding degree of $\langle P \rangle$ is $k = 21$.

7. Concluding remarks

Pairings are being used to design elegant solutions to protocol problems, some of which have been open for many years. Many techniques have been developed for generating suitable elliptic curves; see [23] for a comprehensive survey. The fastest algorithms [6, 31, 35] for computing the Tate pairing (and its variants) on these curves have fast implementations on software [2, 19, 30, 50] and hardware [48] platforms, and are competitive with the exponentiation algorithms that are used in traditional discrete logarithm cryptography. Two areas that deserve further investigation are the practicality of implementing various pairing-based protocols at high security levels (see [34]), and the hardness of the BDHP and related problems.

Researchers are also actively investigating the suitability of hyperelliptic curves and other abelian varieties (see [**49, 6, 28, 27**]). Research in pairing-based cryptography will continue to flourish in the coming years, and especially so if protocols such as identity-based encryption see widespread commercial deployment.

References

1. L. Adleman and M. Huang, "Function field sieve methods for discrete logarithms over finite fields", *Information and Computation*, 151 (1999), 5–16.
2. O. Ahmadi, D. Hankerson and A. Menezes, "Software implementation of arithmetic in $\mathbb{F}_{3^m}$", *International Workshop on Arithmetic of Finite Fields (WAIFI 2007)*, Lecture Notes in Computer Science 4547 (2007), 85–102.
3. ANSI X9.62, *Public Key Cryptography for the Financial Services Industry: The Elliptic Curve Digital Signature Algorithm (ECDSA)*, American National Standards Institute, 1999.
4. A. Atkin and F. Morain, "Elliptic curves and primality proving", *Mathematics of Computation*, 61 (1993), 29–68.
5. R. Balasubramanian and N. Koblitz, "The improbability that an elliptic curve has subexponential discrete log problem under the Menezes-Okamoto-Vanstone algorithm", *Journal of Cryptology*, 11 (1998) 141–145.
6. P. Barreto, S. Galbraith, C. Ó hÉigeartaigh, and M. Scott, "Efficient pairing computation on supersingular abelian varieties", *Designs, Codes and Cryptography*, 42 (2007), 239–271.
7. P. Barreto, H. Kim, B. Lynn and M. Scott, "Efficient algorithms for pairing-based cryptosystems", *Advances in Cryptology – CRYPTO 2002*, Lecture Notes in Computer Science, 2442 (2002), 354–368.
8. P. Barreto, B. Lynn and M. Scott, "Efficient implementation of pairing-based cryptosystems", *Journal of Cryptology*, 17 (2004), 321–334.
9. P. Barreto and M. Naehrig, "Pairing-friendly elliptic curves of prime order", *Selected Areas in Cryptography – SAC 2005*, Lecture Notes in Computer Science, 3897 (2006), 319–331.
10. B. den Boer, "Diffie-Hellman is as strong as discrete log for certain primes", *Advances in Cryptology – CRYPTO '88*, Lecture Notes in Computer Science, 403 (1996), 530–539.
11. A. Boldyreva, "Efficient threshold signatures, multisignatures and blind signatures based on the gap-Diffie-Hellman-group signature scheme", *Public Key Cryptography – PKC 2003*, Lecture Notes in Computer Science, 2567 (2003), 31–46.
12. D. Boneh, X. Boyen and H. Shacham, "Short group signatures", *Advances in Cryptology – CRYPTO 2004*, Lecture Notes in Computer Science, 3152 (2004), 41–55.
13. D. Boneh, G. Di Crescenzo, R. Ostrovsky and G. Persiano, "Public key encryption with keyword search", *Advances in Cryptology – EUROCRYPT 2004*, Lecture Notes in Computer Science, 3027 (2004), 506–522.
14. D. Boneh and M. Franklin, "Identity-based encryption from the Weil pairing", *Advances in Cryptology – CRYPTO 2001*, Lecture Notes in Computer Science, 2139 (2001), 213–229. Full version: *SIAM Journal on Computing*, 32 (2003), 586–615.
15. D. Boneh, C. Gentry, H. Shacham and B. Lynn, "Aggregate and verifiably encrypted signatures from bilinear maps", *Advances in Cryptology – EUROCRYPT 2004*, Lecture Notes in Computer Science, 2656 (2003), 416–432.
16. D. Boneh, B. Lynn and H. Shacham, "Short signatures from the Weil pairing", *Advances in Cryptology – ASIACRYPT 2001*, Lecture Notes in Computer Science, 2248 (2001), 514–532. Full version: *Journal of Cryptology*, 17 (2004), 297–319.
17. D. Boneh and A. Silverberg, "Applications of multilinear forms to cryptography", *Contemporary Mathematics*, 324 (2003), 71–90.
18. D. Coppersmith, "Fast evaluation of logarithms in fields of characteristic two", *IEEE Transactions on Information Theory*, 30 (1984), 587–594.
19. A. Devegili, M. Scott and R. Dahab, "Implementing cryptographic pairings over Barreto-Naehrig curves", *Pairing-Based Cryptography – Pairing 2007*, Lecture Notes in Computer Science 4575 (2007), 197–207.
20. W. Diffie and M. Hellman, "New directions in cryptography", *IEEE Transactions on Information Theory*, 22 (1976), 644–654.
21. T. ElGamal, "A public key cryptosystem and a signature scheme based on discrete logarithms", *IEEE Transactions on Information Theory*, 31 (1985), 469–472.

22. FIPS 186, *Digital Signature Standard (DSS)*, Federal Information Processing Standards Publication 186, National Institute of Standards and Technology, 1994.
23. D. Freeman, M. Scott and E. Teske, "A taxonomy of pairing-friendly elliptic curves", Cryptology ePrint Archive Report 2006/372, 2006. Available from http://eprint.iacr.org/2006/372.
24. G. Frey and H. Rück, "A remark concerning m-divisibility and the discrete logarithm in the divisor class group of curves", *Mathematics of Computation*, 62 (1994), 865–874.
25. S. Galbraith, "Pairings", Ch. IX of I. Blake, G. Seroussi and N. Smart, eds., *Advances in Elliptic Curve Cryptography*, Cambridge University Press, 2005.
26. S. Galbraith, K. Harrison and D. Soldera, "Implementing the Tate pairing", *Algorithmic Number Theory: 5th International Symposium, ANTS-V*, Lecture Notes in Computer Science, 2369 (2002), 324–337.
27. S. Galbraith, F. Hess and F. Vercauteren, "Hyperelliptic pairings", *Pairing-Based Cryptography – Pairing 2007*, Lecture Notes in Computer Science, 4575 (2007), 108–131.
28. S. Galbraith, J. McKee and P. Valença, "Ordinary abelian varieties having small embedding degree" *Finite Fields and Their Applications*, 13 (2007), 800–814.
29. D. Gordon, "Discrete logarithms in $GF(p)$ using the number field sieve", *SIAM Journal on Discrete Mathematics*, 6 (1993), 124–138.
30. D. Hankerson, A. Menezes and M. Scott, "Software implementation of pairings", in *Identity-Based Cryptography*, M. Joye and G. Neven, eds., IOS Press, to appear.
31. F. Hess, N. Smart and F. Vercauteren, "The eta pairing revisited", *IEEE Transactions on Information Theory*, 52 (2006), 4595–4602.
32. A. Joux, "A one round protocol for tripartite Diffie-Hellman", *Algorithmic Number Theory: 4th International Symposium, ANTS-IV*, Lecture Notes in Computer Science, 1838 (2000), 385–393. Full version: *Journal of Cryptology*, 17 (2004), 263–276.
33. K. Karabina and E. Teske, "On prime-order elliptic curves with embedding degrees $k=3$, 4 and 6" *Algorithmic Number Theory: 8th International Symposium, ANTS-VIII*, Lecture Notes in Computer Science, 5011 (2008), 102–117.
34. N. Koblitz and A. Menezes, "Pairing-based cryptography at high security levels", *Proceedings of the Tenth IMA International Conference on Cryptography and Coding*, Lecture Notes in Computer Science, 3796 (2005), 13–36.
35. E. Lee, H.-S. Lee and C.-M. Park, "Efficient and generalized pairing computation on abelian varieties", Cryptology ePrint Archive Report 2008/040, 2008. Available from http://eprint.iacr.org/2008/040.
36. F. Luca and I. Shparlinski, "Elliptic curves with low embedding degree", *Journal of Cryptology*, 19 (2006), 553–562.
37. K. Matthews, "The diophantine equation $x^2 - Dy^2 = N$, $D > 1$, in integers", *Expositiones Mathematicae*, 18 (2000), 323–331.
38. U. Maurer and S. Wolf, "The relationship between breaking the Diffie-Hellman protocol and computing discrete logarithms", *SIAM Journal on Computing*, 28 (1999), 1689–1731.
39. A. Menezes, T. Okamoto and S. Vanstone, "Reducing elliptic curve logarithms to logarithms in a finite field", *IEEE Transactions on Information Theory*, 39 (1993), 1639–1646.
40. V. Miller, "The Weil pairing, and its efficient calculation", *Journal of Cryptology*, 17 (2004), 235–261.
41. A. Miyaji, M. Nakabayashi and S. Takano, "New explicit conditions of elliptic curve traces for FR-reduction", *IEICE – Transactions on Fundamentals of Electronics, Communications and Computer Sciences*, E84-A (2001), 1234–1243.
42. R. Mollin, "Simple continued fraction solutions for diophantine equations", *Expositiones Mathematicae*, 19 (2001), 55–73.
43. F. Morain, "Building cyclic elliptic curves modulo large primes", *Advances in Cryptology – EUROCRYPT '91*, Lecture Notes in Computer Science, 547 (1991), 328–336.
44. I. Niven, H. Zuckerman and H. Montgomery, *An Introduction to the Theory of Numbers*, 5th edition, Wiley, 1991.
45. K. Paterson, "Cryptography from pairings", Ch. X of I. Blake, G. Seroussi and N. Smart, eds., *Advances in Elliptic Curve Cryptography*, Cambridge University Press, 2005.
46. K. Paterson and G. Price, "A comparison between traditional public key infrastructures and identity-based cryptography", *Information Security Technical Report*, 8(3) (2003), 57–72.
47. J. Pollard, "Monte Carlo methods for index computation mod p", *Mathematics of Computation*, 32 (1978), 918–924.

48. R. Ronan, M. Keller, C. Murphy and W. Marnane, "Efficient hardware architectures for identity-based encryption", in *Identity-Based Cryptography*, M. Joye and G. Neven, eds., IOS Press, to appear.
49. K. Rubin and A. Silverberg, "Supersingular abelian varieties in cryptology", *Advances in Cryptology – CRYPTO 2002*, Lecture Notes in Computer Science, 2442 (2002), 336–353.
50. M. Scott, "Implementing cryptographic pairings", *Pairing-Based Cryptography – Pairing 2007*, Lecture Notes in Computer Science, 4575 (2007), 177–196.
51. A. Shamir, "Identity-based cryptosystems and signature schemes", *Advances in Cryptology – Proceedings of CRYPTO 84*, Lecture Notes in Computer Science, 196 (1985), 47–53.
52. J. Silverman, *The Arithmetic of Elliptic Curves*, Springer, 1986.
53. E. Verheul, "Evidence that XTR is more secure than supersingular elliptic curve cryptosystems", *Journal of Cryptology*, 17 (2004) 277–296.

DEPARTMENT OF COMBINATORICS AND OPTIMIZATION, UNIVERSITY OF WATERLOO, WATERLOO, ONTARIO, CANADA N2L 3G1

E-mail address: ajmeneze@uwaterloo.ca

Public-Key Cryptanalysis

Phong Q. Nguyen

ABSTRACT. In 1976, Diffie and Hellman introduced the revolutionary concept of public-key cryptography, also known as asymmetric cryptography. Today, asymmetric cryptography is routinely used to secure the Internet. The most famous and most widely used asymmetric cryptosystem is RSA, invented by Rivest, Shamir and Adleman. Surprisingly, there are very few alternatives known, and most of them are also based on number theory. How secure are those asymmetric cryptosystems? Can we attack them in certain settings? Should we implement RSA the way it was originally described thirty years ago? Those are typical questions that cryptanalysts have tried to answer since the appearance of public-key cryptography. In these notes, we present the main techniques and principles used in public-key cryptanalysis, with a special emphasis on attacks based on lattice basis reduction, and more generally, on algorithmic geometry of numbers. To simplify our exposition, we focus on the two most famous asymmetric cryptosystems: RSA and Elgamal. Cryptanalysis has played a crucial rôle in the way cryptosystems are now implemented, and in the development of modern security notions. Interestingly, it also introduced in cryptology several mathematical objects which have since proved very useful in cryptographic design. This is for instance the case of Euclidean lattices, elliptic curves and pairings.

1. Introduction

Public-key cryptography, also called asymmetric cryptography, was invented by Diffie and Hellman [**DH76**] more than thirty years ago. In public-key cryptography, a user U has a pair of related keys (pk, sk): the key pk is public and should be available to everyone, while the key sk must be kept secret by U. The fact that sk is kept secret by a single entity creates an asymmetry, hence the name *asymmetric cryptography*, to avoid confusion with symmetric cryptography where a secret key is always shared by at least two parties, whose roles are therefore symmetric. The alternative (and perhaps more common) name *public-key cryptography* comes from the very existence of a public key: in conventional cryptography, all keys are secret.

1991 *Mathematics Subject Classification.* Primary 94A60, 11T71; Secondary 11H06, 14G50, 68P25.

Key words and phrases. Cryptanalysis, Security, Public-Key Cryptography, Asymmetric Cryptography, Euclidean Lattices, Geometry of Numbers.

Today, public-key cryptography offers incredibly many features ranging from zero-knowledge to electronic voting (see the handbook [**MOV97**]), but we will restrict to its main goals defined in [**DH76**], which are the following two:

- Asymmetric encryption (also called public-key encryption): anyone can encrypt a message to U, using U's public key pk. But only U should be able to decrypt, using his secret key sk.
- Digital signatures: U can sign any message m, using his secret key sk. Anyone can check whether or not a given signature corresponds to a given message and a given public key.

Such basic functionalities are routinely used to secure the Internet. For instance, digital signatures are prevalent under the form of certificates (which are used everyday by Internet browsers), and asymmetric encryption is used to exchange session keys for fast symmetric encryption, such as in the TLS (Transport Layer Security) protocol.

1.1. Hard problems. Both keys pk and sk are related to each other, but it should be computationally hard to recover the secret key sk from the public key pk, for otherwise there would be no secret key. As a result, public-key cryptography requires the existence of hard computational problems. But is there any provably hard computational problem? This is a very hard question underlying the famous $P \neq NP$ conjecture from complexity theory. Instead of trying to settle this major open question, cryptographers have adopted a more down-to-earth approach by trying various candidates over the years: if a computational problem resists the repeated assaults of the research community, then maybe it should be considered hard, although no proof of its hardness is known or sometimes, even expected. Furthermore, it is perhaps worth noting that the $P \neq NP$ conjecture refers to worst-case hardness, while cryptography typically requires average-case hardness. The (potentially) hard problems currently in consideration within public-key cryptography can be roughly classified into two families.

The first family of hard problems involves problems for which there are very few unknowns, but the size of the unknowns must be rather large to guarantee hardness, which makes the operations rather slow compared to symmetric cryptography. The main members of this family are:

- Integer factorization, popularized by RSA [**RSA78**]. The current factorization record for an RSA number (*i.e.* a product of two large primes) is the following factorization [**BBFK05**] of a 200-digit number (663 bits), obtained with the number field sieve (see the book [**CP01**]):

2799783391	1221327870	8294676387	2260162107	0446786955	4285375600
0992932612	8400107609	3456710529	5536085606	1822351910	9513657886
3710595448	2006576775	0985805576	1357909873	4950144178	8631789462
9518723786	9221823983	=	3532461934	4027701212	7260497819
8464368671	1974001976	2502364930	3468776121	2536794232	0005854795
6528088349	×	7925869954	4783330333	4708584148	0059687737
9758573642	1996073433	0341455767	8728181521	3538140930	4740185467

  A related (and not harder) problem is the so-called e-th root problem, which we will discuss when presenting RSA.
- The discrete logarithm problem in appropriate groups, such as:

- Multiplicative groups of finite fields, especially prime fields, like in the DSA signature algorithm [**Nat94**]. The current record for a discrete logarithm computation in a general prime field is 160 digits [**Kle07**], obtained with the number field sieve.
- Additive groups of elliptic curves over finite fields. There are in fact two kinds of elliptic curves in consideration nowadays:
  * Random elliptic curves for which the best discrete logarithm algorithm is the generic square root algorithm. It is therefore no surprise that the current discrete logarithm record for those curves is 109 bits [**HDdL00**].
  * Special elliptic curves (*e.g.* supersingular curves) for which an efficient pairing is available. On the one hand, this decreases the hardness of the discrete logarithm to the case of finite fields (namely, a low-degree extension of the base field of the curve), which implies bigger sizes for the curves, but on the other hand, it creates exciting cryptographic applications such as identity-based cryptography (see [**Men08**] and the book [**BSS04**]).

Interestingly, these problems would theoretically not resist to large-scale quantum computers (as was famously shown by Shor [**Sho99**]), but the feasibility of such devices is still open.

The second family of hard problems involves problems for which there are many small unknowns, but this number of small unknowns must be rather large to guarantee hardness. Such problems are usually related to NP-hard combinatorial problems for which no efficient quantum algorithm is known. The main examples of this family are:

- Knapsacks and lattice problems. In the knapsack problem, the unknowns are bits. The Merkle-Hellman cryptosystem [**MH78**], an early alternative to RSA, was based on the knapsack (or subset sum) problem. Although knapsack cryptosystems have not been very successful (see the survey [**Odl90**]) due to lattice attacks, they have in some sense enjoyed a second coming under the disguise of lattice-based cryptosystems (see the survey [**NS01**]). Of particular interest is the very efficient NTRU cryptosystem [**HPS98**], which offers much smaller keys than other lattice-based or knapsack-based schemes. Knapsacks and lattice problems are tightly connected.
- Coding problems. The McEliece cryptosystem [**McE78**] is a natural cryptosystem based on the hardness of decoding, which has several variants depending on the type of code used. The lattice-based Goldreich-Goldwasser-Halevi cryptosystem [**GGH97, Ngu99**] can be viewed as a lattice-based analogue of the McEliece cryptosystem.
- Systems of multivariate polynomial equations over small finite fields. The Matsumoto-Imai cryptosystem [**MI88**] is the ancestor of what is now known as multivariate cryptography (see the book [**Kob98**]). In order to prevent general attacks based on Gröbner bases, the security parameter must be rather large. All constructions known use a system of equations with a very particular structure, which they try to hide. Like knapsack cryptography, many multivariate schemes have been broken due to their

exceptional structure. The latest example is the spectacular cryptanalysis [**DFSS07**] of the SFLASH signature scheme.

The main drawback with this second family of problems is the overall size of the parameters. Indeed, apart from NTRU [**HPS98**], the size of the parameters for such problems grows at least quadratically with the security parameter. NTRU offers a smaller keysize than the other members of this family because it uses a compact representation, which saves an order of magnitude.

1.2. Cryptanalysis. Roughly speaking, cryptanalysis is the science of codebreaking. We emphasized earlier that asymmetric cryptography required hard computational problems: if there is no hard problem, there cannot be any asymmetric cryptography either. If any of the computational problems mentioned above turns out to be easy to solve, then the corresponding cryptosystems can be broken, as the public key would actually disclose the secret key. This means that one obvious way to cryptanalyze is to solve the underlying algorithmic problems, such as integer factorization, discrete logarithm, lattice reduction, Gröbner bases, *etc*. Here, we mean a study of the computational problem in its full generality.

Alternatively, one may try to exploit the special properties of the cryptographic instances of the computational problem. This is especially true for the second family of hard problems: even though the underlying general problem is NP-hard, its cryptographic instances may be much easier, because the cryptographic functionalities typically require an unusual structure. In particular, this means that maybe there could be an attack which can only be used to break the scheme, but not to solve the underlying problem in general. This happened many times in knapsack cryptography and multivariate cryptography. Interestingly, generic tools to solve the general problem perform sometimes even much better on cryptographic instances (see [**FJ03**] for Gröbner bases and [**GN08b, NS01**] for lattice reduction).

However, if the underlying computational problem turns out to be really hard both in general and for instances of cryptographic interest, this will not necessarily imply that the cryptosystem is secure. First of all, it is not even clear what is meant exactly by the term *secure* or *insecure*. Should an encryption scheme which leaks the first bit of the plaintext be considered secure? Is the secret key really necessary to decrypt ciphertexts or to sign messages? If a cryptosystem is theoretically secure, could there be potential security flaws for its implementation? For instance, if some of the temporary variables (such as pseudo-random numbers) used during the cryptographic operations are partially leaked, could it have an impact on the security of the cryptosystem? This means that there is much more to cryptanalysis than just trying to solve the main algorithmic problems. In particular, cryptanalysts are interested in defining and studying realistic environments for attacks (adaptive chosen-ciphertext attacks, side-channel attacks, *etc*.), as well as the goals of attacks (key recovery, partial information, existential forgery, distinguishability, *etc*.). This is very much related to the development of *provable security*, a very popular field of cryptography. Overall, cryptanalysis usually relies on three types of failures:

> **Algorithmic failures:** The underlying hard problem is not as hard as expected. This could be due to the computational problem itself, or to special properties of cryptographic instances.
> **Design failures:** Breaking the cryptosystem is not as hard as solving the underlying hard problem.

Implementation failures: Exploiting additional information due to implementation mistakes or side-channel attacks. This is particularly relevant to the world of smartcards, and is not well covered by provable security.

Thirty years after the introduction of public-key cryptography, we have a much better understanding of what security means, thanks to the advances of public-key cryptanalysis. It is perhaps worth noting that cryptanalysis also proved to be a good incentive for the introduction of new techniques in cryptology. Indeed several mathematical objects now invaluable in cryptographic design were first introduced in cryptology as cryptanalytic tools, including:

- Euclidean lattices, whose first cryptologic use was the cryptanalysis [**Adl83, Sha82**] of the Merkle-Hellman cryptosystem [**MH78**]. Besides cryptanalysis, they are now used in lattice-based cryptosystems (see the survey [**NS01**]), as well as in a few security proofs [**Sho01, FOPS01, CNS02**].
- Elliptic curves. One might argue that the first cryptologic usage of elliptic curves was Lenstra's ECM factoring algorithm [**Len87**], before the proposal of cryptography based on elliptic curves [**Kob87, Mil87**]: both articles [**Kob87, Mil87**] mention a draft of [**Len87**] in their introduction.
- Pairings, whose first cryptologic use was cryptanalytic [**MOV93**], to prove that the discrete logarithm problem in certain elliptic curves could be reduced efficiently to the discrete logarithm problem in finite fields. See [**Men08**] and the book [**BSS04**] for positive applications of pairings.

1.3. Road Map. In these notes, we intend to survey the main principles and the main techniques used in public-key cryptanalysis. As a result, we will focus on the two most famous (and perhaps simplest) asymmetric cryptosystems: RSA [**RSA78**] and Elgamal in prime fields [**El 85**], which we will recall in Section 2. Unfortunately, this means that we will ignore the rich cryptanalytic literature related to the second family of hard problems mentioned in Section 1.1, as well as that of elliptic-curve cryptography. Another important topic of cryptanalysis which we will not cover is side-channel cryptanalysis (as popularized by [**Koc96, BDL97**]).

In Section 3, we review the main security notions, which we will illustrate by simple attacks in Section 4. In Section 5, we present a class of rather elementary attacks known as square-root attacks. In Section 6, we introduce the theory of lattices, both from a mathematical and a computational point of view, which is arguably the most popular technique in public-key cryptanalysis. This will be needed for Section 7 where we present the vast class of lattice attacks.

2. Textbooks Cryptosystems

In order to explain what is public-key cryptanalysis, it would be very helpful to give examples of attacks. Although plenty of interesting cryptanalyses have been published in the research literature (see the collections of proceedings [**MZ98, IAC04**]), many require a good understanding of the underlying cryptosystem, which may not be very well-known and may be based on unusual techniques. To simplify our exposition, we only present attacks on the two most famous cryptosystems: RSA [**RSA78**] and Elgamal over prime fields [**El 85**]. Both cryptosystems have the additional advantage of being very easy to describe. We refer to these cryptosystems as textbook cryptosystems, because we will consider the original description of those schemes, the one that can be found in most cryptography textbooks, but not the one which is actually implemented in practice nowadays. Cryptanalysis has played a crucial role in the way cryptosystems are now implemented. We now recall briefly how RSA and Elgamal work.

2.1. RSA. The RSA cryptosystem [**RSA78**] is the most widely used asymmetric cryptosystem. It is based on the hardness of factoring large integers.

2.1.1. *Key generation.* The user selects two large primes p and q (of the same bit-length) uniformly at random, so that $N = pq$ is believed to be hard to factor. As previously mentioned, the factoring record for such numbers is currently a 663-bit N. In electronic commerce, the root certificates used by Internet browsers typically use a N of either 1024 or 2048 bits.

Next, the user selects a pair of integers (e, d) such that:

$$(2.1) \qquad ed \equiv 1 \pmod{\phi(N)},$$

where $\phi(N) = (p-1)(q-1)$ is Euler's function: $\phi(N)$ is the number of integers in $\{1, \ldots, N-1\}$ which are coprime with N. The integers e and d are called the RSA exponents: e is the public exponent, while d is the secret exponent. The RSA public key is the pair (N, e), and the RSA secret key is d. The primes p and q do not need to be kept.

There are essentially three ways to select the RSA exponents:

Random exponents: The user selects an integer $d \in \{2, \ldots, \phi(N) - 1\}$ uniformly at random among those which are coprime with $\phi(N)$. The public exponent e is chosen as the inverse of d modulo $\phi(N)$.

Low Public Exponent: To speed up public exponentiation, the user selects a very small e, possibly with low Hamming weight. If e is not invertible modulo $\phi(N)$, then the user selects a new pair (p, q) of primes, otherwise, the secret exponent d is chosen as the inverse of e modulo $\phi(N)$. The most popular choices are $e = 3$ and $e = 2^{16} + 1 = 65537$. Note that e must be odd to have a chance of being invertible modulo $\phi(N)$.

Short Secret Exponent: To speed up private exponentiation, the user selects this time a short d, with a sufficiently long bit-length so that it cannot be exhaustively searched. If d is not invertible modulo $\phi(N)$, a new d is picked. Otherwise, the public exponent e is chosen as the inverse of d modulo $\phi(N)$. This choice of d is however not recommended: it is known that it is provably insecure [**Wie90**] if $d \leq N^{1/4}$, and it is heuristically insecure [**BD99**] if $d \leq N^{1-1/\sqrt{2}} \approx N^{0.292\cdots}$. In such attacks (which we will describe in later sections), one may recover the factorization of N, given only the public key (N, e).

If one knows the factorization of N, then one can obviously derive the secret exponent d from the public exponent e. In fact, it is well-known that the knowledge of the secret exponent d is equivalent to factoring N. More precisely, it was noticed as early as in [**RSA78**] that if one knows the secret key d, then one can recover the factorization of N in probabilistic polynomial time. It was recently proved in [**CM04**] that this can actually be done in deterministic polynomial time. Hence, recovering the RSA secret key is as hard as factoring the RSA public modulus, but this does not necessarily mean that breaking RSA is as hard as factoring.

2.1.2. *Trapdoor permutation.* We denote by $\mathbb{Z}_N$ the ring $\mathbb{Z}/N\mathbb{Z}$, which we represent by $\{0, 1, \ldots, N-1\}$. The main property of the RSA key generation is the congruence (2.1) which implies, thanks to Fermat's little theorem and the Chinese remainder theorem, that the modular exponentiation function $x \mapsto x^e$ is a permutation over $\mathbb{Z}_N$. This function is called the RSA permutation. It is well-known that its inverse is the modular exponentiation function $x \mapsto x^d$, hence the name *trapdoor permutation*: if one knows the trapdoor d, one can efficiently invert the RSA permutation. Without the trapdoor, the inversion problem is believed to be hard, and is known as the e-th root problem (also called the RSA problem): given an integer $y \in \mathbb{Z}_N$ chosen uniformly at random, find $x \in \mathbb{Z}_N$ such that $y \equiv x^e \mod N$. The RSA assumption states that no probabilistic polynomial-time algorithm can solve the RSA problem with non-negligible probability.

It is however unknown if the knowledge of d is necessary to solve the e-th root problem. Maybe there could be an alternative way to invert the RSA permutation, other than raising to the power d. In fact, the work [**BV98**] suggests that the e-th root problem with a small e might actually be easier than factoring.

An important property of the RSA permutation is its multiplicativity. More precisely, for all x and y in $\mathbb{Z}_N$:

$$(2.2) \qquad (xy)^e \equiv x^e y^e \pmod{N}.$$

This homomorphic property will be very useful for certain attacks.

2.1.3. *Asymmetric encryption.* Textbook-RSA encryption is a simple application of the RSA trapdoor permutation, in which encryption is achieved by applying the RSA permutation. More precisely, the set of messages is $\mathbb{Z}_N = \{0, 1, \ldots N-1\}$. To encrypt a message m, one simply raises it to the power e modulo N, which means that the ciphertext is:

$$(2.3) \qquad c = m^e \bmod N.$$

To decrypt the ciphertext c, one simply inverts the RSA permutation:

$$(2.4) \qquad m = c^d \bmod N.$$

This is the way the RSA public-key encryption scheme was originally described in [**RSA78**], and is still described in many textbooks, but this is not the way RSA is now implemented in various products or standards due to security problems, even though the basic principle remains the same. It is now widely accepted that a trapdoor permutation should not be directly used as a public-key encryption scheme: a preprocessing of the messages is required, *e.g.* OAEP (optimal asymmetric encryption) [**BR95, Poi05**]. The attacks we will present in these notes explain why.

It is worth noting that Textbook-RSA encryption is multiplicative like the RSA permutation. If m_1 are m_2 are two messages in $\mathbb{Z}_N$ encrypted as c_1 and c_2 using (2.3), then their product $m_3 = (m_1 m_2) \bmod N$ is encrypted as $c_3 = (c_1 c_2) \bmod N$. In other words, the ciphertext of a product is the product of the ciphertexts.

2.1.4. *Digital signature.* The magical property of RSA is its trapdoor permutation: most public-key cryptosystems known involve a trapdoor one-way function instead (see [**MOV97**]). Fortunately, it is very easy to derive a digital signature scheme from a trapdoor permutation.

In the original description [**RSA78**], the set of messages to sign is $\mathbb{Z}_N = \{0, 1, \ldots, N-1\}$. The signature of a message $m \in \mathbb{Z}_N$ is simply its preimage through the RSA permutation:

$$s = m^d \bmod N. \tag{2.5}$$

To verify that s is the signature of m with the public key (N, e), one checks that $s \in \mathbb{Z}_N$ and that the following congruence holds:

$$m \equiv s^e \pmod{N}. \tag{2.6}$$

Similarly to the asymmetric encryption case, this is not the way RSA signatures are now implemented in various products or standards due to security problems, even though the basic principle remains the same. Again, we will present attacks which explain why. A trapdoor permutation should not be directly used as a digital signature scheme: a hashing-based preprocessing of the messages is required, *e.g.* FDH (full-domain hash) [**BR96, Poi05**] or PSS (probabilistic signature scheme) [**BR96, Poi05**].

It is worth noting that the preprocessing now in use in asymmetric encryption or digital signatures involves a cryptographic hash function. However, when [**RSA78**] was published, no cryptographic hash function was available! This is why many *ad hoc* solutions were developed (and sometimes deployed) in the eighties, with various degrees of success. We will describe attacks on some of those. The RSA standards [**Lab**] currently advocated by the RSA Security company are: RSA-OAEP for asymmetric encryption and RSA-PSS for signatures.

2.2. Elgamal. While there is essentially only one RSA cryptosystem, there is much more flexibility with the Elgamal cryptosystem [**El 85**] based on the hardness of the discrete logarithm problem: it has many variants depending on the group or subgroup used, as well as the encoding of messages and ciphertexts. Here, we only consider the so-called Textbook Elgamal, that is, the basic Elgamal cryptosystem over a prime field $\mathbb{Z}_p$, as originally described in [**El 85**]. Another significant difference with RSA is the gap between the Elgamal asymmetric encryption scheme and the Elgamal digital signature scheme. In RSA, asymmetric encryption and signatures are the two facets of the RSA trapdoor permutation. Because the Elgamal asymmetric encryption scheme involves a trapdoor one-way function based on the Diffie-Hellman key exchange [**DH76**], rather than a trapdoor permutation, it does not naturally lead to an efficient digital signature scheme. The Elgamal signature scheme is quite different from its asymmetric encryption counterpart: it is the ancestor of most discrete-log based signature schemes, such as DSA, ECDSA or Schnorr's signature (see [**MOV97**]).

2.2.1. *Key generation.* The user selects a large random prime p, in such a way that $p-1$ has at least one large prime factor and has known factorization. It is then believed that the discrete logarithm problem in $\mathbb{Z}_p^\times$ is hard. Thanks to the factorization of $p-1$, the user can compute a generator g of the multiplicative group $\mathbb{Z}_p^\times$. There are essentially two ways to select the generator g:

Random generators: This is the recommended option: the generator g is selected uniformly at random among all generators of $\mathbb{Z}_p^\times$.
Small generators: One tries small values for g, such as $g = 2$, to speed up exponentiation with base g. If none works, one picks another prime p.

We will later see that the choice $g = 2$ has dramatic consequences on the security of the Elgamal signature scheme [**Ble96**].

The parameters g and p are public. They can be considered as central parameters, since they can be shared among several users, but if that is the case, it is important that all users are convinced that the parameters have been generated in a random way so that they have no special property.

The user's secret key is an integer x chosen uniformly at random over $\mathbb{Z}_{p-1} = \{0, 1, \ldots, p-2\}$. The corresponding public key is the integer $y \in \mathbb{Z}_p^\times$ defined as:

(2.7) $$y = g^x \pmod{p}.$$

Many variants of Elgamal alternatively use a prime order subgroup, rather than the whole group $\mathbb{Z}_p^\times$. More precisely, they select an element $g \in \mathbb{Z}_p^\times$ of large prime order $q \ll p$: the secret key x is then chosen in $\mathbb{Z}_q$.

2.2.2. *Asymmetric encryption.* The Elgamal asymmetric encryption scheme can be viewed as an application of the Diffie-Hellman key exchange protocol [**DH76**]. In the well-known basic Diffie-Hellman protocol, Alice and Bob do the following to establish a shared secret key:

- Alice selects an integer $a \in \mathbb{Z}_{p-1}$ uniformly at random, and sends $A = g^a$ mod p to Bob.
- Bob selects an integer $b \in \mathbb{Z}_{p-1}$ uniformly at random, and sends $B = g^b$ mod p to Alice.
- The secret key shared by Alice and Bob is $s = g^{ab} \mod p$. Alice may compute s as $s = B^a \mod p$, while Bob may alternatively compute s as $s = A^b \mod p$.

To transform this key exchange protocol into a probabilistic asymmetric encryption scheme, let us view Alice as the user who possesses the pair of keys (x, y) defined in (2.7), so that $(a, A) = (x, y)$, and let us view Bob as the person who wishes to encrypt messages to the user. Bob knows the public key $y = g^x \mod p$. The set of plaintexts is $\mathbb{Z}_p$. To encrypt a message $m \in \mathbb{Z}_p$:

- Bob selects an integer $k \in \mathbb{Z}_{p-1}$ uniformly at random.
- The ciphertext is the pair $(c, d) \in \mathbb{Z}_p^\times \times \mathbb{Z}_p$ defined as

(2.8) $$c = g^k \pmod{p}$$
(2.9) $$d = my^k \pmod{p}$$

To see how decryption works, notice that thanks to the Diffie-Hellman trick, Alice may compute the (virtual) secret $s = g^{xk} = y^k \mod p$ from her secret key x and the first half c of the ciphertext. This is because $s = c^x \mod p$, as if Bob's pair (b, B) in the Diffie-Hellman protocol was (k, c). Once $y^k \mod p$ is known, Alice may recover the message m from the second half d of the ciphertext, by division.

In other words, the first half (2.8) of the ciphertext sets up a one-time Diffie-Hellman secret key $y^k = g^{kx}$. The second half (2.9) of the ciphertext can be viewed as a one-time pad (using modular multiplication rather than a xor) between the the message and the one-time key. Decryption works by recovering this one-time key using the user's secret key, thanks to the Diffie-Hellman trick.

Since Elgamal encryption [**El 85**] is very much related to the Diffie-Hellman key exchange [**DH76**], one may wonder why it did not already appear in [**DH76**]. Perhaps one explanation is that, strictly speaking, public-key encryption as defined in [**DH76**] was associated to a trapdoor permutation, so that it would be easy to derive both encryption and signature: it was assumed implicitly that the set of ciphertexts had to be identical to the set of plaintexts. But Elgamal encryption does not use nor define a trapdoor permutation. The closest thing to a permutation in Elgamal encryption is the following bijection between $\mathbb{Z}_p \times \mathbb{Z}_{p-1}$ and $\mathbb{Z}_p^\times \times \mathbb{Z}_p$:

$$(m, k) \mapsto (c, d) = (g^k, my^k).$$

But the secret key x only helps to partially invert this bijection: given an image (c, d), one knows how to efficiently recover the corresponding m, but not the second half k, which is a discrete logarithm problem. Thus, it cannot be considered as a trapdoor permutation. In some sense, it could be viewed as a partial trapdoor permutation.

We saw two significant differences between Textbook-Elgamal encryption and Textbook-RSA encryption: Elgamal is probabilistic rather than deterministic, and it is not based on a trapdoor permutation. Nevertheless, there is one noticeable thing in common: Elgamal is multiplicative too. Indeed, assume that two plaintexts m_1 and m_2 are encrypted into (c_1, d_1) and (c_2, d_2) (following (2.8) and (2.9)) using respectively the one-time keys k_1 and k_2. In a natural way, one could define the product of ciphertexts as (c_3, d_3) where:

$$c_3 = c_1 c_2 \in \mathbb{Z}_p^\times$$
$$d_3 = d_1 d_2 \in \mathbb{Z}_p$$

Then it can be easily checked that $(c_3, d_3) \in \mathbb{Z}_p^\times \times \mathbb{Z}_p$ would be decrypted as $m_3 = (m_1 m_2) \bmod p$ because it is the ciphertext of m_3 with the one-time key $k_3 = (k_1 + k_2) \bmod p$. Thus, in Textbook-Elgamal as well as Textbook-RSA, the product of ciphertexts is a ciphertext of the product.

2.2.3. *Digital signature.* Surprisingly, the Elgamal signature scheme [**El 85**] has nothing to do with the Elgamal asymmetric encryption scheme [**El 85**]. The only thing in common is the key generation process and the fact that the scheme is probabilistic.

The set of messages is $\mathbb{Z}_p$. To sign a message $m \in \mathbb{Z}_p$:

- The user selects uniformly at random a one-time key $k \in \mathbb{Z}_{p-1}^\times$, that is an integer in $\{0, \ldots, p-2\}$ coprime with $p-1$.
- The signature of m is the pair $(a, b) \in \mathbb{Z}_p^\times \times \mathbb{Z}_{p-1}$ defined as:

(2.10) $$a = g^k \pmod{p}$$
(2.11) $$b = (m - ax)k^{-1} \pmod{p-1}.$$

To verify a given signature (a, b) of a given message m, one checks that $(a, b) \in \mathbb{Z}_p^\times \times \mathbb{Z}_{p-1}$ and that the following congruence holds:

(2.12) $$g^m \equiv y^a a^b \pmod{p}$$

The previous congruence can be equivalently rewritten as:

(2.13) $$m \equiv ax + b \log a \pmod{p-1},$$

where log denotes the discrete log in $\mathbb{Z}_p^\times$ with respect to the base g. This rewriting will prove particularly useful when presenting attacks. Note that if the pair (a, b) has been generated according to (2.10) and (2.11), then $k = \log a$, so that (2.13) follows easily from (2.11).

3. Security Notions

Perhaps one of the biggest achievements of public-key cryptography is the introduction of rigorous and meaningful security notions for both encryption and signatures. Rigorous, because these notions can be formally defined using the language of complexity theory. Meaningful, because the relatively young history of public-key cryptography seems to indicate that they indeed capture the "right" notion of security, as various attacks have shown that (even slightly) weaker notions of security would be insufficient. However, it should be noted that security notions do not take into account implementation issues: in particular, side-channel attacks are not currently covered by provable security.

Since our focus is on cryptanalysis, rather than provable security, we will not properly define all the security notions: we will content ourselves with informal definitions, to convey intuitions more easily, and to keep our presentation light. We refer the interested reader to the lecture notes [**Poi05**] for a more technical treatment.

We would like to insist on the following point. Some of the security notions widely accepted today may look a bit artificial and perhaps too demanding at first sight. In fact, it could be argued that it is the discovery of certain realistic attacks which have convinced the community of the importance of such strong notions of security. In other words, public-key cryptanalysis has helped to find the right notion of security, but it has also helped in the acceptance of strong security notions. For instance, it is arguably Bleichenbacher's practical attack [**Ble98**] which triggered the switch to OAEP for RSA encryption in the PKCS standards [**Lab**], even though chosen-ciphertext attacks on RSA had appeared long before.

Roughly speaking, it is now customary to define security notions using games (see the survey [**Sho04**]): a cryptographic scheme is said to be secure with respect to a certain security notion if a specific game between a challenger and an attacker cannot be won by the attacker with non-negligible probability, where the attacker is modeled as a probabilistic polynomial-time Turing machine with possibly access to oracles: the security notion defines exacly which oracles the attacker has access to. Informally, a security notion consists of two definitions:

- The goal of the attacker. This defines the rules of the game: what is the purpose of the attacker (that is, when is the game won or lost), and how the game is run.
- The means of the attacker. This is where the access to oracles is defined. For instance, in chosen-ciphertext security, the attacker has access to a decryption oracle, which may decrypt any ciphertext apart from the challenge ciphertext.

The oracles may also depend on the security model. For instance, in the well-known random oracle model, a hash function is modeled as an oracle which behaves like a random function.

3.1. Digital Signatures. We start with digital signatures because the "right" security notion is fairly natural here. Of all the possible goals of the attacker, the most important are the following ones:

    Key recovery: The attacker wants to recover the secret key sk of the signer.
    Universal forgery: the attacker wants to be able to sign any message. This is also called a *selective forgery*.

Existential forgery: The attacker wants to exhibit a new signature. By a new signature, one usually means a signature of a new message, but it may also mean a new signature of a message for which a signature was already known, which is meaningful for a probabilistic signature.

Attacks on signature schemes are also classified based on the means available to the attacker:

No-message attacks: the attacker only knows the public key pk of the signer.

Known-message attacks: the attacker knows a list of valid random pairs (message,signature).

Chosen-message attacks: the attacker may ask for signatures of messages of his/her choice. If the requests are not independent, the chosen-message attack is said to be *adaptive*. Of course, depending on the goal of the attacker, there is a natural restriction over the requests allowed: for instance, in a universal forgery, the attacker cannot ask for the signature of the challenge message he has to sign.

We will see that the original description of the main signature schemes only satisfy very weak notions of security. To achieve the strongest notions of security under appropriate assumptions, a preprocessing of the message is required, using hash functions, but it is not mandatory to have a probabilistic signature scheme, which is a noteworthy difference with the situation of asymmetric encryption.

3.2. Asymmetric Encryption. It took cryptographers significantly longer to define the strongest security notions for asymmetric encryption than for digital signatures, which is a sign that things are arguably more complex with encryption. Of all the possible goals of the attacker, the most important are the following ones:

Key recovery: The attacker wants to recover the secret key sk of the user.

Decryption: the attacker wants to be able to decrypt any ciphertext. The encryption scheme is said to be *one-way* if no efficient attacker is able to decrypt a random ciphertext with non-negligible probability. By a random ciphertext, we mean the ciphertext of a plaintext chosen uniformly at random over the plaintext space.

Malleability: Given a list of ciphertexts, the attacker wants to build a new ciphertext whose plaintext is related to the plaintexts of the input ciphertexts.

Distinguisher: The attacker wants to output two distinct messages m_0 and m_1 such that if a challenger encrypts either m_0 or m_1 into c, the attacker would be able to tell which message was encrypted, just by looking at the challenge ciphertext c.

Clearly, if the encryption scheme is deterministic, there is always a trivial distinguisher: one could select any pair of distinct messages m_0 and m_1, and by encrypting both m_0 and m_1, one could tell which one corresponds to the challenge ciphertext. This implies that probabilistic encryption is necessary to satisfy strong security notions.

Attacks on encryption schemes are also classified based on the means available to the attacker:

Chosen-plaintext attacks: the attacker only knows the public key pk of the user, which implies that he may encrypt any plaintext of his choice.

Valid-ciphertext attacks: the attacker can check whether a given ciphertext is valid, that is, that there exists a plaintext which may be encrypted into such a ciphertext. This makes sense when the set of ciphertexts is bigger than the set of plaintexts.

Plaintext-checking attacks: the attacker can check whether a given ciphertext would be decrypted as a given plaintext.

Chosen-ciphertext attacks: the attacker may ask for decryption of ciphertexts of its choice: if the ciphertext is not valid, the attacker will know. If the requests are not independent, the chosen-message attack is said to be *adaptive*. Of course, depending on the goal of the attacker, there is a natural restriction over the requests allowed: for instance, in a chosen-ciphertext distinguisher, the attacker cannot ask for the decryption of the challenge ciphertext.

4. Elementary Attacks

The goal of this section is to illustrate the security notions described in Section 3 by presenting very simple attacks on textbook cryptosystems.

4.1. Digital Signatures. We first start with elementary attacks on textbook digital signatures.

4.1.1. *Textbook-RSA.* We first consider Textbook-RSA. Like any trapdoor permutation used directly as a signature scheme, Textbook-RSA is vulnerable to a no-message existential forgery. Indeed, anyone can select uniformly at random a number $s \in \mathbb{Z}_N$, and compute:

$$(4.1) \qquad m = s^e \bmod N.$$

Then s is a valid signature of the message $m \in \mathbb{Z}_N$. But this existential forgery is far from being a universal forgery, since there is very limited freedom over the choice of m.

However, in the particular case of Textbook-RSA, it is easy to obtain an adaptive chosen-message universal forgery, thanks to the multiplicativity of the RSA permutation. Indeed, assume that we would like to sign a message $m \in \mathbb{Z}_N$. Select $m_1 \in \mathbb{Z}_N$ uniformly at random. If m_1 is not invertible mod N (which is unlikely), then we have found a non-trivial factor of N, which allows us to sign m. Otherwise, we may compute:

$$m_2 = m m_1^{-1} \pmod{N}.$$

We ask the oracle the signatures s_1 and s_2 of respectively m_1 and m_2. Then it is clear by multiplicativity that $s = (s_1 s_2) \bmod N$ is a valid signature of m.

A well-known countermeasure to avoid the previous attacks is to hash the message before signing it, that is, we assume the existence of a cryptographic hash function h from $\{0,1\}^*$ to $\mathbb{Z}_N$. Instead of signing a message $m \in \mathbb{Z}_N$, we sign an arbitrary binary message $m \in \{0,1\}^*$ and replace m by $h(m)$ in both the signing process (2.5) and the verification process (2.6). The resulting RSA signature scheme is known as FDH-RSA for full-domain hash RSA [**BR96**], and it is provably secure in the random oracle model (roughly speaking, this assumes that the hash function is perfect: behaving like a random function), under the RSA assumption. To make sure that the hash function does not create obvious security failures, the hash function is required to be at least *collision-free*, that is, it should be "computationally hard" to output two distinct messages m_0 and m_1 such that $h(m_0) = h(m_1)$.

In the case of Textbook-RSA, the use of a hash function prevented elementary forgeries and even provided a security proof in the random oracle model, but hash functions do not necessarily solve all the security problems by magic, as we will now see with Textbook-Elgamal.

4.1.2. *Textbook-Elgamal.* First, let us see an elementary existential forgery on Textbook-Elgamal. To forge a signature, it suffices to find a triplet $(m, a, b) \in \mathbb{Z}_p \times \mathbb{Z}_p^\times \times \mathbb{Z}_{p-1}$ satisfying (2.13):

$$m \equiv ax + b\log a \pmod{p-1}.$$

Given an arbitrary m, the signer finds a valid pair (a, b) because he/she selects an a for which he/she already knows $\log a$ (this logarithm is the one-time key k) and makes sure it is invertible modulo $p - 1$. Then because the signer knows the secret exponent x, he/she can solve (2.13) for b. But the attacker does not know the secret exponent x in (2.13), so he/she cannot do the same. One way to solve that problem would be to select a in such a way that ax cancels out with $b \log a$. For instance, if we select an a of the form:

$$a = g^B y^C \pmod{p},$$

where B and C are integers, then

$$ax + b\log a \equiv x(a + bC) + bB \pmod{p-1}.$$

So if we select a C coprime with $p - 1$, we can choose b such that:

$$a + bC \equiv 0 \pmod{p-1}.$$

Finally, we select the message m as:

$$m \equiv bB \pmod{p-1}.$$

Our choice of (m, a, b) then satisfies (2.13). We thus have obtained a no-message existential forgery on Textbook-Elgamal. But this forgery, which was first described in [**El 85**], has almost no flexibility over m: we can obtain many forgeries thanks to different choices of (B, C), but each choice of (B, C) gives rise to a unique m. This means that this forgery will be prevented if we hash the message before hashing, like in FDH-RSA.

We now describe another existential forgery on Textbook-Elgamal, which can also be prevented by hashing. However, as opposed to the previous existential forgery, we will later see that this existential forgery can be transformed into a clever universal forgery found by Bleichenbacher [**Ble96**], which cannot therefore be prevented by hashing.

This alternative existential forgery finds a triplet $(m, a, b) \in \mathbb{Z}_p \times \mathbb{Z}_p^\times \times \mathbb{Z}_{p-1}$ satisfying (2.13) by solving the congruence by Chinese remainders separately. Thus, we decompose the modulus $p - 1$ as $p - 1 = qs$ where s is smooth (that is, it has no large prime factor, see [**Sho05**]). The reason why we choose s to be smooth is that it is easy to extract discrete logarithm in a group of smooth order, using Pohlig-Hellman's algorithm (see [**MOV97, Sho05**]). In particular, we do not know how to compute efficiently the discrete-log function log over $\mathbb{Z}_p^\times$, but for any $z \in \mathbb{Z}_p^\times$, we can efficiently compute $(\log z) \bmod s$. We do not know the secret key x, but because we know the public key $y = g^x \bmod p$, we may compute the smooth part $x \bmod s$. Since $p - 1$ is always even, the smooth part s is at least 2.

Because $p - 1 = qs$, the congruence (2.13) would imply the following two congruences:

(4.2) $$m \equiv ax + b\log a \pmod{q}$$
(4.3) $$m \equiv ax + b\log a \pmod{s}$$

Reciprocally, if we could find a triplet (m, a, b) satisfying both (4.2) and (4.3), would it necessarily satisfy (2.13)? The answer would be positive if q and s were coprime, by the Chinese remainder theorem. So let us assume that we put all the smooth part of $p - 1$ into s, so that the smooth number s is indeed coprime with $q = (p-1)/s$.

We do not know $x \bmod q$, so the mod q-congruence (4.2) looks hard to satisfy. However, note that the triplet $(m, a, b) = (m, q, 0)$ is a trivial solution of (4.2) whenever $m \equiv 0 \pmod{q}$. So let us consider any message m such that $m \equiv 0 \pmod{q}$, and set $a = q$. It remains to satisfy the second congruence (4.3). We can compute $\log a \bmod s$, and if we are lucky, it will be invertible mod s, so that we can solve (4.3). Thus, we have obtained a probabilistic existential forgery, which is weakly universal in the sense that if $\log q$ is coprime with s, then we can forge the signature of any message m divisible by q. Like the previous existential forgery, this attack could easily be avoided using a cryptographic hash function, but Bleichenbacher [**Ble96**] found a trick to remove this limitation over m. We now describe Bleichenbacher's attack, with a presentation slightly different from that of [**Ble96**].

We restrict to the simplest form of Bleichenbacher's forgery, which requires that the generator g is smooth and divides $p - 1$: a natural choice would be $g = 2$. Thus, we let $s = g$ where $p - 1 = qs$ and we assume that s is smooth as before. However, we will no longer assume that q and s are coprime, so it will not suffice to work with (4.2) and (4.3) only. Instead, we will work with the congruence (2.13) mod $p - 1$ directly. We can compute $x_0 = x \bmod s$, so that $x = x_0 + sx_1$ where x_1 is unknown. If we let $a = q$, then (2.13) becomes:

(4.4) $$m \equiv ax_0 + b\log a \pmod{p-1}.$$

This congruence looks hard to solve for b since we know $\log a \bmod s$ but not mod $p - 1$. The trick is that the particular choice $a = q$ enables us to compute $\log a$. We claim that $\log a = \log q$ is equal to the integer $k = (p-3)/2 = (p-1)/2 - 1$. To see this:

$$g^k \equiv g^{(p-1)/2} g^{-1} \pmod{p}$$
$$\equiv (-1)g^{-1} \text{ because } g \text{ is generator, so its Legendre symbol is -1.}$$
$$\equiv qsg^{-1} \text{ because } p - 1 = qs.$$
$$\equiv q \text{ because } g = s.$$

It follows that (4.4) can be rewritten as:

(4.5) $$m \equiv ax_0 + bk \pmod{p-1}.$$

It is an elementary fact of number theory that this linear congruence can be solved for b if and only if $\gcd(k, p-1)$ divides $m - ax_0$. To evaluate $\gcd(k, p-1)$, note that:

$$k^2 = ((p-1)/2 - 1)^2 = ((p-1)/2)^2 - (p-1) + 1 \equiv 1 + ((p-1)/2)^2 \pmod{p-1}.$$

We distinguish two cases:
- If $p \equiv 1 \pmod 4$, then $\gcd(k, p-1) = 1$ because the previous congruence becomes $k^2 \equiv 1 \pmod{p-1}$ as $((p-1)/2)^2$ is a multiple of $p-1$. It follows that whatever the value of m, we can always solve (4.5) for b.
- Otherwise, $p \equiv 3 \pmod 4$, and we claim that $\gcd(k, p-1) = 2$. Indeed, this time, we have that $((p-1)/2)^2 \equiv 1 \pmod{p-1}$ rather than 0, which implies that
$$k^2 \equiv 2 \pmod{p-1}.$$
It follows that $\gcd(k, p-1) = 2$ because we already know that it is ≥ 2. Hence, if we assume that m is uniformly distributed modulo $p-1$, then the probability that $\gcd(k, p-1)$ divides $m - ax_0$ is exactly $1/2$. This means that we can solve (4.5) half of the time.

Hence, if the generator is smooth and divides $p-1$, we can either forge a signature on every message if $p \equiv 1 \pmod 4$, or on half of the messages if $p \equiv 3 \pmod 4$. Bleichenbacher describes other attacks on other specific generators in [**Ble96**].

Surprisingly, on the other hand, Pointcheval and Stern [**PS96**] showed at the same conference as [**Ble96**] that a slight modification of the Elgamal signature scheme is provably secure in the random oracle model. Furthermore, Bleichenbacher's attack applied to that modification as well, but there is fortunately no contradiction because the Pointcheval-Stern security proof assumed that the generator g was chosen uniformly at random among all generators of $\mathbb{Z}_p^*$, in which case it is very unlikely that g will be smooth and dividing $p-1$. This suggests the following lesson: one should always carefully look at all the assumptions made by a security proof.

4.2. Asymmetric Encryption.
4.2.1. Textbook-RSA.
We first consider Textbook-RSA. Like any trapdoor permutation used directly as a public-key encryption scheme, Textbook-RSA is vulnerable to brute-force attacks over the plaintext. More precisely, an attacker has access to a plaintext-checking oracle: the attacker can check whether a given ciphertext c would be decrypted as a given plaintext m, by checking if:

(4.6) $$c \equiv m^e \bmod N.$$

In particular, if the set of plaintexts $\mathcal{M}$ (where $m \in \mathcal{M}$) is small, one can decrypt by brute-force: one would simply enumerate all $m' \in \mathcal{M}$ and check whether the ciphertext c corresponds to the plaintext m', in which case $m = m'$. This would be for instance the case if we were encrypting English plaintexts letter by letter. In other words, when the distribution of plaintexts is very different from the uniform distribution over $\mathbb{Z}_N$, (such as when the set of plaintexts $\mathcal{M}$ is a very small subset of $\mathbb{Z}_N$), attacks may arise. Another famous example is the short-message attack. Assume that the plaintexts are in fact very small: for instance, assume that the plaintext m satisfies $0 \leq m \leq N^{1/e}$, (e.g. m is a 128-bit AES key, N a 1024-bit modulus, and $e = 3$). Then the integer m satisfies: $0 \leq m^e \leq N$, which means that the congruence (4.6) is in fact an equality over $\mathbb{Z}$,

$$c = m^e.$$

But it is well-known that solving univariate polynomial equations over $\mathbb{Z}$ can be done in polynomial time: extracting e-th roots over $\mathbb{Z}$ is simply a particular case. In other words, if $0 \leq m \leq N^{1/e}$, then one can recover the plaintext m from (c, N, e)

in polynomial time. To summarize, if the distribution of the plaintext m is the uniform distribution over $\mathbb{Z}_N$, no one currently knows how to recover efficiently the plaintext m from its ciphertext $c = m^e \bmod N$: this is exactly the RSA assumption. But if the distribution of the plaintext m is very different, there are examples for which there exist very efficient attacks.

Another elementary remark is that the RSA permutation provably leaks information. Given $c = m^e \bmod N$ where m has uniform distribution over $\mathbb{Z}_N$, one does not know how to recover m efficiently, but it is easy to recover efficiently one bit of information on the plaintext m. More precisely, because e must be odd (since it is coprime with $\phi(N)$ which is even), the congruence (4.6) implies the following equality of Jacobi symbols:

$$\left(\frac{c}{N}\right) = \left(\frac{m}{N}\right)^e = \left(\frac{m}{N}\right).$$

In other words, one can derive efficiently the Jacobi symbol $\left(\frac{m}{N}\right)$, which provides one bit of information on the plaintext m.

We earlier saw an adaptive chosen-message universal forgery on Textbook-RSA signatures based on the multiplicativity of the RSA permutation. This elementary attack has an encryption analogue: it can be transformed into an adaptive chosen-ciphertext attack. Indeed, assume that we would like to decrypt a ciphertext $c = m^e \bmod N \in \mathbb{Z}_N$: in other words, we would like to recover the plaintext $m \in \mathbb{Z}_N$. Select $m_1 \in \mathbb{Z}_N$ uniformly at random. If m_1 is not invertible mod N (which is unlikely), then we have found a non-trivial factor of N, which of course allows us to decrypt c. Otherwise, we may compute:

$$c_2 = c m_1^{-e} \pmod{N}.$$

We ask the decryption oracle to decrypt the ciphertext c_2: this gives the plaintext $m_2 \in \mathbb{Z}_N$ defined by $c_2 = m_2^e \bmod N$. Then it is clear by multiplicativity that $m = (m_1 m_2) \bmod N$, which allows us to recover the initial plaintext m.

4.2.2. *Textbook-Elgamal.* Textbook-Elgamal is a probabilistic encryption scheme, unlike Textbook-RSA. In particular, there is no access to a plaintext-checking oracle. However, Textbook-Elgamal provably leaks one bit of information on the plaintext, just like Textbook-RSA. Indeed, if g is a generator of $\mathbb{Z}_p^*$, then its Legendre symbol $\left(\frac{g}{p}\right)$ must be equal to -1. In particular, the congruence (2.8) implies that the ciphertext (c, d) of a message m satisfies:

$$\left(\frac{c}{p}\right) = (-1)^k,$$

which discloses the parity of the one-time key k. Furthermore, the congruence (2.9) implies that:

$$\left(\frac{d}{p}\right) = \left(\frac{m}{p}\right)\left(\frac{y}{p}\right)^k.$$

Because d, y and p are public, and since the parity of k is now known, one can compute the Legendre symbol $\left(\frac{m}{p}\right)$, which discloses one bit of information on the plaintext m.

We saw in Section 4.2.1 an adaptive chosen-ciphertext attack on Textbook-RSA encryption based on the multiplicativity of the RSA permutation. Since Textbook-Elgamal is multiplicative as well (see Section 2.2.2), this adaptive chosen-ciphertext attack can trivially be adapted to the Elgamal setting.

The fact that Textbook-RSA encryption is deterministic makes it vulnerable to several elementary attacks, but transforming it into a probabilistic encryption scheme will not prevent all the security problems by magic, as the example of Textbook-Elgamal encryption shows.

5. Square-Root Attacks

Whenever an exhaustive search over a secret key or a plaintext (or any other secret value) is possible, cryptographers often look for improved attacks based on time/memory trade-offs (see [**MOV97, Hel80, Oec03, BBS06**]). Usually, exhaustive search requires negligible memory M and exponential time T. A time/memory trade-off tries to balance those two costs. It is often achieved by splitting the secret value in values of half-size, in which case the new time and space complexity become roughly the square root of the cost of exhaustive search: that is, if T is the running time of exhaustive search, then both the time and space complexities become roughly $\sqrt{T}$. Sometimes, it is possible to further improve the space complexity of such square-root attacks to negligible memory, which is of considerable interest in practice. But among the three square-root attacks we will present, such a memory improvement is only known for the first one, which deals with the discrete logarithm problem.

5.1. The Discrete Logarithm Problem.
As an illustration, consider the discrete logarithm problem used in Textbook-Elgamal. Let p be a prime and g be a generator of $\mathbb{Z}_p^*$. Assume that one is given an integer y satisfying:

(5.1) $$y = g^x \bmod p,$$

where the integer x is secret. The discrete logarithm problem asks to recover x modulo $p-1$. Assume that the secret exponent x satisfies $0 \leq x \leq X$, where the public bound X is much smaller than p: does that make the discrete logarithm easier? Obviously, the simplest method would be to exhaustive search all exponents x such that $0 \leq x \leq X$, and find out which one satisfies (5.1). This costs X group operations with negligible space. A simple time/memory trade-off is obtained by splitting the secret exponent x in two parts. More precisely, the integer x can be written as:

$$x = x_1 + \lfloor \sqrt{X} \rfloor x_2$$

where x_1 are x_2 are two integers satisfying $0 \leq x_1 \leq \lfloor \sqrt{X} \rfloor \leq \sqrt{X}$ and $0 \leq x_2 \leq X/\lfloor \sqrt{X} \rfloor = O(\sqrt{X})$. This enables to rewrite (5.1) as:

$$y \equiv g^{x_1 + \lfloor \sqrt{X} \rfloor x_2} \pmod{p},$$

that is:

(5.2) $$y/g^{\lfloor \sqrt{X} \rfloor x_2} \equiv g^{x_1} \pmod{p}.$$

Reciprocally, any pair (x_1, x_2) satisfying (5.2) gives rise to a solution x of (5.1). This suggests the following time/memory trade-off:

- Precompute the list L of all $g^{x_1} \bmod p$ where $0 \leq x_1 \leq \lfloor\sqrt{X}\rfloor$, and sort the list L to allow binary search. This will cost essentially $O(\sqrt{X}\ln X)$ polynomial-time operations.
- For all integers x_2 such that $0 \leq x_2 \leq X/\lfloor\sqrt{X}\rfloor$, compute $y/g^{\lfloor\sqrt{X}\rfloor x_2} \bmod p$ and find out if it belongs to the list L. If it belongs to L, output the corresponding solution x to (5.1). This will also cost essentially $O(\sqrt{X}\ln X)$ polynomial-time operations.

In other words, we have obtained a time/memory trade-off to solve (5.2) (and therefore (5.1)), which has time and space complexity roughly $O(\sqrt{X}\ln X)$, if we ignore polynomial costs. The method we have just described is known as the baby-step/giant-step method in the literature (see [**MOV97**]). For the discrete logarithm problem, there are improvements to this basic square-root attack which allow to decrease the space requirement to negligible memory: see for instance Pollard's ρ and kangaroo methods in [**CP01, MOV97**], which are based on cycle-finding algorithms such as Floyd's.

5.2. RSA encryption of short messages. Another simple example of square-root attacks is given by Textbook-RSA encryption of short messages with an arbitrary public exponent e, as explained in [**BJN00**]. Let $0 \leq m \leq B$ be a plaintext encrypted as $c = m^e \bmod N$. We assume that the plaintext is small, that is, $B \ll N$. For instance, m could be a 56-bit DES, N a 1024-bit RSA modulus, and $e = 2^{16}+1$. It might happen that m can be split as $m = m_1 m_2$ where m_1 and m_2 are between 0 and roughly $\sqrt{B}$. Splitting probabilities (as well as theoretical results) are listed in [**BJN00**]:

- For example, if $1 \leq m \leq 2^{64}$ has uniform distribution then m can be split as a product $m_1 m_2$ where $1 \leq m_i < 2^{32}$ with probability ≈ 0.18.
- Extending to $1 \leq m_i \leq 2^{33}$ increases the probability to ≈ 0.29, while extending to $1 \leq m_i \leq 2^{34}$ increases the probability to ≈ 0.35.

This suggests the following attack [**BJN00**]:

- Compute all the values $m_1^e \bmod N$ where $1 \leq m_1 \leq A\sqrt{B}$ for some small constant A. These values (together with the corresponding m_1) should be stored in a structure which is easily searched.
- For all values m_2 such that $1 \leq m_2 \leq A'\sqrt{B}$, compute $c/m_2^e \bmod N$ and, for each value, see if this number appears in the earlier structure.
- If a match is found then we have $c/m_2^e \equiv m_1^e \pmod{N}$ in which case $c \equiv (m_1 m_2)^e \pmod{N}$ and therefore, the secret plaintext is $m = m_1 m_2$.

The cost of the attack is essentially $O((A+A')\sqrt{B}\ln B)$ polynomial-time operations.

5.3. RSA with small CRT secret exponents. The square-root attacks we have described are very elementary, but sometimes, square-root attacks can be tricky. A less elementary example is given by Coppersmith's square-root attack on the discrete logarithm problem with sparse exponents: this is a particular case of the discrete logarithm problem when the secret exponent has low Hamming weight. The motivation is that such exponents allow faster exponentiation, and are therefore tempting for certain cryptographic schemes. For more details, Coppersmith's attack is described in [**Sti02**]: it was originally presented in the eighties as a remark on the message security of the Chor-Rivest public-key encryption scheme. Its time and space complexities are roughly the square root of the running time of exhaustive search over all sparse exponents.

A more sophisticated square-root attack applies to RSA with small CRT secret exponent: the attack is vaguely described in [**QL00**] and is attributed to Richard Pinch. The motivation is the following. To speed up RSA decryption or signature generation, one could select a small secret exponent d. But we will see later (in Section 7.1.1) an attack (due to Wiener [**Wie90**]), which recovers the factorization of the RSA modulus N for usual parameters whenever $d = O(N^{1/4})$. And Wiener's attack was improved by Boneh and Durfee [**BD99**] to $d = O(N^{1-1\sqrt{2}/2}) = O(N^{0.292\cdots})$ using lattice-based techniques which we will describe in Section 7.3. A better way to speed up RSA decryption or signature generation is to choose $N = pq$ and e so that the integers d_p and d_q satisfying

$$ed_p \equiv 1 \pmod{p-1} \text{ and } ed_q \equiv 1 \pmod{q-1}$$

are small. If d_p and d_q are both $O(B)$, there is a simple brute-force attack which costs $O(B)$. Namely, assume without loss of generality that $1 < d_p, d_q < B$ with $d_p \neq d_q$, and consider the following:

- Choose a random $1 < m < N$ and set $c = m^e \bmod N$.
  Recall that $c^{d_p} = m^{ed_p} \equiv m \bmod p$.
- For each $1 < i < B$ one can compute
$$\gcd(c^i - m \bmod N, N)$$
and see if we have factored N.
- When $i = d_p \neq d_q$ we have $c^i \equiv m \bmod p$ and $c^i \not\equiv m \bmod q$. Hence the algorithm will succeed.
- The complexity is $\tilde{O}(B)$.

It is natural to seek a square-root attack in this case. Consider what happens if one tries the obvious approach:

- Write $M = \lfloor \sqrt{B} \rfloor$ and $d_p = d_1 + Md_2$ with $0 \leq d_1 < M$, $0 \leq d_2 \leq M+1$.
- One would expect to compute and store a table of 'baby steps' $c^i \bmod N$ for $0 \leq i < M$.
- Then one would expect to compute the giant steps $(c^M)^j \bmod N$ for $0 \leq j \leq M+1$.
- For each new giant step we must test whether there is a match, i.e., a value for i such that $\gcd(c^i(c^M)^j - m, N) \neq 1$.

The problem is that it seems the only way to check this is to run over the entire table of the baby steps and try each one. If this is done then the final complexity is still $\tilde{O}(B)$ rather than the square root.

The following attack reaches the square-root goal:

- Compute the polynomial
$$G(x) = \prod_{j=0}^{M+1} ((c^M)^j x - m) \bmod N.$$
- This computation takes time $\tilde{O}(M)$ and storing $G(x)$ requires space $\tilde{O}(M)$.
- Note that $G(c^{d_1}) \equiv 0 \bmod p$ since
$$(c^M)^{d_2} c^{d_1} \equiv c^d \equiv m \bmod p.$$
- Evaluate $G(x)$ modulo N at c^i for all $0 \leq i < M$.

- This gives a list of M numbers, one of which has a non-trivial gcd with N. One therefore factors N.

However, this method requires the evaluation of $G(x)$ at M points. Since $G(x)$ is a polynomial of degree $M+1$, one might think that this is too expensive, that it would cost $\tilde{O}(M^2)$. Fortunately, there is an algorithm due to Strassen (see the textbook [**JvzGG03**]), which uses the Fast Fourier Transform (FFT) to evaluate a polynomial of degree M at M points in time $\tilde{O}(M)$. Using this algorithm, we eventually obtain a square-root complexity $\tilde{O}(\sqrt{B})$ as announced. Recently, a lattice attack on this problem appeared in [**JM07**], based on techniques which we will describe in Section 7.3.

6. An Introduction to Lattices

6.1. Background. We will consider $\mathbb{R}^n$ with its usual topology of an Euclidean vector space. We will use bold letters to denote vectors, usually in row notation. The Euclidean inner product of two vectors $\mathbf{x} = (x_i)_{i=1}^n$ and $\mathbf{y} = (y_i)_{i=1}^n$ is denoted by:

$$\langle \mathbf{x}, \mathbf{y} \rangle = \sum_{i=1}^n x_i y_i.$$

The corresponding Euclidean norm is denoted by:

$$\|\mathbf{x}\| = \sqrt{x_1^2 + \cdots + x_n^2}.$$

Denote by $B(\mathbf{x}, r)$ the open ball of radius r centered at $\mathbf{x}$:

$$B(\mathbf{x}, r) = \{\mathbf{y} \in \mathbb{R}^n : \|\mathbf{x} - \mathbf{y}\| < r\}.$$

A subset D of $\mathbb{R}^n$ is called *discrete* when it has no limit point, that is: for all $x \in D$, there exists $\rho > 0$ such that $B(x, \rho) \cap D = \{x\}$. As an example, $\mathbb{Z}^n$ is discrete (because $\rho = 1/2$ clearly works), while $\mathbb{Q}^n$ and $\mathbb{R}^n$ are not. The set $\{1/n : n \in \mathbb{N}^*\}$ is discrete, but the set $\{0\} \cup \{1/n : n \in \mathbb{N}^*\}$ is not. Any subset of a discrete set is discrete.

For any ring R, we denote by $\mathcal{M}_{n,m}(R)$ (resp. $\mathcal{M}_n(R)$) the set of $n \times m$ (resp. $n \times n$) matrices with coefficients in R. $GL_n(R)$ denotes the group of invertible matrices in the ring $\mathcal{M}_n(R)$.

For any subset S of $\mathbb{R}^n$, we define the linear span of S, denoted by $\mathrm{span}(S)$, as the minimal vector subspace (of $\mathbb{R}^n$) containing S.

Let $\mathbf{b}_1, \ldots, \mathbf{b}_m$ be in $\mathbb{R}^n$. The vectors $\mathbf{b}_i$'s are said to be *linearly dependent* if there exist $x_1, \ldots, x_m \in \mathbb{R}$ which are not all zero and such that:

$$\sum_{i=1}^m x_i \mathbf{b}_i = 0.$$

Otherwise, they are said to be *linearly independent*.

The Gram determinant of $\mathbf{b}_1, \ldots, \mathbf{b}_m \in \mathbb{R}^n$, denoted by $\Delta(\mathbf{b}_1, \ldots, \mathbf{b}_m)$, is by definition the determinant of the Gram matrix $(\langle \mathbf{b}_i, \mathbf{b}_j \rangle)_{1 \leq i,j \leq m}$. This real number $\Delta(\mathbf{b}_1, \ldots, \mathbf{b}_m)$ is always ≥ 0, and it turns out to be zero if and only if the $\mathbf{b}_i$'s are linearly dependent. The Gram determinant is invariant by any permutation of the m vectors, and by any integral linear transformation of determinant ± 1 such as adding to one of the vectors a linear combination of the others. The Gram determinant has a very useful geometric interpretation: when the $\mathbf{b}_i$'s are linearly independent, $\sqrt{\Delta(\mathbf{b}_1,\ldots,\mathbf{b}_m)}$ is the m-dimensional volume of the parallelepiped spanned by the $\mathbf{b}_i$'s.

6.2. Lattices. We call *lattice* of $\mathbb{R}^n$ any discrete subgroup of $(\mathbb{R}^n,+)$; that is any subgroup of $(\mathbb{R}^n,+)$ which has the discreteness property. Notice that an additive group is discrete if and only if 0 is not a limit point, which implies that a lattice is any non-empty set $L \subseteq \mathbb{R}^n$ stable by subtraction (in other words: for all $\mathbf{x}$ and $\mathbf{y}$ in L, $\mathbf{x} - \mathbf{y}$ belongs to L), and such that $L \cap B(0,\rho) = \{0\}$ for some $\rho > 0$.

With this definition, the first examples of lattices which come to mind are the zero lattice $\{0\}$ and the *lattice of integers* $\mathbb{Z}^n$. Our definition implies that any subgroup of a lattice is a lattice, and therefore, any subgroup of $(\mathbb{Z}^n,+)$ is a lattice. Such lattices are called *integral lattices*. As an example, consider two integers a and $b \in \mathbb{Z}$: the set $a\mathbb{Z} + b\mathbb{Z}$ of all integral linear combinations of a and b is a subgroup of $\mathbb{Z}$, and therefore a lattice; it is actually the set $\gcd(a,b)\mathbb{Z}$ of all multiples of the gcd of a and b. For another example, consider n integers $a_1,\ldots,a_n$, together with a modulus M. Then the set of all $(x_1,\ldots,x_n) \in \mathbb{Z}^n$ such that $\sum_{i=1}^{n} a_i x_i \equiv 0 \pmod{M}$ is a lattice in $\mathbb{Z}^n$ because it is clearly a subgroup of $\mathbb{Z}^n$.

We give a few basic properties of lattices:

PROPOSITION 6.1. *Let L be a lattice in $\mathbb{R}^n$.*

(1) *There exists $\rho > 0$ such that for all $\mathbf{x} \in L$:*
$$L \cap B(\mathbf{x},\rho) = \{\mathbf{x}\}.$$
(2) *L is closed.*
(3) *For all bounded subsets S of $\mathbb{R}^n$, $L \cap S$ is finite.*
(4) *L is countable.*

PROOF. We know that $L \cap B(0,\rho) = \{0\}$ for some $\rho > 0$. Since L is an additive group, we obtain property 1. It follows that any convergent sequence of L is stationary, which proves property 2. If S is a bounded subset, it must be included in some closed ball B. The set $L \cap B$ is closed and bounded, thus compact. Since it is also discrete, it must be finite (by the Borel-Lebesgue theorem), which gives property 3. Since $\mathbb{R}^n$ is the union of all $B(0,r)$ for $r \in \mathbb{N}$, we obtain property 4. □

Notice that a set which satisfies either property 1 or 3 is necessarily discrete, but an arbitrary discrete subset of $\mathbb{R}^n$ does not necessarily satisfy property 1 nor 3. It is the group structure of lattices which allows such additional properties.

6.3. Lattice Bases. Let $\mathbf{b}_1,\ldots,\mathbf{b}_m$ be arbitrary vectors in $\mathbb{R}^n$. Denote by $L(\mathbf{b}_1,\ldots,\mathbf{b}_m)$ the set of all integral linear combinations of the $\mathbf{b}_i$'s:
$$L(\mathbf{b}_1,\ldots,\mathbf{b}_m) = \left\{ \sum_{i=1}^{m} n_i \mathbf{b}_i : n_1,\ldots,n_m \in \mathbb{Z} \right\}$$
This set is a subgroup of $\mathbb{R}^n$, but it is not necessarily discrete. For instance, one can show that $L((1),(\sqrt{2}))$ is not discrete because $\sqrt{2} \notin \mathbb{Q}$. However, notice that if the $\mathbf{b}_i$'s are in $\mathbb{Q}^n$, then $L(\mathbf{b}_1,\ldots,\mathbf{b}_m)$ is discrete, and so is a lattice. When $L = L(\mathbf{b}_1,\ldots,\mathbf{b}_m)$ is a lattice, we say that L is spanned by the $\mathbf{b}_i$'s, and that the $\mathbf{b}_i$'s are *generators*. When the $\mathbf{b}_i$'s are further linearly independent, we say that $(\mathbf{b}_1,\ldots,\mathbf{b}_m)$ is a *basis* of the lattice L, in which case each lattice vector decomposes itself uniquely as an integral linear combination of the $\mathbf{b}_i$'s. Bases and sets of generators are useful to represent lattices, and to perform computations. One will

typically represent a lattice on a computer by some lattice basis, which can itself be represented by a matrix with real coefficients. In practice, one will usually restrict to integral lattices, so that the underlying matrices are integral matrices.

We define the *dimension* or *rank* of a lattice L, denoted by $\dim(L)$, as the dimension d of its linear span denoted by $\mathrm{span}(L)$. The dimension is the maximal number of linearly independent lattice vectors. Any lattice basis of L must have exactly d elements. There always exist d linearly independent lattice vectors, however such vectors do not necessarily form a basis, as opposed to the case of vectors spaces. But the following theorem shows that one can always derive a lattice basis from such vectors:

THEOREM 6.2. *Let L be a lattice of $\mathbb{R}^n$, with dimension d. Let $\mathbf{c}_1, \ldots, \mathbf{c}_d$ be linearly independent vectors of L. There exists a lower triangular matrix $(u_{i,j}) \in \mathcal{M}_d(\mathbb{R})$ such that the vectors $\mathbf{b}_1, \ldots, \mathbf{b}_d$ defined as $\mathbf{b}_i = \sum_{j=1}^{i} u_{i,j} \mathbf{c}_j$ form a basis of L.*

PROOF. We reproduce the proof of [**Sie89**, Theorem 18, p. 45]. Let $1 \leq i \leq d$. Consider the following set:

$$S_i = \left\{ x_i \in]0,1] : \exists x_1, \ldots, x_{i-1} \in \mathbb{R} \text{ such that } \sum_{j=1}^{i} x_j \mathbf{c}_j \in L \right\}.$$

This set is actually finite because $x_i \in S_i$ implies that $x_i \mathbf{c}_i + \sum_{j=1}^{i-1} (x_j - \lfloor x_j \rfloor) \mathbf{c}_j$ belongs to $L \cap B(0, \sum_{j=1}^{i} \|\mathbf{c}_j\|)$ which is finite. And S_i is not empty since it contains 1, therefore it has a smallest element which is strictly positive, and which we denote by $u_{i,i} > 0$. By definition, there exist $u_{i,1}, \ldots, u_{i,i-1} \in \mathbb{R}$ such that $\mathbf{b}_i = \sum_{j=1}^{i} u_{i,j} \mathbf{c}_j \in L$.

It remains to prove that the $\mathbf{b}_i$'s form a basis. Since $u_{i,i} > 0$, the $\mathbf{b}_i$'s are linearly independent. Now, let $\mathbf{y} \in L$. Since the $\mathbf{b}_i$'s are linearly independent, there exist $y_1, \ldots, y_n \in \mathbb{R}$ such that $\mathbf{y} = \sum_{i=1}^{d} y_i \mathbf{b}_i$. Define $\mathbf{x} = \sum_{i=1}^{d} x_i \mathbf{b}_i$ where $x_i = y_i - \lfloor y_i \rfloor$. We have $\mathbf{x} \in L$ and $0 \leq x_i < 1$. Suppose *ad absurdum* that not all the y_i's are integral: let k be the largest index such that $y_k \notin \mathbb{Z}$. Then $x_k > 0$ and $x_i = 0$ if $i > k$. Thus:

$$\mathbf{x} = u_{k,k} x_k \mathbf{c}_k + \sum_{j=1}^{k-1} u_{k,j} x_k \mathbf{c}_j + \sum_{i=1}^{k-1} x_i \sum_{j=1}^{i} u_{i,j} \mathbf{c}_j.$$

Since $0 < x_k < 1$, $0 < u_{k,k} x_k < u_{k,k}$ which contradicts the fact that $u_{k,k}$ is the smallest element of S_k. □

This gives the unconditional existence of lattice bases:

COROLLARY 6.3. *Any lattice of $\mathbb{R}^n$ has at least one basis.*

Thus, even if sets of the form $L(\mathbf{b}_1, \ldots, \mathbf{b}_m)$ may or may not be lattices, all lattices can be written as $L(\mathbf{b}_1, \ldots, \mathbf{b}_m)$ for some linearly independent $\mathbf{b}_i$'s. The converse is easy to prove:

THEOREM 6.4. *Let $\mathbf{b}_1, \ldots, \mathbf{b}_d \in \mathbb{R}^n$ be linearly independent. Then the set $L(\mathbf{b}_1, \ldots, \mathbf{b}_d)$ is a lattice of dimension d.*

PROOF. Let $L = L(\mathbf{b}_1, \ldots, \mathbf{b}_d)$. It suffices to show that 0 is not a limit point of L. Consider the parallelepiped P defined by:

$$P = \left\{ \sum_{i=1}^{d} x_i \mathbf{b}_i : |x_i| < 1 \right\}.$$

Since the $\mathbf{b}_i$'s are linearly independent, $L \cap P = \{0\}$. Besides, there exists $\rho > 0$ such that $B(0, \rho) \subseteq P$, which shows that 0 cannot be a limit point of L. □

Corollary 6.3 together with Theorem 6.4 give an alternative definition of a lattice: a non-empty subset L of $\mathbb{R}^n$ is a lattice if only if there exist linearly independent vectors $\mathbf{b}_1, \mathbf{b}_2, \ldots, \mathbf{b}_d$ in $\mathbb{R}^n$ such that:

$$L = L(\mathbf{b}_1, \ldots, \mathbf{b}_d).$$

This characterization suggests that lattices are discrete analogues of vector spaces.

Lattice bases are characterized by the following elementary result, whose proof is omitted:

THEOREM 6.5. *Let $(\mathbf{b}_1, \ldots, \mathbf{b}_d)$ be a basis of a lattice L in $\mathbb{R}^n$. Let $\mathbf{c}_1, \ldots, \mathbf{c}_d$ be vectors of L: there exists a $d \times d$ integral matrix $U = (u_{i,j})_{1 \leq i,j \leq d} \in \mathcal{M}_d(\mathbb{Z})$ such that $\mathbf{c_i} = \sum_{j=1}^{d} u_{i,j} \mathbf{b}_j$ for all $1 \leq i \leq d$. Then $(\mathbf{c}_1, \ldots, \mathbf{c}_d)$ is a basis of L if and only if the matrix U has determinant ± 1.*

As a result, as soon as the lattice dimension is ≥ 2, there are infinitely many lattice bases.

6.4. Lattice Volume. Let $(\mathbf{b}_1, \ldots, \mathbf{b}_d)$ and $(\mathbf{c}_1, \ldots, \mathbf{c}_d)$ be two bases of a lattice L in $\mathbb{R}^n$. By Theorem 6.5, there exists a $d \times d$ integral matrix $U = (u_{i,j})_{1 \leq i,j \leq d} \in \mathcal{M}_d(\mathbb{Z})$ of determinant ± 1 such that $\mathbf{c_i} = \sum_{j=1}^{d} u_{i,j} \mathbf{b}_j$ for all $1 \leq i \leq d$. It follows that the Gram determinant of those two bases are equal:

$$\Delta(\mathbf{b}_1, \ldots, \mathbf{b}_d) = \Delta(\mathbf{c}_1, \ldots, \mathbf{c}_d) > 0.$$

The *volume* (or *determinant*) of the lattice L is defined as:

$$\text{vol}(L) = \Delta(\mathbf{b}_1, \ldots, \mathbf{b}_d)^{1/2},$$

which is independent of the choice of lattice basis $(\mathbf{b}_1, \ldots, \mathbf{b}_d)$. We prefer the name *volume* to the name *determinant* because of its geometric interpretation: it corresponds to the d-dimensional volume of the parallelepiped spanned by any basis. In the mathematical literature, the lattice volume we have just defined is sometimes alternatively called co-volume, because it is also the volume of the torus $\text{span}(L)/L$. In the important case of full-dimensional lattices where $\dim(L) = n = \dim(\mathbb{R}^n)$, the volume is equal to the absolute value of the determinant of any lattice basis (hence the alternative name determinant).

Given a lattice L, how does one compute the volume of L? If an explicit basis of L is known, this amounts to computing a determinant: for instance, the volume of the hypercubic lattice $\mathbb{Z}^n$ is clearly equal to one. But if no explicit basis is known, there is sometimes another way, due to the following elementary result: if L_1 and L_2 are two lattices of $\mathbb{R}^n$ with the same dimension such that $L_1 \subseteq L_2$, then L_2/L_1 is a finite group of order denoted by $[L_2 : L_1]$ which satisfies

$$\text{vol}(L_1) = \text{vol}(L_2) \times [L_2 : L_1].$$

As an illustration, consider n integers $a_1, \ldots, a_n$, together with a modulus M. We have seen in Section 6.2 that the set L of all $(x_1, \ldots, x_n) \in \mathbb{Z}^n$ such that $\sum_{i=1}^n a_i x_i \equiv 0 \pmod{M}$ is a lattice in $\mathbb{Z}^n$ because it is a subgroup of $\mathbb{Z}^n$. But there seems to be no trivial basis of L. However, note that $L \subseteq \mathbb{Z}^n$ and that the dimension of L is n because L contains all the vectors of the canonical basis of $\mathbb{R}^n$ multiplied by M. It follows that:

$$\mathrm{vol}(L) = [\mathbb{Z}^n : L].$$

Furthermore, the definition of L clearly implies that:

$$[\mathbb{Z}^n : L] = M/\gcd(M, a_1, a_2, \ldots, a_n).$$

Hence:

$$\mathrm{vol}(L) = \frac{M}{\gcd(M, a_1, a_2, \ldots, a_n)}.$$

6.5. Lattice Reduction. A fundamental result of linear algebra states that any finite-dimensional vector space has a basis. We earlier established the analogue result for lattices: any lattice has a basis. In the same vein, a fundamental result of bilinear algebra states that any finite-dimensional Euclidean space has an orthonormal basis, that is, a basis consisting of unit vectors which are pairwise orthogonal. A natural question is to ask whether lattices also have orthonormal bases, or at least, orthogonal bases. Unfortunately, it is not difficult to see that even in dimension two, a lattice may not have an orthogonal basis. Informally, the goal of lattice reduction is to circumvent this problem: more precisely, the theory of lattice reduction shows that in any lattice, there is always a basis which is not that far from being orthogonal. Defining precisely what is meant exactly by not being far from being orthogonal is tricky, so for now, let us just say that such a basis should consist of reasonably short lattice vectors, which implies that geometrically, such vectors are not far from being orthogonal to each other.

6.5.1. *Minkowski's successive minima.* In order to explain what is a reduced basis, we need to define what is meant by short lattice vectors. Let L be a lattice of dimension ≥ 1 in $\mathbb{R}^n$. There exists a non-zero vector $\mathbf{u} \in L$. Consider the closed hyperball B of radius $\|\mathbf{u}\|$, centered at zero. Then $L \cap B$ is finite and contains $\mathbf{u}$, so it must have a shortest non-zero vector. The Euclidean norm of that shortest non-zero vector is called the *first minimum* of L, and is denoted by $\lambda_1(L) > 0$ or $\|L\|$. By definition, any non-zero vector $\mathbf{v}$ of L satisfies: $\|\mathbf{v}\| \geq \lambda_1(L)$. And there exists $\mathbf{w} \in L$ such that $\|\mathbf{w}\| = \lambda_1(L)$: any such $\mathbf{w}$ is called a shortest vector of L, and it is not unique since $-\mathbf{w}$ would also be a shortest vector. The *kissing number* of L is the number of shortest vectors in L: it is upper bounded by some exponential function of the lattice dimension (see [**CS98**]).

If $\mathbf{w}$ is a shortest vector of L, then so is $-\mathbf{w}$. Thus, one must be careful when defining the *second-to-shortest* vector of a lattice. To circumvent this problem, Minkowski [**Min96**] defined the other minima as follows. For all $1 \leq i \leq \dim(L)$, the i-th *minimum* $\lambda_i(L)$ is defined as the minimum of $\max_{1 \leq j \leq i} \|\mathbf{v}_j\|$ over all i linearly independent lattice vectors $\mathbf{v}_1, \ldots, \mathbf{v}_i \in L$. Clearly, the minima are increasing: $\lambda_1(L) \leq \lambda_2(L) \leq \cdots \leq \lambda_d(L)$. And it is not difficult to see that there always exist linearly independent lattice vectors $\mathbf{v}_1, \ldots, \mathbf{v}_d$ reaching simultaneously the minima, that is $\|\mathbf{v}_i\| = \lambda_i(L)$ for all i. However, surprisingly, as soon as $\dim(L) \geq 4$, such vectors do not necessarily form a lattice basis. The canonical example is the 4-dimensional lattice L defined as the set of all $(x_1, x_2, x_3, x_4) \in \mathbb{Z}^4$

such that $\sum_{i=1}^{4} x_i$ is even. It is not difficult to see that $\dim(L) = 4$ and that all the minima of L are equal to $\sqrt{2}$. Furthermore, it can be checked that the following row vectors form a basis of L:

$$\begin{pmatrix} 1 & -1 & 0 & 0 \\ 1 & 1 & 0 & 0 \\ 1 & 0 & 1 & 0 \\ 1 & 0 & 0 & 1 \end{pmatrix}.$$

The basis proves in particular that $\text{vol}(L) = 2$. However, the following row vectors are linearly independent lattice vectors which also reach all the minima:

$$\begin{pmatrix} 1 & -1 & 0 & 0 \\ 1 & 1 & 0 & 0 \\ 0 & 0 & 1 & 1 \\ 0 & 0 & 1 & -1 \end{pmatrix}.$$

But they do not form a basis, since their determinant is equal to 4: another reason is that for all such vectors, the sum of the first two coordinates is even, and that property also holds for any integral linear combination of those vectors, but clearly not for all vectors of the lattice L. More precisely, the sublattice spanned by those four row vectors has index two in the lattice L.

Nevertheless, in the lattice L, there still exists at least one basis which reaches all the minima simultaneously, and we already gave one such basis. This also holds for any lattice of dimension ≤ 4, but it is no longer true in dimension ≥ 5, as was first noticed by Korkine and Zolotarev in the 19th century, in the language of quadratic forms. More precisely, it can easily be checked that the lattice spanned by the rows of the following matrix

$$\begin{pmatrix} 2 & 0 & 0 & 0 & 0 \\ 0 & 2 & 0 & 0 & 0 \\ 0 & 0 & 2 & 0 & 0 \\ 0 & 0 & 0 & 2 & 0 \\ 1 & 1 & 1 & 1 & 1 \end{pmatrix}$$

has no basis reaching all the minima (which are all equal to two).

6.5.2. *Hermite's constant and Minkowski's theorems.* Now that successive minima have been defined, it is natural to ask how large those minima can be. Hermite [**Her50**] was the first to prove that the quantity $\lambda_1(L)/\text{vol}(L)^{1/d}$ could be upper bounded over all d-rank lattices L. The supremum of $\lambda_1(L)^2/\text{vol}(L)^{2/d}$ over all d-rank lattices L is denoted by γ_d, and called Hermite's constant of dimension d, because Hermite was the first to establish its existence in the language of quadratic forms. The use of quadratic forms explains why Hermite's constant refers to $\max_L \lambda_1(L)^2/\text{vol}(L)^{2/d}$ and not to $\max_L \lambda_1(L)/\text{vol}(L)^{1/d}$. Clearly, γ_d could also be defined as the supremum of $\lambda_1(L)^2$ over all d-rank lattices L of unit volume.

It is known that γ_d is reached, that is: for all $d \geq 1$, there is a d-rank lattice L such that $\gamma_d = \lambda_1(L)^2/\text{vol}(L)^{2/d}$, and any such lattice is called *critical*. But finding the exact value of γ_d is a very difficult problem, which has been central in Minkowski's geometry of numbers. The exact value of γ_d is known only for $1 \leq d \leq 8$ (see the book [**Mar03**] for proofs) and very recently also for $d = 24$ (see [**CK04**]): the values are summarized in the following table.

d	2	3	4	5	6	7	8	24
γ_d	$2/\sqrt{3}$	$2^{1/3}$	$\sqrt{2}$	$8^{1/5}$	$(64/3)^{1/6}$	$64^{1/7}$	2	4
Approximation	1.1547	1.2599	1.4142	1.5157	1.6654	1.8114	2	4

Furthermore, the list of all critical lattices (up to scaling and isometry) is known for each of those dimensions.

However, rather tight asymptotical bounds are known for Hermite's constant. More precisely, we have:
$$\frac{d}{2\pi e} + \frac{\log(\pi d)}{2\pi e} + o(1) \leq \gamma_d \leq \frac{1.744 d}{2\pi e}(1 + o(1)).$$
For more information on the proof of those bounds: see [**MH73**, Chapter II] for the lower bound (which comes from the Minkowski-Hlawka theorem), and [**CS98**, Chapter 9] for the upper bound. Thus, γ_d is essentially linear in d. It is known that $\gamma_d^d \in \mathbb{Q}$ (because there is always an integral critical lattice), but it is unknown if γ_d is an increasing sequence.

Hermite's historical upper bound [**Her50**] on his constant was exponential in the dimension:
$$\gamma_d \leq (4/3)^{(d-1)/2}.$$
The first linear upper bound on Hermite's constant is due to Minkowski, who viewed it as a consequence of his Convex Body Theorem:

THEOREM 6.6 (Minkowski's Convex Body Theorem). *Let L be a full-rank lattice of $\mathbb{R}^n$. Let C be a measurable subset of $\mathbb{R}^n$, convex, symmetric with respect to 0, and of measure $> 2^n \operatorname{vol}(L)$. Then C contains at least a non-zero point of L.*

This theorem is a direct application of the following elementary lemma (see [**Sie89**]), which can be viewed as a generalization of the pigeon-hole principle:

LEMMA 6.7 (Blichfeldt). *Let L be a full-rank lattice in $\mathbb{R}^n$, and F be a measurable subset of $\mathbb{R}^n$ with measure $> \operatorname{vol}(L)$. Then F contains at least two distinct vectors whose difference is in L.*

Indeed, we may consider $F = \frac{1}{2}C$, and the assumption in Theorem 6.6. implies that the measure of F is $> \operatorname{vol}(L)$. From Blichfeldt's lemma, it follows that there exist $\mathbf{x}$ and $\mathbf{y}$ in F such that $\mathbf{x} - \mathbf{y} \in L \setminus \{0\}$. But
$$\mathbf{x} - \mathbf{y} = \frac{1}{2}(2\mathbf{x} - 2\mathbf{y})$$
which belongs to C by convexity, and symmetry with respect to 0. Hence: $\mathbf{x} - \mathbf{y} \in C \cap (L \setminus \{0\})$, which completes the proof of Theorem 6.6.

One notices that the bound on the volumes in Theorem 6.6 is the best possible, by considering
$$C = \left\{ \sum_{i=1}^n x_i \mathbf{b}_i \ : |x_i| < 1 \right\},$$
where the $\mathbf{b}_i$'s form an arbitrary basis of the lattice. Indeed, in this case, the measure of C is exactly $2^n \operatorname{vol}(L)$, but by definition of C, no non-zero vector of L belongs to C.

In Theorem 6.6, the condition on the measure of C is a strict inequality, but it is not difficult to show that the strict inequality can be relaxed to an inequality $\geq 2^n \operatorname{vol}(L)$ if C is further assumed to be compact. By choosing for C a closed hyperball of sufficiently large radius (so that the volume inequality is satisfied), one obtains that any d-dimensional lattice L of $\mathbb{R}^n$ contains a non-zero $\mathbf{x}$ such that
$$\|\mathbf{x}\| \leq 2 \left(\frac{\operatorname{vol}(L)}{v_d} \right)^{\frac{1}{d}},$$

where v_d denotes the volume of the closed unitary hyperball of $\mathbb{R}^d$. Using well-known formulas for v_d, one can derive a linear bound on Hermite's constant, for instance:
$$\forall d, \; \gamma_d \leq 1 + \frac{d}{4}.$$
One can obtain an analogous result for the max-norm:

THEOREM 6.8. *Let L be a d-dimensional lattice. Then there exists a non-zero $\mathbf{x}$ in L such that:*
$$\|\mathbf{x}\|_\infty \leq \operatorname{vol}(L)^{1/d}.$$

Notice that this bound is reached by $L = \mathbb{Z}^d$.

Now that we know how to bound the first minimum, it is natural to ask if a similar bound can be obtained for the other minima. Unfortunately, one cannot hope to upper bound separately the other minima, because the successive minima could be unbalanced. For instance, consider the rectangular 2-rank lattice L spanned by the following row matrix:
$$\begin{pmatrix} \varepsilon & 0 \\ 0 & 1/\varepsilon \end{pmatrix},$$
where $\varepsilon > 0$ is small. The volume of L is one, and by definition of L, it is clear that $\lambda_1(L) = \varepsilon$ and $\lambda_2(L) = 1/\varepsilon$ if $\varepsilon \leq 1$. Here, $\lambda_2(L)$ can be arbitrarily large compared to the lattice volume, while $\lambda_1(L)$ can be arbitrarily small compared to the upper bound given by Hermite's constant.

However, it is always possible to upper bound the geometric mean of the first consecutive minima, as summarized by the following theorem (for an elementary proof, see [**Sie89, MG02**]):

THEOREM 6.9 (Minkowski's Second Theorem). *Let L be a d-rank lattice of $\mathbb{R}^n$. Then for any integer r such that $1 \leq r \leq d$:*
$$\left(\prod_{i=1}^{r} \lambda_i(L)\right)^{1/r} \leq \sqrt{\gamma_d}\, \operatorname{vol}(L)^{1/d}.$$

6.5.3. *Random Lattices.* The upper bound on the first minimum derived from Hermite's constant is only tight for critical lattices, which are very special lattices. One might wonder what happens for more general lattices, say random lattices. But what is a random lattice? Surprisingly, from a mathematical point of view, there is a natural (albeit technically involved) notion of random lattice, which follows from a measure on full-rank lattices with determinant 1 introduced by Siegel [**Sie45**] back in 1945, to provide an alternative proof of the Minkowski-Hlawka theorem; this measure is derived from Haar measures of classical groups. In these lecture notes, no formal definition of random lattices will be needed: we refer the interested reader to the recent articles [**Ajt02, GM03**] which propose efficient ways to generate lattices which are provably random in this sense: see also [**NS06**] for practical considerations. We now list a few important properties of random lattices, to give more intuition on random lattices. We saw in Section 6.5.2 that an n-rank lattice L satisfies:

(6.1) $$\lambda_1(L) \leq \sqrt{\gamma_n}\, \operatorname{vol}(L)^{1/n} \leq \sqrt{1+n/4}\, \operatorname{vol}(L)^{1/n}.$$

Interestingly, a random n-rank lattice L satisfies asymptotically with overwhelming probability (see [**Ajt06**] for a proof):

$$\forall\, 1 \leq i \leq n, \lambda_i(L) \approx \sqrt{\frac{n}{2\pi e}}\, \mathrm{vol}(L)^{1/n}.$$

In particular, the bound on the first minimum derived from Hermite's constant is not that far from being tight in the random case: the ratio between the two upper bounds is bounded independently of the dimension. Thus, even though it is easy to construct lattices for which the first minimum is arbitrarily small compared to Hermite's bound, such lattices are far from being random: the first minimum of random lattices is almost as large as the one of critical lattices. Furthermore, [**Ajt06**] also shows that asymptotically, in a random n-rank lattice L, there exists with overwhelming probability a lattice basis $(\mathbf{b}_1, \ldots, \mathbf{b}_n)$ such that:

$$\forall\, 1 \leq i \leq n, \|\mathbf{b}_i\| \approx \sqrt{\frac{n}{2\pi e}}\, \mathrm{vol}(L)^{1/n}.$$

Such a basis consists of very short vectors, since their norms are close to the successive minima. Thus, there are always nice bases in random lattices.

The previous properties are useful to distinguish specific lattices from random lattices. For instance, in cryptography, one often encounters lattices for which the first minimum is provably much smaller than Hermite's bound (6.1), so such lattices cannot be random, and they might have exceptional properties which can be exploited. And when a lattice is very far from being random, certain computational problems which are hard in the general case may become easy.

6.5.4. *Reduction Notions.* In Section 6.5.3, we saw that random lattices always have nice bases: naturally, one might wonder what happens in the general case. The goal of lattice (basis) reduction is to prove the existence of nice lattice bases in every lattice, and not just random lattices. Such nice bases are called *reduced*, but it is important to stress that there are many notions of reduction. Usually, one first defines a notion of reduction, then shows that there exist bases which are reduced in this sense, and finally proves that bases which are reduced in this sense have interesting properties. In terms of interesting properties, we are interested in both mathematical and computational properties: does it have nice mathematical properties, and is it easy to compute such reduced bases? Computational aspects will only be discussed in the next subsection.

In low dimension ≤ 4, there is one notion of reduction which is arguably better than all the others: the so-called Minkowski reduction. Minkowski defined a natural notion of reduction, for which it is easy to prove that there are Minkowski-reduced bases in all lattices. And Minkowski proved that when the lattice dimension d is ≤ 4, a Minkowski-reduced basis $(\mathbf{b}_1, \ldots, \mathbf{b}_d)$ must satisfy: $\forall i, \|\mathbf{b}_i\| = \lambda_i(L)$, which is arguably the best one can hope for a basis. Furthermore, there is a very natural algorithm to compute such bases, and which is very efficient up to dimension ≤ 4 (see [**NS04**]). However, when the dimension is ≥ 5, among all the reduction notions which are known, none is clearly better than the others. But the best notions of reduction known all provide guarantees on the norm of the basis vectors $\mathbf{b}_1, \ldots, \mathbf{b}_d$, such as upper bounds on the d ratios $\|\mathbf{b}_i\|/\lambda_i(L)$.

Enumerating all the reduction notions known is beyond the scope of these notes. In fact, we will not even define precisely any reduction notion. Instead, we will only present properties of two important notions of reduction (see [**MG02**]): the

Lenstra-Lenstra-Lovász reduction [**LLL82**] (called LLL for short), and the Hermite-Korkine-Zolotarev reduction [**KZ73**] (called HKZ for short). The HKZ reduction is a very strong notion of reduction which is computationally expensive, while the LLL reduction is a weaker notion of reduction which is computationally inexpensive. An HKZ-reduced basis $(\mathbf{b}_1, \ldots, \mathbf{b}_d)$ of a lattice L satisfies for all $1 \leq i \leq d$:

$$\frac{4}{i+3} \leq \left(\frac{\|\mathbf{b}_i\|}{\lambda_i(L)}\right)^2 \leq \frac{i+3}{4}.$$

In particular, $\|\mathbf{b}_1\| = \lambda_1(L)$, and one can see that all the other vectors are very close to the minima. The LLL reduction is a relaxed variant of a notion of reduction proposed by Hermite [**Her50**]: it depends on a factor δ satisfying $\frac{1}{4} < \delta \leq 1$. Historically, the factor chosen in [**LLL82**] was $\delta = 3/4$ for ease of notation, but the closer δ is to 1, the stronger the LLL reduction. An LLL-reduced basis $(\mathbf{b}_1, \ldots, \mathbf{b}_d)$ with factor δ of a lattice L satisfies (see [**LLL82**]):

(1) $\|\mathbf{b}_1\| \leq \alpha^{(d-1)/4} (\operatorname{vol} L)^{1/d}$, where $\alpha = 1/(\delta - \frac{1}{4})$.
(2) For all $1 \leq i \leq d$, $\|\mathbf{b}_i\| \leq \alpha^{(d-1)/2} \lambda_i(L)$.
(3) $\|\mathbf{b}_1\| \times \cdots \times \|\mathbf{b}_d\| \leq \alpha^{d(d-1)/4} \operatorname{vol} L$.

Note that for the historical choice $\delta = 3/4$ of [**LLL82**], we have $\alpha = 2$. Interestingly, for the optimal choice $\delta = 1$, we obtain $\alpha = 4/3$, in which case the previous inequality (1) matches Hermite's exponential bound on Hermite's constant. The vectors of an LLL-reduced basis are thus at most exponentially far from the minima.

We stress that we have not even defined the LLL or HKZ reductions: we only listed a few properties of those reductions. We have not even proved that any lattice must have LLL-reduced bases and HKZ-reduced bases (which holds): typically, the existence of reduced bases is established by means of an algorithm (efficient or not). We will discuss computational aspects of lattice reduction in the next subsection.

6.6. Computational Aspects. In this section, we discuss computational aspects of lattices. More information can be found in [**MG02, GLS93**]. We would like to emphasize that there is a well-known gap between theory and practice: one should be very careful when interpreting theoretical or practical results.

6.6.1. *Computational Model.* When dealing with complexity aspects, we assume implicitly that the lattices under consideration are rational lattices given explicitly by a basis, that is a matrix with rational coefficients: the cost of the algorithm will be measured with respect to the size of this matrix, that is, the maximal bit-length of the numerator and denominator of the coefficients, as well as the numbers of rows and columns of the matrix. From a practical point of view, all the parameters of the matrix are important. Naturally, a lattice algorithm will be said to be polynomial-time if its running time is polynomial in the size of the matrix representing the lattice. Since any rational lattice can easily be transformed into an integral lattice by an appropriate scaling, we can assume without loss of generality that the input lattices are integral lattices.

One may wonder about alternative representations of lattices. For instance, if one is only given a set of generators of an integral lattice, a classical result states that one can compute in polynomial time a basis of the lattice (see [**GLS93**]). More generally, a lattice may be given only implicitly, and the first task is to efficiently find a basis. For instance, the set of integral solutions to a system of linear equations over the integers is a lattice: a classical result states that one can compute in polynomial time a basis of that lattice from the system of equations (see [**GLS93**]).

Complexity results assume that there is a main parameter, and the hardness refers to when that parameter grows to infinity. In the case of lattices, the main parameter is the lattice dimension: the other parameters (bit-length of the matrix entries and the dimension of the space) are then assumed to be polynomial in the lattice dimension. In fixed lattice dimension, all lattice problems become easy.

6.6.2. *Lattice Problems.* There are many computational problems related to lattices, which can be roughly classified in two categories: those which are easy, and those which are believed to be hard.

Among the easy lattice problems which can be solved in polynomial time (see [**GLS93**]), one can find:

Membership: Given a basis of a lattice L in $\mathbb{Q}^n$ and a target vector $\mathbf{t} \in \mathbb{Q}^n$, decide if $\mathbf{t} \in L$ or not.
Equality: Given bases of two lattices L_1 and L_2 in $\mathbb{Q}^n$, decide if $L_1 = L_2$.
Inclusion: Given bases of two lattices L_1 and L_2 in $\mathbb{Q}^n$, decide if $L_1 \subseteq L_2$.
Intersection: Given bases of two lattices L_1 and L_2 in $\mathbb{Q}^n$, find a basis of the lattice $L_1 \cap L_2$.

Interestingly, there are lattice problems which seem to be very hard, due to the existence of NP-hardness results (see [**MG02**]). The most famous lattice problem is the *shortest vector problem* (SVP for short): given a basis of a rational lattice L, find $\mathbf{v} \in L$ such that $\|\mathbf{v}\| = \lambda_1(L)$. Because Ajtai [**Ajt98**] proved that SVP is NP-hard under randomized reductions, the existence of efficient algorithms to solve SVP seems unlikely. In fact, the best deterministic SVP algorithm is Kannan's super-exponential algorithm [**Kan83**] which requires $O(d^{d/(2e)+o(d)})$ polynomial operations (and negligible memory) [**HS07, HS08**], where d is the lattice dimension. The probabilistic SVP algorithm of [**AKS01**] improves the running time to $2^{O(d)}$ polynomial operations, but its space requirements become exponential $2^{O(d)}$ (see [**NV08**] for an assessment of the $O()$ constant). In low dimension $d \leq 4$, there is an elegant and very efficient algorithm to solve SVP, which generalizes Lagrange's algorithm (see [**NS04**]). Since SVP seems to be a very hard problem, one often considers approximate versions of SVP. For instance the γ-approximate SVP with $\gamma \in \mathbb{R}$ is: given a basis of a rational lattice L, find a non-zero $\mathbf{v} \in L$ such that $\|\mathbf{v}\| \leq \gamma \lambda_1(L)$. Approximating SVP within a factor γ means solving γ-approximate SVP. Naturally, the bigger γ, the easier γ-approximate SVP. The LLL algorithm [**LLL82**] solves $(4/3)^{d/2}$-approximate SVP in polynomial time (see [**MG02**]). The best polynomial-time deterministic algorithm for approximate-SVP is Gama and Nguyen's algorithm [**GN08a**] (an improvement of [**Sch87, GHGKN06**]) with an appropriate blocksize k, which can solve γ-approximate SVP for $\gamma = \gamma_k^{(d-k)/(k-1)} = 2^{O(d(\log\log d)^2/\log d)}$ for $k = O(\log d/\log\log d)$. The best polynomial-time randomized algorithm for approximate-SVP is Gama and Nguyen's algorithm [**GN08a**] (an improvement of [**Sch87, GHGKN06**]) using the randomized AKS algorithm [**AKS01**] within blocks of size k, which can solve γ-approximate SVP for $\gamma = \gamma_k^{(d-k)/(k-1)} = 2^{O(d(\log\log d)/\log d)}$ for $k = O(\log d)$.

Another famous lattice problem is the *closest vector problem* (CVP for short), also called the *nearest lattice point problem*: given a basis of a rational lattice $L \in \mathbb{Q}^n$ and a target vector $\mathbf{t} \in \mathbb{Q}^n$, find $\mathbf{v} \in L$ minimizing $\|\mathbf{t} - \mathbf{v}\|$, that is, such that $\|\mathbf{t}-\mathbf{v}\| \leq \|\mathbf{t}-\mathbf{w}\|$ for all $\mathbf{w} \in L$. Similarly as for SVP, one defines γ-approximate

CVP as follows: given a basis of a rational lattice $L \in \mathbb{Q}^n$ and a target vector $\mathbf{t} \in \mathbb{Q}^n$, find $\mathbf{v} \in L$ such that $\|\mathbf{t} - \mathbf{v}\| \leq \gamma \|\mathbf{t} - \mathbf{w}\|$ for all $\mathbf{w} \in L$. Note that if one knows a orthogonal basis for the lattice L (such as is the case for $\mathbb{Z}^n$), CVP becomes trivial, but in general, one only knows a weakly-reduced basis, which makes the problem very difficult. CVP was shown to be NP-hard as early as in 1981 [**Emd81**] (for a much simpler "one-line" proof using the knapsack problem, see [**Mic01**]). Babai's nearest plane algorithm [**Bab86**] uses LLL to solve $2(4/3)^{d/2}$-approximate CVP in polynomial time (see [**MG02**]). Using any of [**Sch87, GHGKN06, GN08a**], this can be improved to $2^{O(d(\log \log d)^2 / \log d)}$ in polynomial time, and even further to $2^{O(d \log \log d / \log d)}$ in randomized polynomial time using [**AKS01**], due to Kannan's link between CVP and SVP (see further). For exact CVP, the best algorithm is Kannan's super-exponential algorithm [**Kan83, Kan87b**], with running time $2^{O(d \log d)}$ (see also [**Hel85, HS07**] for an improved constant).

Interestingly, NP-hardness results for SVP and CVP are known to have limits. Goldreich and Goldwasser [**GG98**] showed that approximating SVP or CVP to within $\sqrt{d/\log d}$ cannot be NP-hard, unless the polynomial-time hierarchy collapses.

There are relationships between SVP and CVP. Goldreich et al. [**GMSS99**] showed that CVP cannot be easier than SVP: given an oracle that solves $f(d)$-approximate CVP, one can solve $f(d)$-approximate SVP in polynomial time. Reciprocally, Kannan proved in [**Kan87a**, Section 7] that any algorithm solving $f(d)$-approximate SVP where f is a non-decreasing function can be used to solve $d^{3/2} f(d)^2$-approximate CVP in polynomial time.

In practice, a popular strategy to try to solve CVP when the target vector is very close to the lattice is Kannan's *embedding method* (see [**Kan87b, GGH97, Ngu99, MG02**]), which uses the previous algorithms for SVP and a simple heuristic reduction from CVP to SVP. Namely, given a lattice basis $(\mathbf{b}_1, \ldots, \mathbf{b}_d)$ and a vector $\mathbf{v} \in \mathbb{R}^n$, the embedding method builds the $(d+1)$-dimensional lattice (in $\mathbb{R}^{n+1}$) spanned by the row vectors $(\mathbf{b}_i, 0)$ and $(\mathbf{v}, 1)$. Depending on the lattice, one should choose a coefficient different from 1 in $(\mathbf{v}, 1)$. It is hoped that a shortest vector of that lattice is of the form $(\mathbf{v} - \mathbf{u}, 1)$ where $\mathbf{u}$ is a closest vector (in the original lattice) to $\mathbf{v}$, whenever the distance to the lattice is smaller than the lattice first minimum. This heuristic may fail (see for instance [**Mic98**] for some simple counterexamples), but it can also sometimes be proved, notably in the case of lattices arising from low-density knapsacks (see [**NS05b**]).

Approximating SVP or CVP is often achieved by solving a more general problem: lattice reduction, which is roughly speaking finding a basis close to all the minima.

6.6.3. *Cost of HKZ and LLL Reductions.* The classical results regarding HKZ and LLL reductions are the following:

- It is possible to compute an HKZ-reduced basis of a d-dimensional lattice in $O(d^{O(d)})$ polynomial operations (see [**Kan83, Sch87, HS07**]): note that this running time is super-exponential in d.
- If the reduction factor δ is a rational number such that $1/4 < \delta < 1$, the LLL algorithm [**LLL82**] computes an LLL-reduced basis of factor δ in polynomial time (see also [**NS05a**] for optimized variants). Note that we need $\delta < 1$, in which case $\alpha > 4/3$. In practice, one often uses $\delta = 0.99$ so that $\alpha \approx 4/3$: in [**MG02**], it is even shown how to select δ converging

to 1 while keeping polynomial-time complexity. However, the constant α is typically a worst-case constant: on the average, in practice, it seems that α should be replaced by a smaller constant close to 1.08 for moderate dimension (see [**NS06, GN08b**]).

6.6.4. *Experimental Facts.* For those who are interested in performing experiments, the NTL library [**Sho**] provides an easy-to-use lattice package, which includes efficient implementations of the main lattice reduction algorithms. In low dimension, one can also play with GP/PARI [**BBB**+].

In this section, we discuss what can be expected in practice regarding the solvability of lattice problems: more information can be found in [**GN08b**]. We stress that there is unfortunately no easy rule-of-thumb to predict what one can do or cannot do in practice. In low dimension, say ≤ 60, the most important lattice problems become easy: for instance, exact SVP and CVP can be quickly solved using existing tools. The main reason is that lattice reduction algorithms behave better than their worst-case bounds: see for instance [**NS06**] for the case of LLL, and [**GN08b**] for the case of BKZ. However, as soon as the lattice dimension becomes very high, it is difficult to predict experimental results in advance. Several factors seem to influence the result: the lattice dimension, the input basis, the structure of the lattice, and in the case of CVP, the distance of the target vector to the lattice. What is always true is that one can quickly approximate SVP and CVP up to exponential factors with an exponentiation base very close to 1 (see [**GN08b**] for concrete values of the exponentiation bases), but in high dimension, such exponential factors may not be enough for cryptanalytic purposes, depending on the application. If better approximation factors are required, one should perform experiments to see if existing algorithms are sufficient. If the lattice and the input basis are not exceptional, there is no reason to believe that exact SVP can be solved in very high dimension (say ≥ 300), although one can always give it a try. Furthermore, if the target vector is not unusually close to the lattice, there is also no reason to believe that exact CVP could be solved in very high dimension (say ≥ 300).

One example of unusual lattice structure is when one knows the existence of a non-zero lattice vector much smaller than Hermite's bound: one should compare the norm of that lattice vector with $\sqrt{d}\,\mathrm{vol}(L)^{1/d}$. In this case, one is advised to try existing algorithms in practice, since there is hope: for instance, [**Ngu99**] reported successes for such SVP instances (and CVP instances for which the target vector is unusually close to the lattice, *i.e.* when the distance is much smaller than $\sqrt{d}\,\mathrm{vol}(L)^{1/d}$) in very high dimension; and the experiments of [**GN08b**] suggest that SVP can be solved for lattices L such that $\lambda_2(L)/\lambda_1(L)$ is a not too small fraction of 1.012^d.

7. Lattice Attacks

In this section, we survey the main lattice attacks:

- Section 7.1 presents natural attacks which use lattices of low dimension.
- Section 7.2 presents natural attacks which use lattices of high dimension.
- Section 7.3 presents attacks based on unusually small roots of polynomial equations (or congruences): finding such roots is done using lattices of moderate dimension.

7.1. Low-Dimensional Attacks.

The attacks we will present in this section are fairly representative of attacks based on low-dimensional lattices. Here, the underlying problem which will be tackled by the use of lattices is as follows: assume that we have a linear congruence of the form

$$\sum_{i=1}^{n} a_i x_i \equiv b \pmod{M}, \tag{7.1}$$

where only the x_i's are unknown integers, whereas the integer $a_i \in \mathbb{Z}$, the integer $b \in \mathbb{Z}$ and the modulus M are known. Obviously, if there is no constraint on the size of the x_i's, it is easy to find a solution $(x_1, \ldots, x_n) \in \mathbb{Z}^n$ to (7.1), so we are interested in solutions satisfying special properties, say the size of the x_i's is small. When n is small (say, less than 10), the following holds:

- Lattice reduction can efficiently find a solution $(x_1, \ldots, x_n) \in \mathbb{Z}^n$ such that $x_i = O(M^{1/n})$. Note that this is trivial if $n = 1$. If $b \equiv 0 \pmod{M}$, the problem can be reduced to finding a very short vector in a lattice. If $b \not\equiv 0 \pmod{M}$, the problem can be reduced to finding a very close lattice vector.
- If there is an exceptional solution $(x_1, \ldots, x_n) \in \mathbb{Z}^n$ such that $\prod_{i=1}^{n} x_i$ is much smaller than M, then it can probably be recovered in practice, and perhaps also in theory. More precisely, if $b \equiv 0 \pmod{M}$, it means that there exists an exceptionally short vector in a certain lattice. And if $b \not\equiv 0 \pmod{M}$, it means that there exists a vector in a certain lattice which is unusually close to a certain target vector.

Such results have been applied many times in cryptanalysis.

7.1.1. RSA with small secret exponent.
Consider the usual RSA key generation:

- The public modulus is $N = pq$ where p and q are large primes of about the same bit-length, that of $N^{1/2}$.
- The pair (e, d) of public and secret exponents satisfy the congruence (2.1), and we have $0 \leq e, d \leq N$.

Wiener [**Wie90**] showed that if the secret exponent d is such that $0 \leq d \leq N^{1/4}$, then one can recover p and q in polynomial time from N and e. Wiener's attack was historically presented using continued fractions. Here, we will present a lattice version of this attack, based on a two-dimensional shortest vector problem. Note that this lattice version will only be heuristic, while Wiener's attack is provable: however, in practice, both work as well. Furthermore, this lattice attack is fairly representative of the numerous heuristic cryptanalyses based on low-dimensional lattices.

Because p and q are balanced, we have:

$$\phi(N) = N + O(\sqrt{N}).$$

The congruence (2.1) implies the existence of some $k = O(d)$ such that $e \cdot d = 1 + k(N + O(\sqrt{N}))$, thus:

$$\ell = e \cdot d - kN = O(d\sqrt{N}).$$

Now consider the 2-rank lattice L spanned by the rows of:

$$\begin{pmatrix} e & \sqrt{N} \\ N & 0 \end{pmatrix}$$

Then L contains $\mathbf{t} = d \times$ first row $- k \times$ second row $= (\ell, d\sqrt{N})$, whose norm is $\approx d\sqrt{N}$, while $\text{vol}(L)^{1/2} = N^{3/4}$. Thus, $\mathbf{t}$ is heuristically expected to be the shortest vector of L if $d\sqrt{N} < N^{3/4}$, that is, $d \leq N^{1/4}$. Note however that we do not claim to have proved that $\mathbf{t}$ is the shortest vector: it is only a very reasonable guess. By solving SVP in the 2-rank lattice L, we can hope to find $\mathbf{t}$, and therefore the secret exponent d.

Let us a give a baby example for concreteness. Assume that Alice had selected the primes $p = 6011673201679823947$ and $q = 6987193563793194751$, so that her RSA modulus is:

$$N = 42004724302405294297751453898364502197.$$

The bit-length of N is 125, so let us assume that Alice selected a 30-bit prime at random as her secret exponent, such as $d = 814510573$, so that Wiener's bound $d < N^{1/4}$ is satisfied. Then Alice's public exponent is:

$$e = 17924546723775007116522646995236610637.$$

From the public key (e, N), the attacker computes $\sqrt{N} \approx 6481105176002414967$, and derives the following 2×2 integer matrix:

$$\begin{pmatrix} 17924546723775007116522646995236610637 & 6481105176002414967 \\ 42004724302405294297751453898364502197 & 0 \end{pmatrix}.$$

After running Lagrange's algorithm, the attacker obtains the following reduced basis:

$$\begin{pmatrix} 4518062787607145156653412229 & -5278928690578992864154946091 \\ 2863039538377673408119351098 4 & 2680335050035250893178150689 5 \end{pmatrix}.$$

Notice that the first row vector of the reduced basis is substantially shorter than the second row vector, which proves that the lattice is not random. From the first row vector, the attacker guesses that Alice's secret exponent is:

$$d = 5278928690578992864154946091/6481105176002414967 = 814510573,$$

which is correct!

7.1.2. RSA signatures with constant-based padding. We saw in Section 4.1.1 an adaptive chosen-message universal forgery on Textbook-RSA, thanks to the multiplicativity of the RSA permutation. This forgery shows that one should preprocess the message before signing it, and check the preprocessing when verifying the signature. One early candidate of preprocessing is constant-based padding, which means that we pad the messages by a fixed (public) series of bits before signing, and check that redundancy when verifying a signature. In other words:

- There is a constant P defining the padding.
- A message m to sign is assumed to be small (say, $|m| \leq M$ where M is much smaller than N), and its signature is:

$$s = (P + m)^d \pmod{N}.$$

- A signature s of a message m is checked using the congruence:

$$s^e \equiv P + m \pmod{N}.$$

One further checks that m is sufficiently small, that is, $|m| \leq M$.

The smaller M is, the harder it should be for an attacker to forge signatures.

Assume that we have three messages m_1, m_2 and m_3. Each m_i is signed as:
$$s_i = (P + m_i)^d \pmod{N}.$$
Then $s_1 \equiv s_2 s_3 \pmod{N}$ if and only if $(P+m_1) \equiv (P+m_2)(P+m_3) \pmod{N}$. We claim that given m_3, we can find suitable m_1 and m_2 less than roughly $\sqrt{N}$ using lattice reduction, namely approximating the closest vector problem in dimension two. This leads to a chosen-message universal forgery, provided that the message size is at least half that of N.

We want to solve $(P + m_1) \equiv (P + m_2)(P + m_3) \pmod{N}$, which is of the form $m_1 - m_2 \alpha \equiv \beta \pmod{N}$. Consider the 2-rank lattice L of all $(x,y) \in \mathbb{Z}^2$ such that $x - y\alpha \equiv 0 \pmod{N}$. Notice that $\mathrm{vol}(L) = N$. We can hope to find a lattice vector $\mathbf{u} = (u_1, u_2)$ whose distance to $\mathbf{t} = (\beta, 0)$ is $\approx \mathrm{vol}(L)^{1/2} \approx N^{1/2}$. Then $m_1 = \beta - u_1$ and $m_2 = -u_2$ are both $O(N^{1/2})$. And $m_1 - m_2 \alpha \equiv \beta \pmod{N}$ which leads to a heuristic forgery which works very well in practice. Hence, we have obtained a chosen-message universal forgery up to the bound $M \approx N^{1/2}$. Interestingly, the bound $N^{1/2}$ for the message bound M has been improved to $N^{1/3}$ using four messages by Brier et al. [**BCCN01**] using different lattice-based techniques: Lenstra and Shparlinski [**LS02**] improved the existential forgery of [**BCCN01**] into a universal forgery.

Again, let us give a baby example for concreteness. We take the same RSA modulus N as the example of Section 7.1.1. The constant P is chosen as the first decimal digits of π multiplied by a suitable power of 10:
$$P = 31415926535897932300000000000000000000.$$
We would like to sign the message $m_3 = 2718281828459045235$. This implies that:
$$\beta = P(P + m_3) - P \equiv 28532925287943337534233793526174219074 \pmod{N},$$
and
$$\alpha = P + m_3 \equiv 31415926535897932302718281828459045235 \pmod{N}.$$
So we consider the lattice L of all $(x,y) \in \mathbb{Z}^2$ such that $x - y\alpha \equiv 0 \pmod{N}$. The following 2×2 matrix is clearly a basis of L:
$$\begin{pmatrix} \alpha & 1 \\ N & 0 \end{pmatrix} = \begin{pmatrix} 31415926535897932302718281828459045235 & 1 \\ 42004724302405294297751453898364502197 & 0 \end{pmatrix}.$$
After running the LLL algorithm, we obtain the following reduced basis:
$$\begin{pmatrix} 2840910670399556715 & 3383974095730158874 \\ -8143041377019128593 & 5086004066464213681 \end{pmatrix}.$$
After running Babai's nearest plane algorithm [**Bab86**] on the target vector $\mathbf{t} = (\beta, 0)$, we obtain the following lattice vector
$$\mathbf{u} = (28532925287943337532025597115229231563 \quad 1667092550642276495),$$
which leads to $m_1 = 2208196410944987511$ and $m_2 = -1667092550642276495$. It can be checked that:
$$(P + m_1) \equiv (P + m_2)(P + m_3) \pmod{N}.$$
Note that both $|m_1|$ and $|m_2|$ are less than 2^{61}, whereas the bit-length of m_3 is 62. By comparison, the bit-length of N is 125, so m_1 and m_2 are indeed close to $\sqrt{N}$.

7.1.3. *Elgamal signature in GnuPG.* GnuPG [**GPG**] is a widely deployed software to secure emails: it is present in most distributions of the Linux operating system, and is more or less an open source version of the famous PGP software. Prior to the publication of [**Ngu04**], GnuPG included an implementation of the Elgamal signature, which turned out to be extremely insecure. Namely, Nguyen showed in [**Ngu04**] that after one signature had been released, an attacker could recover the signer's secret key in less than a second on a personal computer. The attack is based on low-dimensional lattices.

First, let us describe the Elgamal signature scheme as implemented in GnuPG, which slightly differs from Textbook Elgamal. The parameters are a large prime p such that $(p-1)/2$ has large factors, and a generator g of $\mathbb{Z}_p^*$. The secret key is a small exponent x less than $p^{3/8}$, and the public key is $y = g^x \pmod{p}$. Messages are preprocessed before being signed, using a usual padding which we omit here. To sign a padded message $m \in \mathbb{Z}_p$:

- Select a small "random" number k coprime with $p-1$, which turns out to be less than $p^{3/8}$.
- The signature is (a,b) where $a = g^k \bmod p$ and $b = (m-ax)k^{-1} \pmod{p-1}$.

The attack [**Ngu04**] works as follows. Assume that a signature (a,b) of a message m is known. We focus on the congruence $b \equiv (m-ax)k^{-1} \pmod{p-1}$ satisfied by the signature (a,b), that is:

(7.2) $$bk + ax \equiv m \pmod{p-1},$$

where both k and x are $\leq p^{3/8}$. Consider the 2-rank lattice L of all $(\alpha, \beta) \in \mathbb{Z}^2$ such that:

$$b\alpha + a\beta \equiv 0 \pmod{p-1}.$$

The volume of L is $\mathrm{vol}(L) = (p-1)/\gcd(a,b,p-1) \approx p$ because a and b are unlikely to have a large gcd. We can easily find integers $u_1, u_2 \in \mathbb{Z}$ such that

$$bu_1 + au_2 \equiv m \pmod{p-1}.$$

Then the lattice vector $\mathbf{t} = (u_1 - k, u_2 - x) \in L$ is unusually close to $\mathbf{u} = (u_1, u_2)$: the distance between $\mathbf{t}$ and $\mathbf{u}$ is less than $p^{3/8}$, which is itself much less than $\mathrm{vol}(L)^{1/2} \approx p^{1/2}$. If $\mathbf{t}$ is indeed the closest lattice vector, then the secret key x is recovered.

The attack is very efficient in practice, and can be made provable if a and b are assumed to be uniformly distributed: for more details, see [**Ngu04**]. Namely, if a and b are assumed to be uniformly distributed, one can prove that L has no unusually short vectors, which implies that when a lattice vector is unusually close to a target vector, any other lattice vector must be sustantially farther away from that target vector.

7.2. High-Dimensional Attacks. As an illustration of attacks based on high-dimensional lattices, we present an important attack which was historically not presented in terms of lattices, but which can interestingly be viewed in terms of lattices in a simple manner. The attack is Bleichenbacher's celebrated chosen-ciphertext attack [**Ble98**] on RSA-PKCS#1 encryption version 1.5, which arguably motivated the use of chosen-ciphertext security in cryptography standards. Bleichenbacher did not use lattices because he wanted to optimize the attack, but the lattice version of the attack is perhaps easier to understand.

In Section 4.2.1, we saw elementary attacks on Textbook RSA encryption which show that messages must be preprocessed prior to raw RSA encryption (raising to the power e modulo N). A natural question arises: which preprocessing should one use? In the nineties, a very popular solution was to use the PKCS#1 v1.5 standard [**Lab**] advocated by the RSA company: for instance, the standard was used in SSL v3.0, which is widely deployed in Internet browsers. The standard specified how to transform a message M, prior to raw RSA encryption (that is, exponentiation to the power e):

- The message m to encrypt is assumed to be much smaller than the RSA modulus N: it will be at least a few bytes less than N.
- This value is then padded as described in PKCS#1 v1.5 block type 02 (see Figure 1): a zero byte is added to the left, as well as as many non-zero random bytes as necessary in such a way that the first two bytes of the final value are 00 02 followed by as many nonzero random bytes as necessary to match the size of the modulus. In other words, the whole value m described in Figure 1 must fit the size of the modulus N.

| 00 | 02 | Non-zero random bytes | 00 | Message M |

FIGURE 1. PKCS#1 v1.5 encryption padding, block type 02.

When decrypting an RSA ciphertext encrypted by the PKCS#1 v1.5 block type 02 standard, one recovers a value m of the form given in Figure 1 and must proceed as follows to recover the message M:

- One first checks that the first two most significant bytes are 00 and 02.
- Next, one removes all the non-zero bytes until one finds a 00 byte.
- The rest must be the message M.

But what if the decryption process failed? For instance, what if the first two most significant bytes of $c^d \pmod{N}$ are not 00 and 02? Such a situation may arise since anybody can submit ciphertexts, and therefore, ciphertexts are not necessarily valid ciphertexts. Bleichenbacher [**Ble98**] noticed that in several implementations of SSL v3.0, the person who decrypts – in real life, a server which receives many messages encrypted with its RSA public key – actually returns an error message when there is a problem during the decryption process. In other words, in this case, an adversary has access to a 0002-oracle: given any $c \in \mathbb{Z}_N$, the 0002-oracle answers whether or not the first two most significant bytes of $c^d \pmod{N}$ are 00 and 02. In [**Ble98**], Bleichenbacher showed how such an oracle enables an adversary to decrypt any RSA ciphertext $c = m^e \pmod{N}$, including those m of the form described in Figure 1. The attack presented in [**Ble98**] is rather technical, so as to minimize the number of queries to the oracle. In these notes, we will present an alternative lattice-based attack, which is simpler to present, but is not intended to be optimal: the main ideas are nevertheless identical.

Assume that there is an RSA public key (N, e), and that a message $m \in \{0, \ldots, N-1\}$ has been encrypted as $c = m^e \pmod{N}$: the ciphertext c is public, but the message m is of course secret. Assume also that one has access to a 0002-oracle $\mathcal{O}$: given any $c' \in \mathbb{Z}_N$, the oracle $\mathcal{O}$ answers whether or not the first two most significant bytes of $c'^d \pmod{N}$ are 00 and 02. We will see how one can recover m using a reasonable number of oracle queries.

First of all, we note that if we select a $c \in \mathbb{Z}_N$ uniformly at random, the probability that the oracle $\mathcal{O}$ answers yes is very close to $1/256^2 = 1/65536$: here, we only say "very close" because N is not exactly a power of two. This suggests to do the following many times:

- Select uniformly at random $r \in \mathbb{Z}_N$.
- Compute $c' = r^e c \pmod{N}$ and send c' to the oracle $\mathcal{O}$.
- If the answer is yes (which should happen with probability $1/65536$), store r: it means that $rm \pmod{N}$ starts with 00 02, because $c' \equiv (rm)^e \pmod{N}$ by multiplicativity of the RSA permutation. Otherwise, start again.

We now know many random integers $r_1, \ldots, r_n$ such that each $r_i m \bmod N$ starts with 00 02, and we would like to recover the message m. If we knew one of the $r_i m \bmod N$ exactly, it would be easy to recover m by dividing by r_i, whose value is known. But here, we only know an approximation of each of the $r_i m \bmod N$: more precisely, if we let $a = 2^{\ell-15}$ where ℓ is the bit-length of N, then a represents the number 0002 shifted to the left $0 \leq (r_i m \bmod N) - a < N/2^{16}$; we can even have a better approximation if we use $a' = a + N/2^{17}$, which implies that:

$$|(r_i m \bmod N) - a'| \leq N/2^{17}.$$

This kind of problem has been dubbed hidden number problem (HNP) by Boneh and Venkatesan [**BV96**]: here, m is the "hidden number". Boneh and Venkatesan [**BV96**] studied the HNP to obtain bit-security results on the Diffie-Hellman key exchange in prime fields. Later, the HNP and variants were applied to cryptanalysis (see [**NS02, NS03**]), namely to attack classical signature schemes based on the discrete logarithm problem when partial information on the one-time keys used during signature generation is leaked.

We will now solve the HNP by viewing it as a lattice closest vector problem. Consider the $(n+1)$-rank lattice L spanned by the following rows:

$$\begin{pmatrix} 1/65536 & r_1 & r_2 & \cdots & r_n \\ 0 & N & 0 & \cdots & 0 \\ \vdots & 0 & N & \ddots & \vdots \\ \vdots & \vdots & \ddots & \ddots & 0 \\ 0 & 0 & \cdots & 0 & N \end{pmatrix}$$

By multiplying the first row by m, and subtracting appropriate multiples of the other rows, one sees that the lattice L contains the vector

$$\mathbf{m} = (m/65536, mr_1 \bmod N, \ldots, mr_n \bmod N).$$

If we could recover the vector $\mathbf{m} \in L$, we would derive the message m. Since each $mr_i \bmod N$ starts with the 00 02 bytes, we have seen that if ℓ denotes the bit-length of N then the constant $a' = 2^{\ell-15} + N/2^{17}$ satisfies:

$$|(r_i m \bmod N) - a'| \leq N/2^{17}.$$

This suggests to define the target vector $\mathbf{t} = (N/2^{17}, a', a', \ldots, a')$. We note that the lattice vector $\mathbf{m}$ is very close to $\mathbf{t}$. Indeed, each coordinate of $\mathbf{m} - \mathbf{t}$ is less than $N/2^{17}$ in absolute value. Hence:

$$\|\mathbf{m} - \mathbf{t}\| \leq N\sqrt{n+1}/2^{17}.$$

Is that distance exceptional? Since $\text{vol}(L) = N^n/65536$ and L has rank $n+1$, a typical lattice distance should be:

$$\sqrt{n+1}(N^n/65536)^{1/(n+1)},$$

which is roughly $\sqrt{n+1}N^{n/(n+1)}$. Thus, one would expect $\mathbf{m} \in L$ to be heuristically the closest vector to $\mathbf{t}$ if:

(7.3) $$N/2^{17} \ll N^{n/(n+1)}.$$

If $\mathbf{m} \in L$ was indeed the closest lattice vector, any CVP oracle would disclose $\mathbf{m}$. However, in general, the closest vector problem can only be solved in practice when the dimension is not too big. So we shouldn't take too large values of n.

We performed experiments on 512-bit and 1024-bit modulus N using the NTL library [Sho]. To try to solve the closest vector problem, we applied Babai's nearest plane algorithm [Bab86] on an LLL-reduced basis and BKZ-reduced bases of blocksize 10 and 20. If N is a 512-bit number, then (7.3) is satisfied as soon as $n+1 \gg 30$. In practice, we were able to recover m within a few seconds when n is roughly greater than 40. This means that the total number of oracle queries is $\approx 40 \times 65536 = 2,621,440$. If N is a 1024-bit number, then (7.3) is satisfied as soon as $n+1 \gg 60$. In practice, we were able to recover m within a few minutes when n is roughly greater than 80. This means that the total number of oracle queries is $\approx 80 \times 65536 = 5,242,880$. Interestingly, the numbers of oracle queries required by the lattice attack are not that much bigger than in the initial (non-lattice) method of Bleichenbacher [Ble98].

7.3. Polynomial Attacks. We now survey an important application of lattice reduction found in 1996 by Coppersmith [**Cop97, Cop01**], and its developments. These results illustrate the power of linearization combined with lattice reduction.

7.3.1. *Univariate modular equations.* Consider Textbook-RSA encryption with a small public exponent e, such as $e = 3$. Recall that a message $m \in \mathbb{Z}_N$ is encrypted as:

$$c = m^e \mod N.$$

We saw in Section 4.2.1 the short-message attack: if $0 \leq m \leq N^{1/e}$, then the short message m can be recovered from c. Can this short-message attack be extended?

For instance, if the message m is the shift of a short message (less than $N^{1/e}$), then the same attack applies, after division (modulo N) by a suitable power of two. More generally, what if only a few consecutive bits of the message m were unknown? Such messages are called stereotyped: many parts of the message are known. This is the case of emails, which include known fields such as the name of the sender, the name of the recipient, *etc.* Formally speaking, we assume that the secret message $m \in \{0, \ldots, N-1\}$ is of the form:

$$m = m_0 + 2^k s,$$

where m_0, s, k are all non-negative integers, but only s is secret: the integers m_0 and k are known. This corresponds to the situation where $m = $ 'known bits' $\|$ 'unknown bits' $\|$ 'known bits', where the $\|$ symbol denotes concatenation. Then the ciphertext c satisfies:

$$c = (m_0 + 2^k s)^e \pmod{N},$$

which, after division by a suitable power of two, can be rewritten as

$$P(s) \equiv 0 \pmod{N},$$

where $P(x) \in \mathbb{Z}[x]$ is a monic polynomial of degree e whose coefficients can all be derived from c, k, m_0 and N.

At first sight, this is just an instance of the general problem of solving univariate polynomial equations modulo some integer N of unknown factorization, which is considered to be hard. Indeed, for some polynomials, the problem is equivalent to the knowledge of the factorization of N. And the particular case of extracting e-th roots modulo N is the problem of decrypting ciphertexts in the RSA cryptosystem, for an eavesdropper. Surprisingly, Coppersmith [**Cop97**] showed using the LLL algorithm that the special problem of finding small roots was easy:

THEOREM 7.1 (Coppersmith). *Let $P(x) \in \mathbb{Z}[x]$ be a monic polynomial of degree δ in one variable, and let N be an integer of unknown factorization. Then one can find in time polynomial in $(\log N, \delta)$ all integers x_0 such that $P(x_0) \equiv 0 \pmod{N}$ and $|x_0| \leq N^{1/\delta}$.*

Before proving Theorem 7.1, let us make a few remarks. Related (but weaker) results appeared in the eighties [**Hås88, VGT88**]. More precisely, Håstad [**Hås88**] presented his result in terms of a system of low-degree modular equations, but he actually studies the same problem, and his approach proves a weaker version of Theorem 7.1 with the smaller bound $N^{2/(\delta(\delta+1))}$ instead of $N^{1/\delta}$. Incidentally, Theorem 7.1 implies that the number of roots less than $N^{1/\delta}$ is polynomial, which was also proved in [**KS94**] (using elementary techniques).

Theorem 7.1 is easy to prove if $P(x)$ is of the form $P(x) = x^\delta + c$: this is what we used in the short-message attack against Textbook-RSA. Can we hope to improve the bound $N^{1/\delta}$ to say $C \times N^{1/\delta}$? It is not difficult to see that we can do so if we multiply the polynomial running-time of Theorem 7.1 by C, but the new running-time is then exponential in $\log C$: namely, one splits the roots interval of length $2C \times N^{1/\delta}$ into roughly C intervals of length $2N^{1/\delta}$. Unfortunately, if one would like to keep a polynomial running-time, one cannot hope to improve the (natural) bound $N^{1/\delta}$ for all polynomials and all moduli N. Indeed, for the polynomial $P(x) = x^\delta$ and $N = p^\delta$ where p is prime, the roots of P mod N are the multiples of p. Thus, one cannot hope to find all the small roots (slightly) beyond $N^{1/\delta} = p$, because there are simply too many of them. This suggests that even an SVP-oracle (instead of an approximate-SVP algorithm like LLL) should not improve Theorem 7.1 in general, as evidenced by the proof of Theorem 7.1: the approximation factor provided by LLL does not play a significant role, because the lattices considered by the proof have a huge volume (compared to their dimension). It was noticed in [**BN00**] that if one only looks for the smallest root mod N, an SVP-oracle can improve the bound $N^{1/\delta}$ for very particular moduli (namely, squarefree N of known factorization, without too small factors). Note that in such cases, finding modular roots can still be difficult, because the number of modular roots can be exponential in the number of prime factors of N. Coppersmith discusses potential improvements in [**Cop01**]. For instance, the condition $P(X)$ being monic can replaced by the gcd of the coefficients of $P(X)$ and N being equal to 1.

Theorem 7.1 has many applications. The historical application was to attack RSA encryption when a very small public exponent is used (see [**Bon99**] for a survey). Later applications include Chinese remaindering in the presence of noise [**BN00**], and surprisingly, a few security proofs of factoring-based cryptographic schemes (see [**Sho01, Bon01**]). We already saw the cryptanalytic application to stereotyped messages, which generalized the short-message attack: if there are less than $(\log N)/e$ unknown consecutive bits in the message m, then the whole message m can be recovered in polynomial time from its ciphertext $c = m^e$ (mod N) and the public key (N, e). A less direct application is the random pad: to prevent elementary attacks on RSA, rather than applying the PKCS#1 v1.5 padding, one could simply append random bytes to a message m, before raising it to the power e modulo N. More precisely the ciphertext of a message $m \ll N$ is $c = (m\|r)^e$ (mod N), where r is a sequence of bits chosen uniformly at random for each encryption. If the same message $m \ll N$ is encrypted twice, an adversary may collect the ciphertexts $c_1 = (m\|r_1)^e$ (mod N) and $c_2 = (m\|r_2)^e$ (mod N). Coppersmith [**Cop97**] noticed that by computing the resultant of those two polynomials in (m, r_1, r_2), one obtains a univariate polynomial congruence modulo N of degree e^2, satisfied by $r_1 - r_2$. Thus, if the random sequence r has less than $\log(N)/(e^2)$ bits, then one can recover $r_1 - r_2$, which eventually leads to the recovery of the message m using other techniques (see [**CFPR96**]).

We now sketch a proof of Theorem 7.1, in the spirit of Howgrave-Graham [**HG97**], who simplified Coppersmith's original proof by working in the dual lattice of the lattice originally considered by Coppersmith. More details can be found in the survey [**Cop01**]. Coppersmith's method reduces the problem of finding small modular roots to the (easy) problem of solving polynomial equations over $\mathbb{Z}$. More precisely, it applies lattice reduction to find an integral polynomial equation satisfied by all small modular roots of P. The intuition is to linearize all the equations of the form $x^i P(x)^j \equiv 0$ (mod N^j) for appropriate integral values of i and j. Such equations are satisfied by any solution of $P(x) \equiv 0$ (mod N). Small solutions x_0 will give rise to unusually short solutions to the resulting linear system. To transform modular equations into integer equations, we will use the elementary fact that any sufficiently small integer must be zero. More precisely, we will use the following elementary lemma[1], with the notation $\|r(x)\| = \sqrt{\sum a_i^2}$ for any polynomial $r(x) = \sum a_i x^i \in \mathbb{Q}[x]$:

LEMMA 7.2. *Let $r(x) \in \mathbb{Q}[x]$ be a polynomial of degree $< n$ and let X be a positive integer. Suppose $\|r(xX)\| < 1/\sqrt{n}$. If $r(x_0) \in \mathbb{Z}$ with $|x_0| \leq X$, then $r(x_0) = 0$ holds over the integers.*

PROOF. If $|x_0| \leq X$, then the Cauchy-Schwarz inequality ensures that:

$$r(x_0)^2 = \left(\sum_{i=0}^{n-1} r_i x_0^i\right)^2 = \left(\sum_{i=0}^{n-1} r_i X^i (x_0/X)^i\right)^2$$

$$\leq \left(\sum_{i=0}^{n-1} (r_i X^i)^2\right) \times \left(\sum_{i=0}^{n-1} (x_0/X)^{2i}\right)$$

$$\leq \|r(xX)\|^2 \times n$$

Thus, if we further have $\|r(xX)\| < 1/\sqrt{n}$, then $|r(x_0)| < 1$. Hence, if $r(x_0) \in \mathbb{Z}$, it must be zero. □

---

[1] A similar lemma is used in [**Hås88**]. Note also the resemblance with [**LLL82**, Prop. 2.7].

We would like to apply Lemma 7.2 to a suitable polynomial $r(x) \in \mathbb{Q}[x]$, that is, a polynomial satisfying:
- Property 1: $\|r(xX)\| < 1/\sqrt{1 + \deg r}$. In other words, the vector corresponding to the polynomial $r(xX)$ must be short.
- Property 2: $r(x_0) \in \mathbb{Z}$ whenever $P(x_0) \equiv 0 \pmod{N}$ and $x_0 \in \mathbb{Z}$.

If we find such a polynomial $r(x) \in \mathbb{Q}[x]$, then by solving the equation $r(x_0) = 0$ over $\mathbb{Z}$, we will find in polynomial time all the integers $x_0 \in \mathbb{Z}$ such that $P(x_0) \equiv 0 \pmod{N}$ and $|x_0| \leq X$. And if X is sufficiently close to $N^{1/\delta}$, say $N^{1/\delta} = O(X)$, then Theorem 7.1 would follow.

But how can we find such a polynomial $r(x) \in \mathbb{Q}[x]$? An obvious candidate is $q(x) = P(x)/N \in \mathbb{Q}[x]$, which clearly satisfies Property 2. But it is unclear whether $q(x)$ would satisfy Property 1. Other natural choices would be all the polynomials of the form $q_{u,v}(x) = x^u (P(x)/N)^v \in \mathbb{Q}[x]$ where u and v are non-negative integers. Such polynomials satisfy Property 2, just like $q(x)$, but they are also unlikely to satisfy Property 1. There are however many other candidates: notice that any integral linear combination of the $q_{u,v}(x)$'s satisfies Property 2, and maybe one such combination could satisfy Property 1. This suggests to find $r(x) \in \mathbb{Q}[x]$ satisfying Lemma 7.2 among all integral linear combinations of the $q_{u,v}(x)$'s: this is reminiscent of finding short vectors in a lattice.

Since there is an infinite number of $q_{u,v}(x)$'s, it might be useful to restrict to polynomials of bounded degree, where the bound is a parameter which we will select in an appropriate manner. More precisely, let us consider a non-negative integer h, as well as the $n = (h+1)\delta$ polynomials $q_{u,v}(x) = x^u (P(x)/N)^v \in \mathbb{Q}[x]$, where $0 \leq u \leq \delta - 1$ and $0 \leq v \leq h$. Now, we would like to find a short vector in the lattice corresponding to the $q_{u,v}(xX)$'s. More precisely, define the $n \times n$ matrix M whose i-th row consists of the coefficients of $q_{u,v}(xX)$, starting by the low-degree terms, where $v = \lfloor (i-1)/\delta \rfloor$ and $u = (i-1) - \delta v$. Notice that the i-th row represents a polynomial $q_{u,v}(xX)$ of degree $i - 1$, whose leading coefficient is $X^u (X^\delta/N)^v = X^{i-1}/N^v$. Hence, the matrix M is lower triangular, and a simple calculation leads to:
$$\det(M) = X^{n(n-1)/2} N^{-nh/2}.$$

Let us now apply an LLL-reduction to the full-dimensional lattice spanned by the rows of M. The first vector of the reduced basis corresponds to a non-zero polynomial of the form $r(xX)$, and has Euclidean norm $\|r(xX)\|$. The theoretical bounds of the LLL algorithm ensure that:
$$\|r(xX)\| \leq 2^{(n-1)/4} \det(M)^{1/n} = 2^{(n-1)/4} X^{(n-1)/2} N^{-h/2}.$$

Recall that we need $\|r(xX)\| \leq 1/\sqrt{n}$ to apply Lemma 7.2. Hence, for a given choice of h, the method is guaranteed to find modular roots x_0 up to the bound X if the bound satisfies:
$$X \leq \frac{1}{\sqrt{2}} N^{h/(n-1)} n^{-1/(n-1)}.$$

The limit of the upper bound, when h grows to ∞, is $\frac{1}{\sqrt{2}} N^{1/\delta}$. Thus, we would like to select a sufficiently large h so that the bound X satisfies $N^{1/\delta} = O(X)$, but on the other hand, we need to keep the running time of the algorithm polynomial by restricting to sufficiently small values of h, with respect to $\log N$ and δ. Fortunately, both requirements are compatible: Theorem 7.1 follows from an appropriate choice of h as a function of $\log N$ and δ.

The algorithm of Theorem 7.1 is practical: see [**CNS99, HG98**] for experimental results. In practice, the optimal choice of parameters depends very much on the implementation of the lattice reduction algorithm: rather than fix the bound X, and choose h and n accordingly, one should select the lattice rank n, and compute the theoretical bound X which is guaranteed. In order to find the value of n which offers the best trade-off between the running time and the size of the bound X, one should perform a series of experiments with existing implementations of lattice reduction algorithms.

7.3.2. *The gcd generalization.* Interestingly, Theorem 7.1 can be viewed as a particular case of the following gcd result:

THEOREM 7.3. *Let $P(x) \in \mathbb{Z}[x]$ be a monic polynomial of degree δ in one variable, and let N be an integer of unknown factorization. Let $\alpha \in \mathbb{Q}$ such that $0 \leq \alpha \leq 1$. Then one can find in time polynomial in $(\log N, \delta)$ and the bit-size of α all integers x_0 such that $\gcd(P(x_0), N) \geq N^\alpha$ and $|x_0| \leq N^{\alpha^2/\delta}$.*

Strictly speaking, Theorem 7.3 only appeared explicitly in [**May03, May04**] where it was attributed to Coppersmith. However, it was earlier presented in several workshop/summer school talks (such as SAC 2001), and could be considered as a folklore theorem: the result was implicit in [**BDHG99, Bon00**]; the particular case $P(x)$ of degree 1 was stated and proved in [**HG01**], and the proof of [**HG01**] also works for the general case. Blömer and May [**BM05**, Cor. 14] proved a slightly different result where there are two modifications in the statement of Theorem 7.3: one replaces the assumption $P(x)$ monic by the weaker assumption that the gcd of the coefficients of $P(x)$ is coprime with N, and one replaces the property $\gcd(P(x_0), N) \geq N^\alpha$ by the stronger property: $P(x_0) \geq N^\alpha$ and $P(x_0)$ divides N.

Note that Theorem 7.1 is simply the case $\alpha = 1$ in Theorem 7.3. By choosing different values of α, one obtains interesting applications [**BDHG99, Bon00, HG01, CM04**]. To give a flavour of the applications, let us present two examples:

Factoring with a hint: Consider an RSA modulus $N = pq$ where p and q have the same size. Assume that we know half of the most significant bits of p: for instance, one could imagine that half of the bits are given by the identity of the user, so that it would not be necessary to store them. Thus, we know an integer p_0 such that $p = p_0 + \varepsilon$ where ε is an unknown integer such that $0 \leq \varepsilon \lesssim N^{1/4}$. Consider the polynomial $P(x) = p_0 + x$. Then $\gcd(P(\varepsilon), N) = p \gtrsim N^{1/2}$ with $\varepsilon \leq N^{1/4}$. By applying Theorem 7.3 with $\alpha = 1/2$, we obtain ε and therefore factor N in polynomial time. Such a result was first proved by Coppersmith [**Cop97**], but not using Theorem 7.3. Rather, Coppersmith [**Cop97**] applied an analogue of Theorem 7.1 to bivariate equations over the integers, which we discuss in Section 7.3.4. We assumed that the (half) unknown bits of p were the least significant bits of p: by tweaking the polynomial $P(x)$, one can apply Theorem 7.3 to easily prove the more general result where the unknown bits of p are located at an arbitrary position (such as most significant bits, or middle bits), as while as they are all consecutive (not split among several blocks). More precisely, we may write $p = p_0 + \varepsilon 2^k$ where p_0 and k are known, which leads us to consider $P(x) = cp_0 + x$ where c is chosen as the inverse of 2^k modulo N.

Factoring of $N = p^r q$: Assume that $N = p^r q$ where r is large, and p and q need not be prime. Assume that we know an approximation p_0 of p : $p = p_0 + \varepsilon$. Consider the polynomial $P(x) = (p_0+x)^r$. Then $\gcd(P(\varepsilon), N) = p^r$ is very large. By a careful application of Theorem 7.3, Boneh, Durfee and Howgrave-Graham [**BDHG99**] proved that all numbers $N = p^r q$ where $r > \log p$ and $\log q = O(\log p)$ can be factored in time polynomial in $\log N$. In such a case, a sufficiently good approximation p_0 of p can be found in polynomial time by brute force: because r is large, we do not need a very good approximation.

We will not give a complete proof of Theorem 7.3: see [**HG01, May03**] for more details. Rather, we will give the main argument, compared to Theorem 7.1. In Theorem 7.1, we used the fact that every sufficiently small integer was zero, in order to transform a polynomial congruence modulo N into a polynomial equation over $\mathbb{Z}$. Theorem 7.3 relies on the fact that every sufficiently small rational with bounded denominator must be zero. More precisely, the proof considers again an integral linear combination $r(x) \in \mathbb{Q}[x]$ of the polynomials $q_{u,v}(x) = x^u (P(x)/N)^v$ with the constraint $0 \leq v \leq h$. If the gcd of $P(x_0)$ with N is $\geq N^\alpha$, then $Q(x_0)$ is not necessarily an integer like in the proof of Theorem 7.1: However, the rational number $Q(x_0)$ then has denominator $\leq N^{h(1-\alpha)}$. Thus, this rational number is therefore zero if it is $< 1/N^{h(1-\alpha)}$. This still reduces the problem to finding short lattice vectors, but the proof is more technical: namely, because the bound on the short vector depends here on the parameter h, we need to find the right balance between all the parameters used by the algorithm.

7.3.3. *Multivariate modular equations.* Interestingly, Coppersmith [**Cop97**] noticed that Theorem 7.1 can be heuristically extended to multivariate polynomial modular equations. Assume for instance that one would like to find all small roots of $P(x, y) \equiv 0 \pmod{N}$, where $P(x, y)$ has total degree δ and has at least one monic monomial $x^\alpha y^{\delta-\alpha}$ of maximal total degree. If one could obtain two algebraically independent integral polynomial equations satisfied by all sufficiently small modular roots (x, y), then one could compute (as resultant) a univariate integral polynomial equation satisfied by x, and hence find efficiently all small (x, y). To find such equations, one can use an analogue of Lemma 7.2 to bivariate polynomials, with the (natural) notation $\|r(x,y)\| = \sqrt{\sum_{i,j} a_{i,j}^2}$ for $r(x,y) = \sum_{i,j} a_{i,j} x^i y^j$:

LEMMA 7.4. *Let $r(x, y) \in \mathbb{Q}[x, y]$ be a sum of at most w monomials. Assume $\|r(xX, yY)\| < 1/\sqrt{w}$ for some $X, Y \geq 0$. If $r(x_0, y_0) \in \mathbb{Z}$ with $|x_0| < X$ and $|y_0| < Y$, then $r(x_0, y_0) = 0$ holds over the integers.*

By analogy, one chooses a parameter h and select $r(x, y)$ as a linear combination of the polynomials $q_{u_1, u_2, v}(x, y) = x^{u_1} y^{u_2} (P(x, y)/N)^v$, where $u_1 + u_2 + \delta v \leq h\delta$ and $u_1, u_2, v \geq 0$ with $u_1 < \alpha$ or $u_2 < \delta - \alpha$. Such polynomials have total degree less than $h\delta$, and therefore are linear combinations of the $n = (h\delta + 1)(h\delta + 2)/2$ monic monomials of total degree $\leq \delta h$. Due to the condition $u_1 < \alpha$ or $u_2 < \delta - \alpha$, such polynomials are in bijective correspondence with the n monic monomials (associate to $q_{u_1, u_2, v}(x, y)$ the monomial $x^{u_1 + v\alpha} y^{u_2 + v(\delta - \alpha)}$). One can represent the polynomials as n-dimensional vectors in such a way that the $n \times n$ matrix consisting of the $q_{u_1, u_2, v}(xX, yY)$'s (for some ordering) is lower triangular with coefficients $N^{-v} X^{u_1 + v\delta} y^{u_2 + v(\delta - \alpha)}$ on the diagonal.

Now consider the first two vectors $r_1(xX, yY)$ and $r_2(xX, yY)$ of an LLL-reduced basis of the lattice spanned by the rows of that matrix. Since the rational $q_{u_1,u_2,v}(x_0, y_0)$ is actually an integer for any root (x_0, y_0) of $P(x, y)$ modulo N, we need $\|r_1(xX, yY)\|$ and $\|r_2(xX, yY)\|$ to be less than $1/\sqrt{n}$ to apply Lemma 7.4. A (tedious) computation of the triangular matrix determinant enables to prove that $r_1(x, y)$ and $r_2(x, y)$ satisfy that bound when $XY < N^{1/\delta - \varepsilon}$ and h is sufficiently large. Thus, one obtains two integer polynomial bivariate equations satisfied by all small modular roots of $P(x, y)$.

The problem is that, although such polynomial equations are linearly independent as vectors, they might be algebraically dependent, making the method heuristic. This heuristic assumption is unusual: many lattice-based attacks are heuristic in the sense that they require traditional lattice reduction algorithms to behave like SVP-oracles. An important open problem is to find sufficient conditions to make Coppersmith's method provable for bivariate (or multivariate) equations: see [**BJ07**] for recent progress on this question. Note that the method cannot work all the time. For instance, the polynomial $x - y$ has clearly too many roots over $\mathbb{Z}^2$ and hence too many roots modulo any N (see [**Cop97**] for more general counterexamples).

Such a result may enable to prove several attacks which are for now, only heuristic. Indeed, there are applications to the security of the RSA encryption scheme when a very low public exponent or a low private exponent is used (see [**Bon99**] for a survey), and related schemes such as the KMOV cryptosystem (see [**Ble97**]). In particular, the experimental evidence of [**BD99, Ble97, DN00**] shows that the method is very effective in practice for certain polynomials.

Let us make a few remarks. In the case of univariate polynomials, there was basically no choice over the polynomials $q_{u,v}(x) = x^u (P(x)/N)^v$ used to generate the appropriate univariate integer polynomial equation satisfied by all small modular roots. There is much more freedom with bivariate modular equations. Indeed, in the description above, we selected the indices of the polynomials $q_{u_1,u_2,v}(x, y)$ in such a way that they corresponded to all the monomials of total degree $\leq h\delta$, which form a triangle in $\mathbb{Z}^2$ when a monomial $x^i y^j$ is represented by the point (i, j). This corresponds to the general case where a polynomial may have several monomials of maximal total degree. However, depending on the shape of the polynomial $P(x, y)$ and the bounds X and Y, other regions of (u_1, u_2, v) might lead to better bounds.

Assume for instance $P(x, y)$ is of the form $x^{\delta_x} y^{\delta_y}$ plus a linear combination of $x^i y^j$'s where $i \leq \delta_x$, $j \leq \delta_y$ and $i + j < \delta_x + \delta_y$. Intuitively, it is better to select the (u_1, u_2, v)'s to cover the rectangle of sides $h\delta_x$ and $h\delta_y$ instead of the previous triangle, by picking all $q_{u_1,u_2,v}(x, y)$ such that $u_1 + v\delta_x \leq h\delta_x$ and $u_2 + v\delta_y \leq h\delta_y$, with $u_1 < \delta_x$ or $u_2 < \delta_y$. One can show that the polynomials $r_1(x, y)$ and $r_2(x, y)$ obtained from the first two vectors of an LLL-reduced basis of the appropriate lattice satisfy Lemma 7.4, provided that h is sufficiently large, and the bounds satisfy $X^{\delta_x} Y^{\delta_y} \leq N^{2/3 - \varepsilon}$. Boneh and Durfee [**BD99**] applied similar and other tricks to a polynomial of the form $P(x, y) = xy + ax + b$. This allowed better bounds than the generic bound, leading to improved attacks on RSA with low secret exponent (see also [**DN00**] for an extension to the trivariate case, useful when the RSA primes are unbalanced). More precisely, recall that the RSA exponents d and e are such that $e \cdot d \equiv 1 \mod \phi(N)$. Since $\phi(N) = (p-1)(q-1) = N + 1 - p - q = N + 1 - s$, where $s = p + q \approx N^{1/2}$ there exists k such that $e \cdot d + k(N + 1 - s) = 1$. We obtain a bivariate polynomial congruence with unknowns k and s:

$$k(N+1-s) \equiv 1 \pmod{e},$$

which is of the form $P(x,y) = xy+ax+b$ as mentioned previously. Here, $s \approx N^{1/2}$ is relatively small. If d is small, then so will be the unknown integer k. By optimizing Coppersmith's technique to this polynomial, Boneh and Durfee [**BD99**] showed that one can heuristically factor the RSA modulus $N = pq$ from the public key (N,e) if $d \leq N^{1-1/\sqrt{2}} \approx N^{0.292}$, which improved the bound $N^{0.25}$ of Wiener [**Wie90**] (see Section 7.1.1). The bound can be improved if p and q are unbalanced [**DN00**].

7.3.4. *Multivariate integer equations.* The general problem of solving multivariate polynomial equations over $\mathbb{Z}$ is also hard, as integer factorization is a special case. Coppersmith [**Cop97**] showed that a similar (albeit more technical) lattice-based approach can be used to find small roots of bivariate polynomial equations over $\mathbb{Z}$:

THEOREM 7.5 (Coppersmith). *Let $P(x,y)$ be a polynomial in two variables over $\mathbb{Z}$, of maximum degree δ in each variable separately, and assume the coefficients of P are relatively prime as a set. Let X,Y be bounds on the desired solutions x_0, y_0. Define $\hat{P}(x,y) = P(Xx, Yy)$ and let D be the absolute value of the largest coefficient of $\hat{P}$. If $XY < D^{2/(3\delta)} 2^{-14\delta/3}$, then in time polynomial in $(\log D, \delta)$, we can find all integer pairs (x_0, y_0) such that $P(x_0, y_0) = 0$, $|x_0| < X$ and $|y_0| < Y$.*

Again, the method extends heuristically to more than two variables, and there can be improved bounds depending on the shape[2] of the polynomial (see [**Cop97**]). Theorem 7.5 was introduced to factor in polynomial time an RSA–modulus $N = pq$ provided that half of the (either least or most significant) bits of either p or q are known (see [**Cop97, Bon00, BDF98**]). This was sufficient to break an ID-based RSA encryption scheme proposed by Vanstone and Zuccherato [**VZ95**]. Boneh *et al.* [**BDF98**] provide another application, for recovering the RSA secret key when a large fraction of the bits of the secret exponent is known. However, none of the applications cited above happen to be "true" applications of Theorem 7.5: it was later realized in [**HG98, BDHG99**] that those results could alternatively be obtained from Theorem 7.3, which is the gcd generalization of Theorem 7.1.

The main idea of the proof of Theorem 7.5 is to find another bivariate integer polynomial equation satisfied by the small roots. Surprisingly, it is possible to do so using lattice reduction while making sure that this new equation is algebraically independent from the first equation. Then, by computing a resultant, and solving univariate polynomial equations over $\mathbb{Z}$, one can deduce all the small roots.

The original proof by Coppersmith can be found in [**Cop97**]. Coron [**Cor07**] found an alternative method inspired by Theorem 7.1. Blömer and May [**BM05**] showed a general method to adapt the bounds of Theorem 7.5 depending on the shape of the polynomial $P(x,y)$. In particular, they showed that Theorem 7.1 can actually follow from Theorem 7.5. Surprisingly, Theorem 7.3 does not seem to follow from Theorem 7.5, though Blömer and May [**BM05**] are able to show that a result close to Theorem 7.3 can be viewed as a corollary of Theorem 7.5.

---

[2]The coefficient $2/3$ is natural from the remarks at the end of the previous section for the bivariate modular case. If we had assumed P to have total degree δ, the bound would be $XY < D^{1/\delta}$.

Acknowledgements

We would like to thank Steven Galbraith, Alexander May, Igor Shparlinski, Damien Stehlé and Frederik Vercauteren for helpful discussions and comments on drafts of these notes.

References

[Adl83] L. M. Adleman, *On breaking generalized knapsack publick key cryptosystems*, Proc. of 15th STOC, ACM, 1983, pp. 402–412.

[Ajt98] M. Ajtai, *The shortest vector problem in L_2 is NP-hard for randomized reductions*, Proc. of 30th STOC, ACM, 1998, Available at [**ECC**] as TR97-047.

[Ajt02] M. Ajtai, *Random lattices and a conjectured 0-1 law about their polynomial time computable properties*, Proc. of FOCS 2002, IEEE, 2002, pp. 13–39.

[Ajt06] M. Ajtai, *Generating random lattices according to the invariant distribution*, Draft of March, 2006.

[AKS01] M. Ajtai, R. Kumar, and D. Sivakumar, *A sieve algorithm for the shortest lattice vector problem*, Proc. 33rd STOC, ACM, 2001, pp. 601–610.

[Bab86] L. Babai, *On Lovász lattice reduction and the nearest lattice point problem*, Combinatorica **6** (1986), 1–13.

[BBB+] C. Batut, K. Belabas, D. Bernardi, H. Cohen, and M. Olivier, *PARI/GP computer package version 2*, Université de Bordeaux I.

[BBFK05] F. Bahr, M. Boehm, J. Franke, and T. Kleinjung, *Factorization of RSA-200*, Public announcement on May 9th., 2005.

[BBS06] Elad Barkan, Eli Biham, and Adi Shamir, *Rigorous bounds on cryptanalytic time/memory tradeoffs*, Advances in Cryptology – Proc. CRYPTO '06, Lecture Notes in Computer Science, vol. 4117, Springer, 2006, pp. 1–21.

[BCCN01] E. Brier, C. Clavier, J.-S. Coron, and D. Naccache, *Cryptanalysis of RSA signatures with fixed-pattern padding.*, Proc. CRYPTO '01, LNCS, vol. 2139, IACR, Springer-Verlag, 2001, pp. 433–439.

[BD99] D. Boneh and G. Durfee, *Cryptanalysis of RSA with private key d less than $N^{0.292}$*, Proc. of Eurocrypt '99, LNCS, vol. 1592, IACR, Springer-Verlag, 1999, pp. 1–11.

[BDF98] D. Boneh, G. Durfee, and Y. Frankel, *An attack on RSA given a small fraction of the private key bits*, Proc. of Asiacrypt '98, LNCS, vol. 1514, Springer-Verlag, 1998, pp. 25–34.

[BDHG99] D. Boneh, G. Durfee, and N. A. Howgrave-Graham, *Factoring $n = p^r q$ for large r*, Proc. of Crypto '99, LNCS, vol. 1666, IACR, Springer-Verlag, 1999.

[BDL97] D. Boneh, R. A. DeMillo, and R. J. Lipton, *On the importance of checking cryptographic protocols for faults*, Proc. of Eurocrypt '97, LNCS, vol. 1233, IACR, Springer-Verlag, 1997, pp. 37–51.

[BJ07] Aurélie Bauer and Antoine Joux, *Toward a rigorous variation of Coppersmith's algorithm on three variables*, Advances in Cryptology - Proc. EUROCRYPT '07, Lecture Notes in Computer Science, vol. 4515, Springer, 2007, pp. 361–378.

[BJN00] D. Boneh, A. Joux, and P. Q. Nguyen, *Why textbook ElGamal and RSA encryption are insecure*, Proc. of Asiacrypt '00, LNCS, vol. 1976, IACR, Springer-Verlag, 2000.

[Ble96] D. Bleichenbacher, *Generating ElGamal signatures without knowing the secret key*, Proc. of Eurocrypt '96, LNCS, vol. 1070, IACR, Springer-Verlag, 1996, Corrected version available from the author, pp. 10–18.

[Ble97] _____, *On the security of the KMOV public key cryptosystem*, Proc. of Crypto '97, LNCS, vol. 1294, IACR, Springer-Verlag, 1997, pp. 235–248.

[Ble98] _____, *Chosen ciphertext attacks against protocols based on the RSA encryption standard PKCS #1*, Proc. of Crypto '98, LNCS, vol. 1462, IACR, Springer-Verlag, 1998, pp. 1–12.

[BM05] J. Blömer and A. May, *A tool kit for finding small roots of bivariate polynomials over the integers.*, Advances in Cryptology - Proc. of EUROCRYPT 2005, Lecture Notes in Computer Science, vol. 3494, Springer, 2005, pp. 251–267.

[BN00]   D. Bleichenbacher and P. Q. Nguyen, *Noisy polynomial interpolation and noisy Chinese remaindering*, Proc. of Eurocrypt '00, LNCS, vol. 1807, IACR, Springer-Verlag, 2000.

[Bon99]   D. Boneh, *Twenty years of attacks on the RSA cryptosystem*, Notices of the AMS **46** (1999), no. 2, 203–213.

[Bon00]   _____, *Finding smooth integers in short intervals using CRT decoding*, Proc. of 32nd STOC, ACM, 2000.

[Bon01]   _____, *Simplified OAEP for the RSA and Rabin functions*, Proc. of Crypto '01, LNCS, IACR, Springer-Verlag, 2001.

[BR95]   M. Bellare and P. Rogaway, *Optimal asymmetric encryption*, Proc. of Eurocrypt '94, LNCS, vol. 950, IACR, Springer-Verlag, 1995, pp. 92–111.

[BR96]   _____, *The exact security of digital signatures - how to sign with RSA and Rabin*, Proc. of Eurocrypt '96, LNCS, vol. 1070, IACR, Springer-Verlag, 1996, pp. 399–416.

[BSS04]   I. F. Blake, G. Seroussi, and N. Smart, *Advances in elliptic curve cryptography*, London Mathematical Society Lecture Note Series, vol. 317, Cambridge University Press, 2004.

[BV96]   D. Boneh and R. Venkatesan, *Hardness of computing the most significant bits of secret keys in Diffie-Hellman and related schemes*, Proc. of Crypto '96, LNCS, IACR, Springer-Verlag, 1996.

[BV98]   _____, *Breaking RSA may not be equivalent to factoring*, Proc. of Eurocrypt '98, LNCS, vol. 1233, Springer-Verlag, 1998, pp. 59–71.

[CFPR96]   D. Coppersmith, M. K. Franklin, J. Patarin, and M. K. Reiter, *Low-exponent RSA with related messages*, Proc. of Eurocrypt '96, LNCS, vol. 1070, IACR, Springer-Verlag, 1996, pp. 1–9.

[CK04]   H. Cohn and A. Kumar, *The densest lattice in twenty-four dimensions*, Electron. Res. Announc. Amer. Math. Soc. **10** (2004), 58–67 (electronic).

[CM04]   J.-S. Coron and A. May, *Deterministic polynomial time equivalence of computing the RSA secret key and factoring*, Cryptology ePrint Archive: Report 2004/208. Appeared in J. Cryptology, 2007., 2004.

[CNS99]   C. Coupé, P. Q. Nguyen, and J. Stern, *The effectiveness of lattice attacks against low-exponent RSA*, Proc. of PKC'99, LNCS, vol. 1431, Springer-Verlag, 1999.

[CNS02]   D. Catalano, P. Q. Nguyen, and J. Stern, *The hardness of Hensel lifting: the case of RSA and discrete logarithm*, Proc. of Asiacrypt '02, LNCS, vol. 2501, IACR, Springer-Verlag, 2002, pp. 299–310.

[Cop97]   D. Coppersmith, *Small solutions to polynomial equations, and low exponent RSA vulnerabilities*, J. of Cryptology **10** (1997), no. 4, 233–260, Revised version of two articles from Eurocrypt '96.

[Cop01]   _____, *Finding small solutions to small degree polynomials*, Proc. of CALC '01, LNCS, Springer-Verlag, 2001.

[Cor07]   J.-S. Coron, *Finding small roots of bivariate integer polynomial equations: A direct approach*, Advances in Cryptology - Proc. of CRYPTO 2007, Lecture Notes in Computer Science, vol. 4622, Springer, 2007, pp. 379–394.

[CP01]   R. Crandall and C. Pomerance, *Prime numbers – a computational perspective*, Springer-Verlag, 2001.

[CS98]   J.H. Conway and N.J.A. Sloane, *Sphere packings, lattices and groups*, Springer-Verlag, 1998, Third edition.

[DFSS07]   V. Dubois, P.-A. Fouque, A. Shamir, and J. Stern, *Practical cryptanalysis of SFLASH*, Advances in Cryptology – Proceedings of CRYPTO '07, LNCS, vol. 4622, Springer-Verlag, 2007.

[DH76]   W. Diffie and M. E. Hellman, *New directions in cryptography*, IEEE Trans. Inform. Theory **IT-22** (1976), 644–654.

[DN00]   G. Durfee and P. Q. Nguyen, *Cryptanalysis of the RSA schemes with short secret exponent from Asiacrypt '99*, Proc. of Asiacrypt '00, LNCS, vol. 1976, IACR, Springer-Verlag, 2000.

[ECC]   ECCC, http://www.eccc.uni-trier.de/eccc/, The Electronic Colloquium on Computational Complexity.

[El 85]   T. El Gamal, *A public key cryptosystem and a signature scheme based on discrete logarithms*, IEEE Trans. Inform. Theory **31** (1985), 469–472.

[Emd81]   P. van Emde Boas, *Another NP-complete problem and the complexity of computing short vectors in a lattice*, Tech. report, Mathematische Instituut, University of Amsterdam, 1981, Report 81-04. Available at http://turing.wins.uva.nl/~peter/.

[FJ03]   J.C. Faugère and A. Joux, *Algebraic cryptanalysis of hidden field equation (HFE) cryptosystems using Gröbner bases*, Proc. of Crypto '03, LNCS, vol. 2729, Springer-Verlag, 2003, pp. 44–60.

[FOPS01] E. Fujisaki, T. Okamoto, D. Pointcheval, and J. Stern, *RSA–OAEP is secure under the RSA assumption*, Proc. of Crypto '01, LNCS, IACR, Springer-Verlag, 2001.

[GG98]   O. Goldreich and S. Goldwasser, *On the limits of non-approximability of lattice problems*, Proc. of 30th STOC, ACM, 1998, Available at [**ECC**] as TR97-031.

[GGH97]   O. Goldreich, S. Goldwasser, and S. Halevi, *Public-key cryptosystems from lattice reduction problems*, Proc. of Crypto '97, LNCS, vol. 1294, IACR, Springer-Verlag, 1997, Available at [**ECC**] as TR96-056., pp. 112–131.

[GHGKN06] N. Gama, N. Howgrave-Graham, H. Koy, and P. Q. Nguyen, *Rankin's constant and blockwise lattice reduction*, Proc. of Crypto '06, LNCS, vol. 4117, Springer-Verlag, 2006, pp. 112–130.

[GLS93]   M. Grötschel, L. Lovász, and A. Schrijver, *Geometric algorithms and combinatorial optimization*, Springer-Verlag, 1993.

[GM03]   D. Goldstein and A. Mayer, *On the equidistribution of Hecke points*, Forum Mathematicum **15** (2003), 165–189.

[GMSS99] O. Goldreich, D. Micciancio, S. Safra, and J.-P. Seifert, *Approximating shortest lattice vectors is not harder than approximating closest lattice vectors*, Information Processing Letters **71** (1999), 55–61, Available at [**ECC**] as TR99-002.

[GN08a]   N. Gama and P. Q. Nguyen, *Finding short lattice vectors within Mordell's inequality*, STOC '08 – Proc. 40th ACM Symposium on the Theory of Computing, ACM, 2008.

[GN08b]   _____, *Predicting lattice reduction*, Advances in Cryptology – Proc. EUROCRYPT '08, Lecture Notes in Computer Science, vol. 4965, Springer, 2008.

[GPG]   GPG, *The GNU privacy guard*, http://www.gnupg.org.

[Hås88]   J. Håstad, *Solving simultaneous modular equations of low degree*, SIAM J. Comput. **17** (1988), no. 2, 336–341, Preliminary version in Proc. of Crypto '85.

[HDdL00] R. Harley, D. Doligez, D. de Rauglaudre, and X. Leroy, *Ecc2k-108 challenge solved*, Public announcement on April 4th., 2000.

[Hel80]   M. E. Hellman, *A cryptanalytic time-memory tradeoff*, IEEE Trans. Inform. Theory **26** (1980), 401–406.

[Hel85]   B. Helfrich, *Algorithms to construct Minkowski reduced and Hermite reduced bases*, Theoretical Computer Science **41** (1985), 125–139.

[Her50]   C. Hermite, *Extraits de lettres de M. Hermite à M. Jacobi sur différents objets de la théorie des nombres, deuxième lettre*, J. Reine Angew. Math. **40** (1850), 279–290, Also available in the first volume of Hermite's complete works, published by Gauthier-Villars.

[HG97]   N. A. Howgrave-Graham, *Finding small roots of univariate modular equations revisited*, Cryptography and Coding, LNCS, vol. 1355, Springer-Verlag, 1997, pp. 131–142.

[HG98]   _____, *Computational mathematics inspired by RSA*, Ph.D. thesis, University of Bath, 1998.

[HG01]   _____, *Approximate integer common divisors*, Proc. of CALC '01, LNCS, Springer-Verlag, 2001.

[HPS98]   J. Hoffstein, J. Pipher, and J.H. Silverman, *NTRU: a ring based public key cryptosystem*, Proc. of ANTS III, LNCS, vol. 1423, Springer-Verlag, 1998, Additional information at http://www.ntru.com, pp. 267–288.

[HS07]   Guillaume Hanrot and Damien Stehlé, *Improved analysis of kannan's shortest lattice vector algorithm*, Advances in Cryptology - Proc. CRYPTO 2007, Lecture Notes in Computer Science, vol. 4622, Springer, 2007, pp. 170–186.

[HS08]   _____, *Worst-case hermite-korkine-zolotarev reduced lattice bases*, CoRR **abs/0801.3331** (2008).

[IAC04]   IACR, *Advances in cryptology 1998–2003*, Springer-Verlag, 2004, Electronic Proceedings of the Eurocrypt, Crypto, Asiacrypt, FSE and PKC Conferences.

[JM07]   Ellen Jochemsz and Alexander May, *A polynomial time attack on RSA with private CRT-exponents smaller than 0.073*, Advances in Cryptology – Proc. CRYPTO '07, Lecture Notes in Computer Science, vol. 4622, Springer, 2007, pp. 395–411.

[JvzGG03] Joachim' J. von zur Gathen and J. Gerhard, *Modern computer algebra*, second ed., Cambridge University Press, Cambridge, 2003.

[Kan83]   R. Kannan, *Improved algorithms for integer programming and related lattice problems*, Proc. of 15th STOC, ACM, 1983, pp. 193–206.

[Kan87a]   ———, *Algorithmic geometry of numbers*, Annual review of computer science **2** (1987), 231–267.

[Kan87b]   ———, *Minkowski's convex body theorem and integer programming*, Math. Oper. Res. **12** (1987), no. 3, 415–440.

[Kle07]   T. Kleinjung, *Discrete logarithms in GF(p) – 160 digits*, Public announcement on Feb. 5th., 2007.

[Kob87]   N. Koblitz, *Elliptic curve cryptosystems*, Math. Comp. **48** (1987), 203–209.

[Kob98]   ———, *Algebraic aspects of cryptography*, Springer-Verlag, 1998.

[Koc96]   P. C. Kocher, *Timing attacks on implementations of Diffie-Hellman, RSA, DSS, and other systems*, Proc. of Crypto '96, LNCS, vol. 1109, IACR, Springer-Verlag, 1996, pp. 104–113.

[KS94]   S. V. Konyagin and T. Seger, *On polynomial congruences*, Mathematical Notes **55** (1994), no. 6, 596–600.

[KZ73]   A. Korkine and G. Zolotareff, *Sur les formes quadratiques*, Math. Ann. **6** (1873), 336–389.

[Lab]   RSA Laboratories, *The public-key cryptography standards (PKCS)*, Available at http://www.rsasecurity.com/rsalabs.

[Len87]   H. W. Lenstra, Jr., *Factoring integers with elliptic curves*, Ann. of Math. **126** (1987), 649–673.

[LLL82]   A. K. Lenstra, H. W. Lenstra, Jr., and L. Lovász, *Factoring polynomials with rational coefficients*, Mathematische Ann. **261** (1982), 513–534.

[LS02]   A. K. Lenstra and I. Shparlinski, *Selective forgery of RSA signatures with fixed-pattern padding.*, Proc. of PKC '02, Lecture Notes in Computer Science, vol. 2274, Springer, 2002, pp. 228–236.

[Mar03]   J. Martinet, *Perfect lattices in Euclidean spaces*, Grundlehren der Mathematischen Wissenschaften, vol. 327, Springer-Verlag, Berlin, 2003.

[May03]   A. May, *New RSA vulnerabilities using lattice reduction methods*, Ph.D. thesis, University of Paderborn, 2003.

[May04]   ———, *Secret exponent attacks on RSA-type schemes with moduli $n = p^r q$*, Public Key Cryptography – Proc. of PKC 2004, Lecture Notes in Computer Science, vol. 2947, Springer, 2004, pp. 218–230.

[McE78]   R. J. McEliece, *A public-key cryptosystem based on algebraic number theory*, Tech. report, Jet Propulsion Laboratory, 1978, DSN Progress Report 42-44.

[Men08]   A. Menezes, *An introduction to pairing-based cryptography*, AMS, 2008, In this book.

[MG02]   D. Micciancio and S. Goldwasser, *Complexity of lattice problems: A cryptographic perspective*, Kluwer Academic Publishers, 2002.

[MH73]   J. Milnor and D. Husemoller, *Symmetric bilinear forms*, Springer-Verlag, 1973.

[MH78]   R. Merkle and M. Hellman, *Hiding information and signatures in trapdoor knapsacks*, IEEE Trans. Inform. Theory **IT-24** (1978), 525–530.

[MI88]   T. Matsumoto and H. Imai, *Public quadratic polynominal-tuples for efficient signature-verification and message-encryption*, Proc. of Eurocrypt '88, LNCS, vol. 330, Springer-Verlag, 1988, pp. 419–453.

[Mic98]   D. Micciancio, *On the hardness of the shortest vector problem*, Ph.D. thesis, Massachusetts Institute of Technology, 1998.

[Mic01]   ———, *The hardness of the closest vector problem with preprocessing*, IEEE Trans. Inform. Theory **47** (2001), no. 3, 1212–1215.

[Mil87]   V. Miller, *Use of elliptic curves in cryptography*, Proc. of Crypto '85, LNCS, vol. 218, IACR, Springer-Verlag, 1987, pp. 417–426.

[Min96]   H. Minkowski, *Geometrie der Zahlen*, Teubner-Verlag, Leipzig, 1896.

[MOV93]   A. Menezes, T. Okamoto, and S. A. Vanstone, *Reducing elliptic curve logarithms to logarithms in a finite field*, IEEE Trans. Inform. Theory **39** (1993), no. 5, 1639–1646.

[MOV97] A. Menezes, P. Van Oorschot, and S. Vanstone, *Handbook of applied cryptography*, CRC Press, 1997, Freely available on the Internet.
[MZ98]   K. S. McCurley and C. D. Ziegler, *Advances in cryptology 1981–1997*, Springer-Verlag, 1998, Electronic Proceedings of the Eurocrypt and Crypto Conferences.
[Nat94] National Institute of Standards and Technology (NIST), *FIPS publication 186: Digital signature standard*, May 1994.
[Ngu99] P. Q. Nguyen, *Cryptanalysis of the Goldreich-Goldwasser-Halevi cryptosystem from Crypto '97*, Proc. of Crypto '99, LNCS, vol. 1666, IACR, Springer-Verlag, 1999, pp. 288–304.
[Ngu04] _____, *Can we trust cryptographic software? Cryptographic flaws in GNU Privacy Guard v1.2.3.*, Advances in Cryptology - Proc. EUROCRYPT 2004, Lecture Notes in Computer Science, vol. 3027, Springer, 2004, pp. 555–570.
[NS01]   P. Q. Nguyen and J. Stern, *The two faces of lattices in cryptology*, Cryptography and Lattices – Proc. CALC '01, LNCS, vol. 2146, Springer-Verlag, 2001, pp. 146–180.
[NS02]   P. Q. Nguyen and I. E. Shparlinski, *The insecurity of the digital signature algorithm with partially known nonces.*, J. Cryptology **15** (2002), no. 3, 151–176.
[NS03]   _____, *The insecurity of the elliptic curve digital signature algorithm with partially known nonces.*, Des. Codes Cryptography **30** (2003), no. 2, 201–217.
[NS04]   P. Q. Nguyen and D. Stehlé, *Low-dimensional lattice basis reduction revisited (extended abstract)*, Proc. of the 6th Algorithmic Number Theory Symposium (ANTS VI), LNCS, vol. 3076, Springer-Verlag, 2004, pp. 338–357.
[NS05a] _____, *Floating-point LLL revisited*, Proc. of Eurocrypt 2005, LNCS, vol. 3494, Springer-Verlag, 2005, pp. 215–233.
[NS05b] Phong Q. Nguyen and Jacques Stern, *Adapting density attacks to low-weight knapsacks*, Advances in Cryptology – Proceedings of ASIACRYPT '05, LNCS, vol. 3788, Springer-Verlag, 2005, pp. 41–58.
[NS06]   P. Q. Nguyen and D. Stehlé, *LLL on the average*, Proc. of ANTS-VII, LNCS, vol. 4076, Springer-Verlag, 2006.
[NV08]   P. Q. Nguyen and T. Vidick, *Sieve algorithms for the shortest vector problem are practical*, J. of Mathematical Cryptology **2** (2008), no. 2, 181–207.
[Odl90] A. M. Odlyzko, *The rise and fall of knapsack cryptosystems*, Cryptology and Computational Number Theory, Proc. of Symposia in Applied Mathematics, vol. 42, A.M.S., 1990, pp. 75–88.
[Oec03] Philippe Oechslin, *Making a faster cryptanalytic time-memory trade-off*, Advances in Cryptology – Proc. CRYPTO '03, Lecture Notes in Computer Science, vol. 2729, Springer, 2003, pp. 617–630.
[Poi05] D. Pointcheval, *Provable security for public key schemes*, pp. 133–185, Birkhäuser Verlag, 2005.
[PS96]   D. Pointcheval and J. Stern, *Security proofs for signature schemes*, Proc. of Eurocrypt '96, LNCS, vol. 1070, IACR, Springer-Verlag, 1996, pp. 387–398.
[QL00]   G. Qiao and K.-Y. Lam, *RSA signature algorithm for microcontroller implementation.*, Proc. of CARDIS '98, Lecture Notes in Computer Science, vol. 1820, Springer-Verlag, 2000, pp. 353–356.
[RSA78] R. L. Rivest, A. Shamir, and L. M. Adleman, *A method for obtaining digital signatures and public-key cryptosystems*, Communications of the ACM **21** (1978), no. 2, 120–126.
[Sch87] C. P. Schnorr, *A hierarchy of polynomial lattice basis reduction algorithms*, Theoretical Computer Science **53** (1987), 201–224.
[Sha82] A. Shamir, *A polynomial time algorithm for breaking the basic Merkle-Hellman cryptosystem*, Proc. of 23rd FOCS, IEEE, 1982, pp. 145–152.
[Sho]   V. Shoup, *Number Theory C++ Library (NTL)*, Available at http://www.shoup.net/ntl/.
[Sho99] Peter W. Shor, *Polynomial-time algorithms for prime factorization and discrete logarithms on a quantum computer*, SIAM Rev. **41** (1999), no. 2, 303–332 (electronic). MR MR1684546 (2000e:11159)
[Sho01] V. Shoup, *OAEP reconsidered*, Proc. of Crypto '01, LNCS, IACR, Springer-Verlag, 2001.

[Sho04] _____, *Sequences of games: a tool for taming complexity in security proofs*, Cryptology ePrint Archive: Report 2004/332, 2004.

[Sho05] _____, *A computational introduction to number theory and algebra*, Cambridge University Press, 2005, Also available on the Internet.

[Sie45] C. L. Siegel, *A mean value theorem in geometry of numbers*, Annals of Mathematics **46** (1945), no. 2, 340–347.

[Sie89] C. L. Siegel, *Lectures on the geometry of numbers*, Springer-Verlag, 1989.

[Sti02] D. R. Stinson, *Some baby-step giant-step algorithms for the low hamming weight discrete logarithm problem.*, Math. Comput. **71** (2002), no. 237, 379–391.

[VGT88] B. Vallée, M. Girault, and P. Toffin, *How to guess ℓ-th roots modulo n by reducing lattice bases*, Proc. of AAEEC-6, LNCS, vol. 357, Springer-Verlag, 1988, pp. 427–442.

[VZ95] S. A. Vanstone and R. J. Zuccherato, *Short RSA keys and their generation*, J. of Cryptology **8** (1995), no. 2, 101–114.

[Wie90] M. Wiener, *Cryptanalysis of short RSA secret exponents*, IEEE Trans. Inform. Theory **36** (1990), no. 3, 553–558.

INRIA. ÉCOLE NORMALE SUPÉRIEURE, DÉPARTEMENT D'INFORMATIQUE; 45, RUE D'ULM, F–75005 PARIS.

E-mail address: http://www.di.ens.fr/~pnguyen/

Pseudorandom Number Generators from Elliptic Curves

Igor E. Shparlinski

ABSTRACT. We give a survey of several recently suggested constructions of generating sequences of pseudorandom points on elliptic curves. Such constructions are of interest for both classical and elliptic curve cryptography and are also of intrinsic mathematical interest. We also explain some main underlying ideas behind the proofs, pose several open questions and outline several directions for further research.

1. Introduction

1.1. Motivation. There is a vast literature devoted to generating pseudorandom numbers using arithmetic of finite fields and residue rings, see [**60, 61, 62, 63, 73, 83**] and references therein. Here we consider a reasonably new source of pseudorandom numbers which is based on using the group structure of elliptic curves over finite fields. We remark that the idea of using elliptic curves as a source of randomness is not new and dates back to [**44**]. However here we consider different constructions which also have a different emphasis. Besides intrinsic mathematical interest, there are two main reasons motivating such constructions:

- Many standard pseudorandom number generators based on finite fields and residue rings have proved to be insecure or at least to require great care in their use, see [**5, 6, 7, 12, 13, 20, 30, 31, 33, 43, 47, 50**]. However the recent result of [**37**] shows that pseudorandom number generators on elliptic curves are not immune to this kind of attack and should also be used with great care.
- Many cryptographic protocols explicitly require generation of random points on a given elliptic curve, see [**2, 9**].

It should be noted that usually there is nothing too exciting in the constructions themselves, which in most of the cases are merely straightforward analogues of well-known constructions over finite fields (however, see Section 3.6 for a more elliptic-curve-specific construction). Typically, the most interesting part lies in the analysis and in proving various results about their period, distribution and other properties.

Here we give a survey of several recently proposed constructions together with a representative sample of the results which have been obtained and of the ideas which have been used. We also propose several open questions and directions for

---

1991 *Mathematics Subject Classification.* 11G05, 11K45, 11T23, 11T71.

further research. Some of these questions can probably be solved by a rather straight forward extension of already known results, but some may require principally new approaches.

1.2. Acknowledgement. This paper is an updated and extended version of the survey [75]. The author is very grateful to World Scientific for generous permission to re-use the material of [75].

This work was supported in part by ARC grant DP0881473.

2. Preliminaries

2.1. Notation. For a prime power q and a positive integer m, we use $\mathbb{F}_q$ to denote a finite field of q elements and $\mathbb{Z}/m\mathbb{Z}$ to denote the residue ring modulo m.

The implied constants in the symbols 'O', '$\ll$' and '$\gg$' may occasionally, where obvious, depend on the real positive numbers ε and δ or some other explicitly described "fixed" parameters, but are absolute otherwise. We recall that the notations $U = O(V)$, $U \ll V$, and $V \gg U$ are all equivalent to the assertion that the inequality $|U| \le cV$ holds for some constant $c > 0$. We also use the symbol $o(1)$ to denote a function which tends to 0 and depends only on ε, δ and other parameters.

For a real $x > 0$ we use $\log x$ to denote the binary logarithm of x.

2.2. Basic Facts on Elliptic Curves. Let $\mathbf{E}$ be an elliptic curve defined over $\mathbb{F}_q$, given by an *affine Weierstraß equation* of the form

$$(1) \qquad Y^2 + (a_1 X + a_3)Y = X^3 + a_2 X^2 + a_4 X + a_6,$$

with coefficients $a_1, a_2, a_3, a_4, a_6 \in \mathbb{F}_q$, such that the partial derivatives $a_1 Y - 3X^2 - a_2 X - a_4$ and $2Y + a_1 X + a_3$ do not vanish simultaneously at points of the curve $(x, y) \in \mathbf{E}(\overline{\mathbb{F}}_q)$ over the algebraic closure $\overline{\mathbb{F}}_q$ of $\mathbb{F}_q$, see [8, 79]. We put $h(X) = a_1 X + a_3$ and $f(X) = X^3 + a_2 X^2 + a_4 X + a_6$, thus the Weierstraß equation becomes

$$Y^2 + h(X)Y - f(X) = 0.$$

If p is the characteristic of $\mathbb{F}_q$ then For $p > 2$ one can always take $h = 0$ and for $p > 3$ also $a_2 = 0$; for $p = 2$ at least one of a_1, a_3 must be nonzero. In this case (1) takes form

$$(2) \qquad Y^2 = X^3 + aX + b,$$

for some $a, b \in \mathbb{F}_q$ with $4a^3 + 27b^2 \ne 0$.

We recall that the set $\mathbf{E}(\mathbb{F}_q)$ of $\mathbb{F}_q$-rational points forms an abelian group of order which satisfies the Hasse–Weil inequality

$$(3) \qquad |\#\mathbf{E}(\mathbb{F}_q) - q - 1| \le 2q^{1/2},$$

and with the *point at infinity* $\mathcal{O}$ as the neutral element of this group (which does not have affine coordinates), see [2, 8, 51, 79] for this and other general properties of elliptic curves.

We use $\oplus$ to denote the group operation. For example, $Q \oplus \mathcal{O} = Q$ for any point $Q \in \mathbf{E}(\mathbb{F}_q)$.

It is well-known that the group of $\mathbb{F}_q$-rational points $\mathbf{E}(\mathbb{F}_q)$ is of the form

$$\mathbf{E}(\mathbb{F}_q) \cong \mathbb{Z}/L\mathbb{Z} \times \mathbb{Z}/M\mathbb{Z},$$

where the integers L and M are uniquely determined with $M \mid L$. We also recall (although we do not use this fact) that the *Weil pairing* implies that $M \mid q - 1$.

For a point $Q \in \mathbf{E}(\mathbb{F}_q)$ we use $x(Q)$ and $y(Q)$ to denote its components, that is, $Q = (x(Q), y(Q))$.

2.3. Some Important Characteristics of Pseudorandom Number Generators.
There are several important criteria which a good sequence of pseudorandom numbers should satisfy. However here we concentrate only on its *period*, *discrepancy* and *linear complexity*.

Certainly any decent sequence of pseudorandom numbers should have a large period. In fact, it has turned out that most of the known bounds on the discrepancy and linear complexity are nontrivial only if the corresponding sequence is of sufficiently large period.

For a sequence of N points in the s-dimensional unit cube $[0,1)^s$

(4) $$\Gamma = \{(\gamma_{1,n}, \ldots \gamma_{s,n}) \in [0,1)^s, \quad 1 \le n \le N\}$$

its discrepancy $\Delta(\Gamma)$ is defined as

$$\Delta(\Gamma) = \sup_{B \subseteq [0,1)^s} \left| \frac{T_\Gamma(B)}{N} - |B| \right|,$$

where $T_\Gamma(B)$ is the number of points of Γ in the box

$$B = [\alpha_1, \beta_1) \times \ldots \times [\alpha_s, \beta_s) \subseteq [0,1)^s$$

and the supremum is taken over all such boxes, see [**22, 49**] for exhaustive treatments of this subject. It is easy to see that the discrepancy is a quantitative measure of uniformity of distribution of sequences, and thus good pseudorandom sequences should (after an appropriate scaling) have a small discrepancy.

Given a sequence $s_0, \ldots, s_{N-1}$ of N elements of a ring $\mathcal{R}$ we call its linear complexity the smallest value of ℓ for which

$$s_{n+\ell} = c_{\ell-1} s_{n+\ell-1} + \ldots + c_0 s_n, \qquad n = 0, \ldots, N - \ell - 1,$$

with some coefficients $c_0, \ldots, c_{\ell-1} \in \mathcal{R}$. We use the convention that the linear complexity is 0 if $s_0 = s_1 = \ldots = s_{N-1} = 0$ and N if $s_0 = s_1 = \ldots = s_{N-2} = 0$ but $s_{N-1} \ne 0$. If s_n is an infinite sequence which is periodic with period T, then the linear complexity of the first N elements stabilizes at $N = 2T$.

The linear complexity is an important cryptographic characteristic of sequences and provides information on the predictability and thus suitability for cryptography. Linear complexity of various sequences of cryptographic interest has been studied in a vast number of works, see [**21, 73**] and references therein.

3. Constructions

3.1. General Conventions.
As we have mentioned, the constructions presented here are direct analogues of the corresponding constructions over finite fields and residue rings.

We always assume that the elliptic curve $\mathbf{E}$ is defined over a prime field $\mathbb{F}_p$ which is represented by the elements of the set $\{0, 1, \ldots, p-1\}$. For example, if $Q \in \mathbf{E}(\mathbb{F}_p)$ then we treat $x(Q)/p$ as a rational number in a unit interval $[0,1]$.

The more general case of arbitrary finite fields $\mathbb{F}_q$ can be considered without any substantial difficulties (however some of the results depends on how the field is given).

3.2. Linear Congruential Generator on Elliptic Curves, EC-LCG.

For a given point $G \in \mathbf{E}(\mathbb{F}_p)$, the **EC-LCG** is defined as the sequence:

$$U_n = G \oplus U_{n-1} = nG \oplus U_0, \qquad n = 1, 2, \ldots, \tag{5}$$

where $U_0 \in \mathbf{E}(\mathbb{F}_q)$ is the "initial value".

The **EC-LCG** generator has been suggested in [38] and than studied in a number of papers [4, 24, 34, 35, 39].

3.3. Power Generator on Elliptic Curves, EC-PG.

For a given point $G \in \mathbf{E}(\mathbb{F}_p)$ and an integer $e \geq 2$, the **EC-LCG** is defined as the sequence:

$$W_n = eW_{n-1} = e^n G, \qquad n = 1, 2, \ldots, \tag{6}$$

where $W_0 \in \mathbf{E}(\mathbb{F}_q)$ is the "initial value".

The **EC-PG** generator has been introduced and studied in [53], see also [25].

3.4. Naor-Reingold Generator on Elliptic Curves, EC-NRG.

For a given point $G \in \mathbf{E}(\mathbb{F}_p)$ of order t and a k-dimensional an integer vector $\mathbf{a} = (a_1, \ldots, a_k) \in (\mathbb{Z}/t\mathbb{Z})^k$, the **EC-NRG** is defined as the sequence:

$$F_{\mathbf{a}}(n) = a_1^{\nu_1} \ldots a_k^{\nu_k} G, \qquad n = 1, 2, \ldots, \tag{7}$$

where $n = \nu_1 \ldots \nu_k$ is the bit representation of n, $0 \leq n \leq 2^k - 1$.

The **EC-NRG** generator has been introduced and studied in [72, 78] and is a full analogue of the original construction of [59] described over a finite field.

Since this construction is more complicated than the other two, we give a numerical example. Let $G \in \mathbf{E}(\mathbb{F}_p)$ be of order $t = 19$, $k = 5$ and $\mathbf{a} = (3, 2, 5, 3, 4)$. Then,

$$\begin{aligned}
F_{\mathbf{a}}(0) &= 3^0 2^0 5^0 3^0 4^0 G = G, \\
F_{\mathbf{a}}(1) &= 3^0 2^0 5^0 3^0 4^1 G = 4G, \\
F_{\mathbf{a}}(2) &= 3^0 2^0 5^0 3^1 4^0 G = 3G, \\
F_{\mathbf{a}}(3) &= 3^0 2^0 5^0 3^1 4^1 G = 12G, \\
&\ldots \quad \ldots \\
F_{\mathbf{a}}(11) &= 3^0 2^1 5^0 3^1 4^1 G = 24G = 5G, \\
&\ldots \quad \ldots \\
F_{\mathbf{a}}(31) &= 3^1 2^1 5^1 3^1 4^1 G = 360G = 18G.
\end{aligned}$$

Note that in the above computation we have used that $19G = \mathcal{O}$, the point at infinity.

3.5. Subset-Sum Generator on Elliptic Curves, EC-SSG.

Let $u(n)$ be a linear recurrence sequence of elements of $\mathbb{F}_2$ of order k, that is,

$$u(n+k) + c_{k-1}u(n+k-1) + \ldots + c_1 u(n+1) + c_0 u(n) = 0, \qquad n = 1, 2, \ldots,$$

for some $c_0, \ldots, c_{k-1} \in \mathbb{F}_2$, $c_0 \neq 0$, see [57, Chapter 8].

Following [23], given k points $G_1, \ldots, G_k \in \mathbf{E}(\mathbb{F}_p)$, we define the **EC-SSG** as the sequence:

$$S_n = \sum_{j=1}^{k} u(n+j-1) G_j, \qquad n = 1, 2, \ldots, \tag{8}$$

where the summation symbol refers to the group operation on $\mathbf{E}$, see also [31].

This construction is an elliptic curve analogue of the subset sum generator over finite fields and residue rings, which has been introduced in [**71**] and studied in [**19, 31, 32, 69, 70**].

3.6. Frobenius Endomorphism Generator on Elliptic Curves, EC-FEG.

Here we outline yet another approach to generating pseudorandom points on elliptic curves which is based on different ideas and has been intensively studied in the literature, see [**2, 36, 45, 52, 54, 58, 80, 81**] and references therein. The underlying idea of this approach is to make an effective use of the Frobenius endomorphism. Although these sequences have never been explicitly suggested as sources of pseudorandom numbers, they can certainly be used for this purpose.

We explain this construction in the simplest case of *Koblitz curves* $\mathbf{E}_a$ defined over $\mathbb{F}_2$ by an equation of the form

$$(9) \qquad Y^2 + XY = X^3 + aX^2 + 1,$$

where $a \in \mathbb{F}_2$, which have been introduced in [**45**]. This construction produces points over binary fields $\mathbb{F}_{2^r}$ which can be interpreted as r-bit strings, which in turn can be used to produce pseudorandom numbers (if, for example, these strings are used as binary digits).

Several other curves can also be used in a similar fashion, see [**2, 36, 52, 54, 58, 80, 81**].

Let r be a sufficiently large positive integer. Then we fix a point $G \in \mathbf{E}_a(\mathbb{F}_{2^r})$ of order t.

We now consider the set of vectors

$$\mathcal{N}_k = \{(\nu_1, \ldots, \nu_k) \in \{0, \pm 1\}^k \mid \nu_j \nu_{j+1} = 0\},$$

that is, the set of vectors with coordinates 0 and ± 1 without two consecutive nonzero coordinates.

It is known, see [**11**], that

$$(10) \qquad \#\mathcal{N}_k = \frac{4}{3} 2^k + O(1).$$

It is not hard to show that every integer n has a representation of the form

$$(11) \qquad n = \sum_{j=0}^{k-1} \nu_j 2^j$$

with some $\mathbf{n} = (\nu_0, \ldots, \nu_{k-1}) \in \mathcal{N}_k$, where $k = \log n + O(1)$, but it is more natural to index the points which we are about to construct by vectors $\mathbf{n} \in \mathcal{N}_k$ rather than by the corresponding integers, since the points $G_\mathbf{n}$ can be arranged in a sequence by ordering the vectors $\mathbf{n} \in \mathcal{N}_k$ lexicographically.

Let σ be the *Frobenius endomorphism*, acting on points $(x, y) \in \mathbb{F}_{2^r}^2$ as

$$\sigma((x, y)) = (x^2, y^2).$$

Clearly, if $Q \in \mathbf{E}_a(\mathbb{F}_{2^r})$ then $\sigma(Q) \in \mathbf{E}_a(\mathbb{F}_{2^r})$ as well.

For $k \leq r$ we consider the points

$$(12) \qquad G_\mathbf{n} = \sum_{j=0}^{k-1} \nu_j \sigma^j(G), \qquad \mathbf{n} = (\nu_0, \ldots, \nu_{k-1}) \in \mathcal{N}_k,$$

(as in (8), the summation symbol refers to the group operation on the elliptic curve).

As we have mentioned, now these points can be used as a sequence by arranging $\mathbf{n} = (\nu_0, \ldots, \nu_{k-1}) \in \mathcal{N}_k$ in some prescribed order, for example, lexicographically or by the size of the integers n given by (11).

We remark that a similar construction can also be implemented with elements of the multiplicative group $\mathbb{F}_{2^r}^*$. That is, instead of the points (12), one can consider the points

$$g_\mathbf{n} = \prod_{j=0}^{k-1} \left(\sigma^j(g)\right)^{\nu_j}, \qquad \mathbf{n} = (\nu_0, \ldots, \nu_{k-1}) \in \mathcal{N}_k,$$

for some fixed element $g \in \mathbb{F}_{2^r}^*$. However, its full advantages can only be seen on elliptic curves. To demonstrate this, we observe the following important features of the construction (12):

- it does not involve any doubling of points, which is more expensive than addition of distinct points on elliptic curves (while in a finite field multiplication and squaring both cost about the same);
- it involves subtraction which costs the same as addition (while in a finite field division is more expensive than multiplication).

3.7. Some Other Constructions. We note that after [44], there have been several other suggestions and approaches to extracting pseudorandomness from elliptic curves, see also [14, 18, 41, 65, 66, 67, 68]. However, these methods and results have a slightly different focus and we do not discuss them in this paper.

We note that graphs based on random walks on the graphs from supersingular elliptic curves from [64], have been suggested as sources of hash-functions, see [15, 16] In these graphs, the nodes are labelled supersingular elliptic curves and nodes are connected if there is low degree isogeny between the corresponding curves. It is shown in [64] that this construction produces a very important type of graphs which are known as *Ramanujan graphs*. The underlying ideas are very interesting and maybe can lead to some new pseudorandom number generators.

We also note that in [77] elliptic curves are used to produce new examples of so-called pseudorandom graphs, see [40, 48] for surveys of pseudorandom graphs. The results of [77] are based on the estimate of [46] which has been presented as Lemma 2. Such graphs can be of use for various cryptographic applications such as hash functions, see [82, 84].

4. Main Tools

4.1. Discrepancy and Exponential Sums. Typically the bounds on the discrepancy of a sequence are derived from bounds of exponential sums with elements of this sequence. The relation is made explicit in the celebrated *Koksma–Szüsz inequality*, see Theorem 1.21 of [22], which we present it in the following form.

LEMMA 1. *There exists an absolute constant $C > 0$ such that, for any integer $L > 1$ and any sequence Γ of N points (4) the discrepancy $\Delta(\Gamma)$ satisfies the following bound:*

$$\Delta(\Gamma) < C^s \left(\frac{1}{L} + \frac{1}{N} \sum_{\substack{0 \le a_1, \ldots, a_s \le L \\ a_1 + \ldots + a_s > 0}} \prod_{j=1}^{s} \frac{1}{a_j + 1} \left| \sum_{n=1}^{N} \exp\left(2\pi i \sum_{j=1}^{s} a_j \gamma_{j,n}\right) \right| \right).$$

For estimation of the corresponding exponential sums with various sequences of pseudorandom numbers, the following bound from [46] has been used, which in turn is a generalization of the classical bound of [10] (and is also obtained using several auxiliary results from [10]).

LEMMA 2. *For any subgroup $\mathcal{H} \in \mathbf{E}(\mathbb{F}_q)$ and any rational function $f(X,Y) \in \mathbb{F}_q(X,Y)$ of degree d which is not constant on $\mathbf{E}$, the bound*

$$\sum_{Q \in \mathcal{H}}{}^{*} \psi(f(Q)) = O(p^{1/2})$$

holds, where ψ is a nontrivial additive character of $\mathbb{F}_q$ and $\sum^{*}$ means the the poles of $f(X,Y)$ are excluded from the summation.

In particular, choosing $f(X,Y) = X$ or $f(X,Y) = Y$ in Lemma 2 we obtain nontrivial bounds with exponential sums with $x(Q)$ and $y(Q)$, respectively.

Lemma 2, combined with Lemma 6 in Section 4.2, yields the following estimate which, for example, forms the basis of the argument in [53]. Namely, it is used in the proofs of Theorems 15 and 25 below.

LEMMA 3. *Fix integers $1 \leq d_1 < \ldots < d_s \leq D$ and fix $c_1, \ldots, c_s \in \mathbb{F}_q$ with $c_s \neq 0$. Let $\mathbf{E}$ be an ordinary elliptic curve defined over $\mathbb{F}_q$. Then the following bound holds:*

$$\max_{\chi \in \mathcal{X}^*} \left| \sum_{\substack{Q \in \mathcal{H} \\ Q \neq \mathcal{O}}} \psi\left(\sum_{i=1}^{s} c_i x(d_i Q)\right) \right| = O\left(sD^2 q^{1/2}\right),$$

where ψ is a nontrivial additive character of $\mathbb{F}_q$ and $\mathcal{H}$ is an arbitrary subgroup of $\mathbf{E}(\mathbb{F}_q)$ of order $t = \#\mathcal{H}$ such that

$$\gcd(t, d_1 \cdots d_s) = 1.$$

In some applications one also needs estimates of certain bilinear sums. The following estimate is derived in [77] from a version of Lemma 6 in Section 4.2 and the classical bounds of exponential sums along a curve from [10].

LEMMA 4. *Let ψ be a nontrivial additive character. Let $\mathcal{U}$ and $\mathcal{V}$ be arbitrary sets of $\mathbf{E}(\mathbb{F}_q)$ and let $\rho(U)$ and $\vartheta(V)$ be arbitrary bounded complex functions supported on $\mathcal{U}$ and $\mathcal{V}$, respectively, with*

$$|\rho(U)| \leq 1, \ u \in \mathcal{U}, \quad \text{and} \quad |\vartheta(V)| \leq 1, \ v \in \mathcal{V}.$$

Then for any fixed integer $\nu \geq 1$ we have

$$\sum_{U \in \mathcal{U}} \sum_{V \in \mathcal{V}} \rho(U) \vartheta(V) \psi(x(U \oplus V))$$

$$\ll (\#\mathcal{U})^{1-1/2\nu} (\#\mathcal{V})^{1/2} q^{1/2\nu} + (\#\mathcal{U})^{1-1/2\nu} \#\mathcal{V} q^{1/4\nu},$$

where ψ is a nontrivial additive character of $\mathbb{F}_q$ and the implied constant depends only on ν.

It is easy to see that the bound in Lemma 4 is nontrivial whenever

$$\#\mathcal{U} > q^{1/2+\varepsilon} \quad \text{and} \quad \#\mathcal{V} > q^{\varepsilon}$$

for some fixed $\varepsilon > 0$. A variant of this bound is used in [55] in the proof of Theorem 23.

Some other bilinear sums with points on elliptic curves have been estimated in [1, 3], these estimates can also be used to study the discrepancy of the **EC-PG**, see Section 6.2.

4.2. Nonvanishing of Some Rational Functions of Elliptic Curves.

In many applications one needs to apply Lemma 2 to much more general functions than $f(X,Y) = X$ or $f(X,Y) = Y$ in the above example. Then the main difficulty in such applications is to show that such functions satisfy the conditions of Lemma 2.

For example, in [39] the following very general class of functions has been considered. Let H be a place of degree d of **E** and let

$$\mathcal{F} = \{f_1, \ldots, f_r\} \tag{13}$$

be a set of $r \geq 1$ rational functions in $\mathbb{F}_p(\mathbf{E})$ with pole divisors of the form

$$(f_i)_\infty = (i + \delta)(H), \qquad 1 \leq i \leq r, \tag{14}$$

where

$$\delta = \begin{cases} 1, & \text{if } d = 1, \\ 0, & \text{if } d \geq 2. \end{cases}$$

Since **E** has genus one, such functions exist by the *Riemann-Roch theorem*. We define $\rho = r + \delta$.

For $r = 2$ and $H = \mathcal{O}$ a natural example (which we have already mentioned in the above) is given by $f_1(P) = x(P)$ and $f_2(P) = y(P)$, where $P = (x(P), y(P)) \neq \mathcal{O}$. In particular, $d = 1$, $\rho = 3$ for this example.

Furthermore, let $\mathcal{M}_{r,s}(\mathbb{F}_p)$ denote the set of all nonzero $r \times s$ matrices

$$C = (c_{i,j})_{1 \leq i \leq r, 1 \leq j \leq s}$$

over $\mathbb{F}_p$.

For a matrix $C \in \mathcal{M}_{r,s}(\mathbb{F}_p)$, a set $\mathcal{F}$ of functions (13) and a generic point Q on **E** we consider the function

$$\mathcal{L}_{C,\mathcal{F}}(Q) = \sum_{i=1}^{r} \sum_{j=1}^{s} c_{i,j} f_i(W_j \oplus Q),$$

as a function in the function field $\mathbb{F}_p(\mathbf{E})$.

The following result of [39] shows that $\mathcal{L}_{C,\mathcal{F}}(Q)$ does not vanish.

LEMMA 5. *For any point $G \in \mathbf{E}(\mathbb{F}_p)$ of order t and any matrix $C \in \mathcal{M}_{r,s}(\mathbb{F}_p)$ with $s \leq t$ and any set $\mathcal{F}$ of functions (13) satisfying (14):*

- *The function $\mathcal{L}_{C,\mathcal{F}}(Q)$ is not constant.*
- *The cyclic group $\langle G \rangle$ generated by the point G contains at most $sd\rho$ zeros of $\mathcal{L}_{C,\mathcal{F}}(Q)$.*
- *If $H \in \langle G \rangle \oplus W_0$ then $\langle G \rangle$ contains at most s poles of $\mathcal{L}_{C,\mathcal{F}}(Q)$, which are of the form $H \ominus W_j$ for $1 \leq j \leq s$, and no poles otherwise.*

Lemma 5, combined with Lemma 1 and Lemma 2, plays a central role in the proof of Theorem 13 below. A variant of Lemma 5 is also given in [55].

For some applications functions with different structure become relevant, but first we need to recall the definition of division polynomials on elliptic curves (for more details see for example [2, 8, 51, 79].)

Assume that **E** is given by (1). We put $b_2 = a_1^2 + 4a_2$, $b_4 = a_1 a_3 + 2a_4$, $b_6 = a_3^2 + 4a_6$, and $b_8 = a_1^2 a_6 + 4a_2 a_6 - a_1 a_3 a_4 + a_2 a_3^2 - a_4^2$.

The *division polynomials* $\psi_m(X,Y) \in \mathbb{F}_q[X,Y]/(Y^2 + h(X)Y - f(X))$, $m \geq 0$, are recursively defined by the relations

$$\begin{aligned}
\psi_0 &= 0, \\
\psi_1 &= 1, \\
\psi_2 &= 2Y + h(X), \\
\psi_3 &= 3X^4 + b_2 X^3 + 3b_4 X^2 + 3b_6 X + b_8, \\
\psi_4 &= (2X^6 + b_2 X^5 + 5b_4 X^4 + 10b_6 X^3 + 10b_8 X^2 + (b_2 b_8 - b_4 b_6)X \\
&\quad + (b_4 b_8 - b_6^2))\psi_2, \\
\psi_{2k+1} &= \psi_{k+2}\psi_k^3 - \psi_{k-1}\psi_{k+1}^3, \quad k \geq 2, \\
\psi_{2k} &= \psi_k(\psi_{k+2}\psi_{k-1}^2 - \psi_{k-2}\psi_{k+1}^2)/\psi_2, \quad k \geq 3.
\end{aligned}$$

Note that $\psi_m(X,Y) \in \psi_2(X,Y)\mathbb{F}_q[X]$ if q is odd and m is even and $\psi_m(X,Y) \in \mathbb{F}_q[X]$ is a univariate polynomial otherwise.

Therefore, since

$$\psi_2^2(X,Y) = 4f(X) + h^2(X),$$

we have

$$\psi_m^2(X,Y), \psi_{m-1}(X,Y)\psi_{m+1}(X,Y) \in \mathbb{F}_q[X].$$

In particular, we may write $\psi_{2k+1}(X)$ and $\psi_m^2(X)$.

The division polynomials are used to compute multiples of a point. Let $Q = (x,y) \neq \mathcal{O}$, then the first coordinate of mQ is given by

$$x(mQ) = \frac{\vartheta_m(x)}{\psi_m^2(x)},$$

where

$$\vartheta_m(X) = X\psi_m^2 - \psi_{m-1}\psi_{m+1}.$$

The zeros of the denominator $\psi_m^2(X)$ are exactly the first coordinates of the non-trivial m-torsion points, that is, the points $Q = (x,y) \in \overline{\mathbb{F}}_q^2$ on $\mathbf{E}$ with $mQ = \mathcal{O}$.

The following statement from [53] deals with linear combinations of multiples of a point G. It is similar to [78, Lemma 6] (which treats the special case of $D < p = q$). In fact the degree bounds are straight forward, only the non-vanishing of the polynomials is not immediately obvious.

LEMMA 6. *Fix integers $1 \leq d_1 < \ldots < d_s \leq D$ and fix elements $c_1, \ldots, c_s \in \mathbb{F}_q$ with $c_s \neq 0$. Let $\mathbf{E}$ be an ordinary elliptic curve defined over $\mathbb{F}_q$. Let us consider the following rational function*

$$L(X) = \sum_{i=1}^{s} c_i \frac{\vartheta_{d_i}(X)}{\psi_{d_i}^2(X)} \in \mathbb{F}_q(X).$$

There are nonzero polynomials $H_1, H_2 \in \mathbb{F}_q[X]$ with $\deg H_1, \deg H_2 < sD^2$ such that

$$L(X) = \frac{H_1(X)}{H_2(X)}.$$

Furthermore, $L(X)$ has a pole of multiplicity one.

A combination of Lemma 2 and Lemma 6 implies Lemma 3, which we have presented in Section 4.1.

5. Periodic Structure

5.1. Period of EC-LCG. It is clear that the period T of the sequence (5) is equal to the order $T = t$ of G. This naturally leads to the question of estimating how often this order is large.

Denote by $\mathcal{T}_p$ the set of all triples (a, b, G), where $a, b \in \mathbb{F}_p$ are such that $4a^3 + 27b^2 \neq 0$ and G is a point on the corresponding curve $\mathbf{E}_{a,b}(\mathbb{F}_p)$, given by (2). From (3) we see that

$$\#\mathcal{T}_p = \left(p^2 + O(p)\right)\left(p + O(p^{1/2})\right) \sim p^3.$$

The following result, showing that typically the period of (5) is large has been established in [**74**].

THEOREM 7. *For any prime $p \geq 5$, $\delta > 0$ and $\varepsilon > 0$ the number of triples $(a, b, G) \in \mathcal{T}_p$ such that the period T of the sequence (5) satisfies the inequality*

$$T < p^{1-\delta}$$

is at most $O\left(\#\mathcal{T}_p p^{-2\delta/3+\varepsilon}\right)$.

5.2. Period of EC-PG. The period T of the sequence (5) is equal to the multiplicative order of e modulo the order t of G (provided that $\gcd(e, t) = 1$) and thus is a little harder to control.

Given an arbitrary $X \geq 2$, we denote by $\mathcal{S}(X)$ the set of all quintuples of the form (p, a, b, e, G), where $p \in [X/2, X]$ is prime, $a, b \in \mathbb{F}_p$ are such that $4a^3 + 27b^2 \neq 0$, G is a point of order t on the corresponding curve $\mathbf{E}_{a,b}(\mathbb{F}_p)$, given by (2) and $e \in [1, \#\mathbf{E}_{a,b}(\mathbb{F}_p) - 1]$ is an integer with $\gcd(e, t) = 1$. We see that

$$\#\mathcal{S}(X) = \sum_{X/2 \leq p \leq X} \sum_{(a,b,G) \in \mathcal{T}_p} \frac{\varphi(t_p(a, b, G))}{t_p(a, b, G)} \#\mathbf{E}_{a,b}(\mathbb{F}_p).$$

It has been shown in [**74**] that

$$\frac{X^5}{\log X} \gg \#\mathcal{S}(X) \gg \frac{X^5}{\log X \log \log X}.$$

The following result from [**74**] shows that "on average" over all parameters from $\mathcal{S}(X)$ the period of (6) is still large.

THEOREM 8. *For any sufficiently large X, any $\varepsilon > 0$ and $\Delta = \varepsilon \log X$, the number of quintuples $(p, a, b, e, G) \in \mathcal{S}(X)$ such that the period T of the sequence (5) satisfies the inequality*

$$T < p \exp(-\Delta)$$

is at most $O\left(\#\mathcal{S}(X) \exp\left(-0.39 \left(\Delta \log \Delta\right)^{1/3}\right)\right)$.

5.3. Period of EC-NRG. Certainly, any lower bound on the linear complexity of this sequence (for example, see Theorem 27 below) implies the same lower bound on the period. However, one can get better estimates.

In particular, the period T of the sequence (7) has never been studied in [**42**] (in fact, even in more general settings which cover both the sequence (7) and the Naor-Reingold generator over finite fields).

We however notice that if, for example, $a_1 = \ldots = a_{k-r} = 1$ then obviously

$$F_{\mathbf{a}}(n) = F_{\mathbf{a}}(n + 2^r), \qquad 0 \leq n \leq 2^k - 2^r - 1,$$

thus in this case the period of the sequence $F_{\mathbf{a}}(n)$ is at most 2^r. This shows that only "statistical" results which apply to almost all (but not all) vectors $\mathbf{a} = (\mathbb{Z}/t\mathbb{Z})^k$ are possible.

It is shown in [**42**] that the size of the set of such "bad" vectors $\mathbf{a} = (\mathbb{Z}/t\mathbb{Z})^k$ can be estimated very precisely.

Since the sequence (7) is defined only on the final segment $n = 0, \ldots, 2^k - 1$, it is natural to define its period as the smallest positive integers T such that

$$F_{\mathbf{a}}(n+T) = F_{\mathbf{a}}(n), \qquad 0 \leq n < 2^k - T.$$

THEOREM 9. *Let G be a point of order t and let $\mathcal{A}(G,k)$ be the set of vectors $\mathbf{a} = (\mathbb{Z}/t\mathbb{Z})^k$ such that the period T of the sequence (7) satisfies $T < 2^{k-1}$. Then*

$$\#\mathcal{A}(G,k) = t^{k-2} + O\left(t^{k-3+o(1)}\right).$$

One can also continue the sequence (7) periodically with period 2^k. This case is considered in [**42**] as well.

5.4. Period of EC-SSG. Since every linear recurrence sequence $u(n)$ of order k over $\mathbb{F}_2$ is periodic with period $\tau \leq 2^k - 1$ then the **EC-SSG** given by (8) is also periodic with some period $T \mid \tau$. Most likely $T = \tau$. However it is also conceivable that $T < \tau$ and it is certainly an interesting question to describe the cases when this may happen.

QUESTION 10. *Give sufficiently broad conditions that guarantee that the period of the **EC-SSG** given by (8) is the same as the period of the underlying linear recurrence sequence $u(n)$.*

5.5. Period of EC-FEG. This question is not so clearly formulated for the **EC-FEG** as there are many ways to fix the order in which this points are taken. However we notice that no matter in what order the points are chosen, if they form a sequence of period T then at least one point $Q \in \mathbf{E}_a(\mathbb{F}_{2^r})$ should appear at least $\#\mathcal{N}_k/T$ times.

We now however present the following result of [**54**], which gives an upper bound on the multiplicity of appearance among the points (12) of an arbitrary point $Q \in \mathbf{E}_a(\mathbb{F}_{2^r})$.

THEOREM 11. *Let $G \in \mathbf{E}_a(\mathbb{F}_{2^r})$ be of prime order t, where $a \in \mathbb{F}_2$. For any integers k and s with $1 \leq s \leq k$ and $2^s \leq t/8$, and for every point $Q \in \mathbf{E}_a(\mathbb{F}_{2^r})$ the number of points $G_{\mathbf{n}}$ given by (12) with $G_{\mathbf{n}} = Q$, where $\mathbf{n} \in \mathcal{N}_k$, does not exceed $\#\mathcal{N}_{k-s}$.*

In particular, the bound of Theorem 11 implies that if $2^k < t/8$ then the points $G_{\mathbf{n}}$ are all distinct. For larger values of k choosing

$$s = \lfloor \log t \rfloor - 3,$$

from (10) we conclude that for any point $Q \in \mathbf{E}_a(\mathbb{F}_{2^r})$ the number of representations $G_{\mathbf{n}} = Q$, with $\mathbf{n} \in \mathcal{N}_k$ is $O(2^k t^{-1})$. Therefore, in this case, the period T of any sequence arranged from the points (12) satisfies $T \gg t$.

The condition of primality of t is quite adequate and in fact natural for cryptographic applications. Still, obtaining more general results would certainly be of interest.

QUESTION 12. *Obtain an analogue of of Theorem 11 for points G of arbitrary order t.*

On the other hand, there are extensions of Theorem 11 to more general fields and elements of the ideal class group of hyperelliptic curves, see [**54**] for more details.

5.6. Ideas Behind the Proofs. Theorems 7 and 8 are based on some elementary number theory and also bounds from [**28**] on the cardinality of the set of integers $n \leq x$ for which the value of the Carmichael function $\lambda(n)$ is atypically small. A result of [**56**] about the number of elliptic curves E over $\mathbb{F}_q$ with a given number of points $\mathbf{E}(\mathbb{F}_q)$ is used too.

The proof of Theorem 9 is based on the careful examination of the structure of possible periods of the sequence (7) and classification of the corresponding vectors $\mathbf{a} = (\mathbb{Z}/t\mathbb{Z})^k$.

The proof of Theorem 11 uses some facts about resultants in the residue ring $\mathbb{Z}/t\mathbb{Z}$. This is why it does not immediately extend to points G of composite order t, see Question 12.

6. Discrepancy

6.1. Discrepancy of EC-LCG. Let U_n be the sequence given by (5) for $G \in \mathbf{E}(F_p)$, where the elliptic curve $\mathbf{E}$ is defined over $\mathbb{F}_p$ and p is prime.

For an integer $s \geq 1$ we consider the $2s$-dimensional points

$$(15) \quad \left(\frac{x(U_n)}{p}, \frac{y(U_n)}{p}, \ldots, \frac{x(U_{n+s-1})}{p}, \frac{y(U_{n+s-1})}{p} \right).$$

The following result is a special partial case of a more general estimate from [**39**].

THEOREM 13. *Assume that $\mathbf{E}$ is an elliptic curve over $\mathbb{F}_p$ where p is prime and t is the order of $G \in \mathbf{E}(\mathbb{F}_p)$. Then for the $2s$-dimensional discrepancy D_s of the points (15) for $n = 1, \ldots, t$ the following bound holds:*

$$D_s = O(t^{-1} p^{1/2} (\log p)^s).$$

Clearly the bound is nontrivial only if $t \geq p^{1/2} (\log p)^s$, but as we have seen in Theorem 7 this holds for most of the random choices of the parameters.

It is very plausible that the same method can produce a similar bound (probably only with an extra factor of $\log p$) on the $2s$-dimensional discrepancy of the points (15) taken over a part of the period, however this has not been worked out.

QUESTION 14. *Prove the bound $O(t^{-1} p^{1/2} (\log p)^{s+1})$ on the $2s$-dimensional discrepancy of the set of points (15) for $n = 1, \ldots, N$ and any integer $N \leq t$.*

As we have mentioned, one can find in [**39**] a more general bound which applies to points constructed by using other functions defined on points on elliptic curves, rather than just $x(Q)$ and $y(Q)$.

Finally, in [**17**] taking the Legendre symbol of some fixed rational function on the points of the sequence given by (5) has been suggested as the source of pseudorandom bits.

6.2. Discrepancy of EC-PG.
The discrepancy of the points associated with the sequence (6) has been estimated in [53].

THEOREM 15. *Assume that* $\mathbf{E}$ *is an elliptic curve over* $\mathbb{F}_p$ *where* p *is prime and* t *is the order of* $G \in \mathbf{E}(\mathbb{F}_p)$. *Let* T *be the period of the sequence* (6). *Then for any fixed integer* $\nu \geq 1$, *the discrepancy* D *of the points*
$$\frac{x(W_n)}{p}, \qquad n = 1, \ldots, T,$$
the following bound holds:
$$D = O\left(T^{-(3\nu+2)/2\nu(\nu+2)} t^{(\nu+1)/\nu(\nu+2)} p^{1/4(\nu+2)} \log p\right).$$

The optimal choice of ν depends on the relation between T, t and p. For example, if $T = p^{1+o(1)}$, which is typically the case (see Theorem 8), then $\nu = 1$ is the optimal choice which leads to the bound $D = O\left(p^{-1/12+o(1)}\right)$.

On the other hand, if $T \geq t^{2/3} q^{1/6+\varepsilon}$ for some fixed $\varepsilon > 0$, then taking sufficiently large ν makes the bound of Theorem 15 nontrivial.

A nontrivial upper bound on the discrepancy of the points (6) for $n = 1, \ldots, N$, where $N \leq T$ has been given in [25].

We remark that an alternative way of estimating exponential sums, and thus the discrepancy for the sequence (6) is given in [3], which however seems to lead to weaker estimates.

We however do not see any plausible approaches to estimating the multidimensional discrepancy (on full or a part of the period) in the style of Theorem 13.

QUESTION 16. *Obtain a nontrivial bound on the s-dimensional discrepancy of the points*
$$\left(\frac{x(W_n)}{p}, \ldots, \frac{x(W_{n+s-1})}{p}\right)$$
for $n = 1, \ldots, N$, *where* $N \leq t$.

As we have mentioned, even the case $N = t$ is of interest and seems to require new ideas to be resolved.

6.3. Discrepancy of EC-NRG.
We now turn our attention to the sequence $F_{\mathbf{a}}(n)$ given by (7). The following result has been obtained in [72].

THEOREM 17. *Assume that* $\mathbf{E}$ *is an elliptic curve over* $\mathbb{F}_p$ *where* p *is prime Let* $G \in \mathbf{E}(\mathbb{F}_p)$ *be of prime order* t. *Then for any* $\delta > 0$, *for a random vector* $\mathbf{a}$ *chosen uniformly from* $(\mathbb{Z}/t\mathbb{Z})^k$ *and the sequence* $F_{\mathbf{a}}(n)$ *given by* (7), *with probability at least* $1 - \delta$ *discrepancy* $D_{\mathbf{a}}$ *of the points*
$$\frac{x(F_{\mathbf{a}}(n))}{p}, \qquad n = 0, \ldots, 2^k - 1,$$
the following bound holds:
$$D_{\mathbf{a}} = O\left(\delta^{-1} B(k, t, p) \log^2 p\right),$$
where
$$B(n, l, p) = 2^{-k/2} + 3^{k/2} 2^{-k} t^{-1/2} p^{1/4} + k^{1/2} t^{-1/2} + t^{-1} p^{1/2}.$$

It is easy to check that the bound of Theorem 17 is nontrivial beginning with
$$t \geq \max\left\{p^{1/2+\varepsilon}, k^{1+\varepsilon}\right\}$$
with any fixed $\varepsilon > 0$. It is natural to select k of order $\log p$ (thus the definition domain of $F_{\mathbf{a}}$ and the value domain are of approximately the same size) the second term can be dropped. In fact, in the most interesting case when k is about the bit length of p, thus $k = \log p + O(1)$ we obtain $B(k,t,p) \ll B(t,p)$ where
$$B(t,p) = \begin{cases} t^{-1/2}p^{1/2-\gamma/2}, & \text{if } l \geq p^\gamma; \\ t^{-1}p^{1/2}, & \text{if } t < p^\gamma; \end{cases}$$
and $\gamma = 2.5 - \log 3 = 0.9150\ldots$.

We now mention several open questions.

QUESTION 18. *Obtain a nontrivial upper bound on the discrepancy of the points*
$$\frac{x(F_{\mathbf{a}}(n))}{p}, \qquad n = 1, \ldots, N,$$
where $N < 2^k$.

In principle, the method of proof of Theorem 17 should apply to Question 18, however optimizing some parameters which occur in the proof, in order to get the best possible bound within this approach, can be more complicated in this case as one more parameter, the segment length N, enters the picture.

The next question is more of theoretic value, since in most of the practical applications of the sequence (7), only t is chosen to be prime anyway (for example, see [59]). Still, to complete the picture, and maybe to gain more understanding about the **EC-NRG** we pose it here.

QUESTION 19. *Extend Theorem 17 to points G of composite order t.*

Finally, we conclude with a question to which the method of (7) does not immediately apply (even for $N = 2^k$) and which we believe is harder than Questions 18 and 19.

QUESTION 20. *Obtain a nontrivial bound on the s-dimensional discrepancy of the points*
$$\left(\frac{x(F_{\mathbf{a}}(n))}{p}, \ldots, \frac{x(F_{\mathbf{a}}(n+s-1))}{p}\right), \qquad n = 0, \ldots, N-1,$$
where $N < 2^k$.

6.4. Discrepancy of EC-SSG.
The following result has been given in [23].

THEOREM 21. *Assume that $\mathbf{E}$ is an elliptic curve over $\mathbb{F}_p$ where p is prime and let $u(n)$ be a linear recurrence sequence of elements of $\mathbb{F}_2$ of order k and period τ, whose characteristic polynomial $Z^k + c_{k-1}Z^{k-1} + \ldots + c_1 Z + c_0 \in \mathbb{F}_2[Z]$ is irreducible over $\mathbb{F}_2$. Then for any $\delta > 0$, for all but $O(\delta p^k)$ choices of k points $G_1, \ldots, G_k \in \mathbf{E}(\mathbb{F}_p)$, the discrepancy $D_{G_1,\ldots,G_k}(N)$ of the points*
$$\frac{x(S_n)}{p}, \qquad n = 1, \ldots, N,$$
where the sequence S_n is given by (8), satisfies the bound
$$D_{G_1,\ldots,G_k}(N) = O\left(\delta^{-1}\min\{N^{-1/2}, p^{-1/4}\}\log^3 p\right),$$

for every $N \leq \tau$.

Certainly obtaining a higher-dimensional analogue of Theorem 21 is a very important task, which is likely to require some new ideas.

QUESTION 22. *Estimate the s-dimensional discrepancy of the points*
$$\left(\frac{x(S_n)}{p}, \ldots, \frac{x(S_{n+s-1})}{p}\right), \quad n = 1, \ldots, N,$$
where the sequence S_n *is given by* (8).

We remark that for the finite field analogue of **EC-SSG** such estimates of multidimensional discrepancy are given in [**19, 32**] (within the same approach as for the one-dimensional case), but in the settings of elliptic curves multidimensional seems to be more difficult.

6.5. Discrepancy of EC-FEG.
Since the **EC-FEG** produces points over $\mathbb{F}_{2^r}$, it makes sense to redefine the notion of discrepancy in this case.

Let $\mathbf{E}_a$ be a Koblitz curve given by (9) with some $a \in \mathbb{F}_2$.

Let $\omega_1, \ldots, \omega_r$ be a fixed basis of $\mathbb{F}_{2^r}$ over $\mathbb{F}_2$. For a fixed subset $\mathcal{J} \subseteq \{1, \ldots, r\}$ and a vector $\mathbf{c} = (c_j)_{j \in \mathcal{J}}$ with $c_j \in \mathbb{F}_2$, we denote by $T_k(\mathcal{J}, \mathbf{c})$ the number of $\mathbf{n} \in \mathcal{N}_k$ for which the coordinate of $x(G_{\mathbf{n}})$ at the jth position is c_j for every $j \in \mathcal{J}$, where $G_{\mathbf{n}}$ is given by (12).

It is rather straightforward to express the deviation of $T_k(\mathcal{J}, \mathbf{c})$ from its expected value $\#\mathcal{N}_k 2^{-\#\mathcal{J}}$ in terms of character sums, which leads to the following result.

THEOREM 23. *Assume that* $\mathbf{E}_a$ *is a Koblitz curve* (9), *where* $a \in \mathbb{F}_2$. *Let* $G \in \mathbf{E}_a(\mathbb{F}_{2^r})$ *be of prime order* t. *Then for any integer* $k \geq 1$ *the bound*
$$\max_{\mathcal{J}, \mathbf{c}} \left| T_k(\mathcal{J}, \mathbf{c}) - \#\mathcal{N}_k 2^{-\#\mathcal{J}} \right| \ll \#\mathcal{N}_k \left(2^{r/4\nu} t^{-1/2\nu} + 2^{r(\nu+1)/4\nu^2 - k/2\nu} \right)$$
holds with any fixed integer
$$\nu \geq \frac{r}{2k},$$
where the implied constant depends only on ν.

6.6. Ideas Behind the Proofs.
All of the above results rely on estimates of relevant exponential sums combined with Lemma 1.

The proof of Theorem 13 follows immediately from the bound of Lemma 2 coupled with Lemma 5.

Lemma 3 is important for the proof of Theorem 15, which also follows the approach which originates from [**26, 27, 29**]. The same technique is also used in [**25**], but is also augmented by some other arguments (which vary depending on whether the length of the segment N is close to T or much smaller). As we have said, the method of [**3**] is different.

In addition to Lemma 2, the proofs of Theorems 17 and 21 make use of averaging in a substantial way, as well as some combinatorial arguments.

The proof of Theorem 23 is based on a combination of a variant of Lemma 5 with some techniques used to estimate bilinear sums of the same kind as in Lemma 4.

7. Linear Complexity

7.1. Linear Complexity of EC-LCG.
The following estimate is a special partial case of a much more general result from [39].

THEOREM 24. *Assume that* $\mathbf{E}$ *is an elliptic curve over* $\mathbb{F}_p$ *where* p *is prime Let* $G \in \mathbf{E}(\mathbb{F}_p)$ *be of prime order* t. *The linear complexity* $L(N)$ *of the sequence of* $x(U_n)$, $n = 1, \ldots, N$, *where the sequence* U_n *given by* (5), *satisfies*

$$L(N) \geq \begin{cases} \min\{N/3, t/3\}, & \text{if } \mathcal{O} = U_0, \\ \min\{N/4, t/3\}, & \text{if } \mathcal{O} \in \langle G \rangle \oplus U_0, \\ \min\{N/3, t/2\}, & \text{otherwise}, \end{cases}$$

where $\langle G \rangle$ *is the subgroup of* $\mathbf{E}(\mathbb{F}_p)$ *generated by* G.

Probably the constants in the denominators can be improved slightly, but overall the bound is quite satisfactory.

7.2. Linear Complexity of EC-PG.
Unfortunately for the **EC-PG** the lower bound, obtained in [53] is more modest.

THEOREM 25. *Assume that* $\mathbf{E}$ *is an elliptic curve over* $\mathbb{F}_p$ *where* p *is prime and* t *is the order of* $G \in \mathbf{E}(\mathbb{F}_p)$. *Let* T *be the period of the sequence* (6). *The linear complexity* L *of the sequence of* $x(W_n)$, $n = 1, \ldots, 2T$, *where the sequence* W_n *given by* (5), *satisfies*

$$L \gg T t^{-2/3}.$$

As we have mentioned in Section 2.3, the linear complexity of any periodic sequence of period T achieves it largest value at the interval of length $2T$. However shorter intervals are of interest too.

QUESTION 26. *Obtain a nontrivial bound lower bound on the the linear complexity of the sequence of* $x(W_n)$, $n = 1, \ldots, N$, *for* $N \leq 2T$.

7.3. Linear Complexity of EC-NRG.
The following result is shown in [78].

THEOREM 27. *Assume that* $\mathbf{E}$ *is an elliptic curve over* $\mathbb{F}_p$ *where* p *is prime Let* $G \in \mathbf{E}(\mathbb{F}_p)$ *be of prime order* t. *Suppose that* $\gamma > 0$ *and* k *are chosen to satisfy*

$$k \geq (2 + \gamma) \log l.$$

Then for any $\delta > 0$ *and sufficiently large* t, *the linear complexity* $L_\mathbf{a}$ *of the sequence of* $x(F_\mathbf{a}(n))$, $n = 0, \ldots, 2^k - 1$, *where the sequence* $F_\mathbf{a}(n)$ *given by* (7), *satisfies*

$$L_\mathbf{a} \gg \min\{t^{1/3-\delta}, t^{\gamma-3\delta} \log^{-2} t\}$$

for all except $O(t^{k-\delta})$ *vectors* $\mathbf{a} \in (\mathbb{Z}/t\mathbb{Z})^k$.

Typically the bit length of p and l are of the same order as n. Thus

$$\log p \sim \log l \sim n.$$

In the most interesting case, the parameter k is the bit length of p, that is, $k \sim \log p$. In this case Theorem 27 implies a lower bound on $L_\mathbf{a}$ which is exponential in k, if $t \leq p^{1/2-\varepsilon}$ for some $\varepsilon > 0$. On the other hand the uniformity of distribution results of Theorem 17 are nontrivial for $t \geq p^{1/2+\varepsilon}$. Thus, unfortunately, these results characterizing different aspects of randomness in the **EC-NRG** do not overlap.

QUESTION 28. *Obtain a nontrivial bound lower bound on the the linear complexity of the sequence of* $x(F_\mathbf{a}(n))$, $n = 0, \ldots, 2^k - 1$, *for* $k \sim \log p$ *and* $t \geq p^{1/2}$.

Studying the linear complexity of the **EC-NRG** in parts of the period is of ultimate interest as well.

QUESTION 29. *Obtain a nontrivial lower bound on the the linear complexity of the sequence of $x(F_{\mathbf{a}}(n))$, $n = 0, \ldots, N$, for $N < 2^k$.*

7.4. Linear Complexity of EC-SSG. In the finite field setting some results have been obtained in [**69, 70**] however even in this case many basic questions about the linear complexity of are widely open and definitely deserve more attention. So it is not surprising that essentially nothing is known the linear complexity of the **EC-SSG**. The problem does not seem unapproachable and probably some nontrivial lower bounds can be obtained. As the first step one can study the linear complexity on the full period.

QUESTION 30. *Prove lower bounds on the linear complexity of the sequence $x(S_n)$, $n = 1, \ldots, \tau$, obtained from the points (8), where τ is the period of the underlying linear recurrence sequence $u(n)$.*

7.5. Linear Complexity of EC-FEG. As in the case of the period estimates, discussed in Section 5.5, the order in which the points (12) are arranged is certainly important for the linear complexity of the resulting sequence. There are unfortunately no results for any of the natural orderings.

QUESTION 31. *Prove lower bounds on the linear complexity of the sequences obtained from the points (12) arranged lexicographically or by the size of the integers n given by (11).*

7.6. Ideas Behind the Proofs. Most of the proofs use the following idea: if the linear complexity of the corresponding sequence is low, it usually leads to a certain identity between linear combinations of rational functions of controlled degree. After this bounds on the number of zeros of such linear combinations can be applied. For example Lemma 5 and Lemma 6 are used in the proofs of Theorem 24 and Theorem 25, respectively.

8. Further Perspectives

Most of the previous constructions are essentially direct analogues of the constructions already well-known in finite fields. However there are several other ways to extend them to elliptic curves. For example, instead of the sequence (7) one can consider the sequence

$$H_n = \sum_{j=1}^{k} \nu_j G_j, \qquad n = 1, 2, \ldots,$$

for given k points $G_1, \ldots, G_k \in \mathbf{E}(\mathbb{F}_p)$, where $n = \nu_1 \ldots \nu_k$ is the bit representation of n and, as in (8), the summation symbol refers to the group operation on **E**. This sequence is similar two both the **EC-NRF** and the **EC-SSG** but is not equivalent to either of them.

The construction of the **EC-FEG** is more specific for elliptic curves than the other constructions of this paper (and, as we have mentioned, is more efficient there) but can also be used on elements of finite fields.

There are however operations which have no analogue for elements of finite fields. More specifically, we mean the Weil and other types of pairing, see [**2, 8, 79**] for the description of different types of pairing and cryptographic applications.

Certainly, one can also expect more applications of the idea of using the Frobenius endomorphism. So, we conclude with the following general question.

QUESTION 32. *Study whether the ideas used in the previous constructions can be combined with the idea of using the Frobenius endomorphism and Weil pairing and thus lead to new pseudorandom number generators of cryptographic and mathematical interest.*

Yet another interesting direction has already been mentioned in Section 3.7:

QUESTION 33. *Study whether the ideas of* [**15, 16**] *may lead to some efficient and reliable pseudorandom number generators.*

Hyperelliptic and other curves of genus $g \geq 2$, and their Jacobians, can also be used in this area. Despite some results in this direction (see [**54, 65, 66**]) this line of research has never been studied systematically. In fact, the basic underlying ingredient of many results for pseudorandom generators on elliptic curves, the bound of exponential sums from [**46**], is missing in the case of curves of genus $g \geq 2$. So extending this bound should probably be the first step. On the other hand, in many cases the classical bound of [**10**] can already be sufficient.

References

[1] O. Ahmadi and I. E. Shparlinski, 'On the sum-product problem on elliptic curves', *Preprint*, 2008, 1-13.
[2] R. Avanzi, H. Cohen, C. Doche, G. Frey, T. Lange and K. Nguyen, *Elliptic and hyperelliptic curve crytography: Theory and practice*, CRC Press, 2005.
[3] W. D. Banks, J. B. Friedlander, M. Garaev and I. E. Shparlinski, 'Double character sums over elliptic curves and finite fields,' *Pure and Appl. Math. Quart.*, **2** (2006), 179–197.
[4] P. Beelen and J. Doumen, 'Pseudorandom sequences from elliptic curves', *Finite Fields with Applications to Coding Theory, Cryptography and Related Areas*, Springer-Verlag, Berlin, 2002, 37–52.
[5] S. R. Blackburn, D. Gomez-Perez, J. Gutierrez and I. E. Shparlinski, 'Predicting the inversive generator', *Lect. Notes in Comp. Sci.*, Springer-Verlag, Berlin, **2898** (2003), 264–275.
[6] S. R. Blackburn, D. Gomez-Perez, J. Gutierrez and I. E. Shparlinski, 'Predicting nonlinear pseudorandom number generators', *Math. Comp.*, **74** (2005), 1471–1494.
[7] S. R. Blackburn, D. Gomez-Perez, J. Gutierrez and I. E. Shparlinski, 'Reconstructing noisy polynomial evaluation in residue rings', *J. of Algorithms*, **61** (2006), 47–90.
[8] I. Blake, G. Seroussi and N. Smart, *Elliptic curves in cryptography*, London Math. Soc., Lecture Note Series, **265**, Cambridge Univ. Press, 1999.
[9] I. Blake, G. Seroussi and N. Smart, *Advances in elliptic curves in cryptography*, London Math. Soc., Lecture Note Series, **317**, Cambridge Univ. Press, 2005.
[10] E. Bombieri, 'On exponential sums in finite fields', *Amer. J. Math.*, **88** (1966), 71–105.
[11] W. Bosma, 'Signed bits and fast exponentiation', *J. Théorie des Nombres Bordeaux*, **13** (2001), 27–41.
[12] J. Boyar, 'Inferring sequences produced by pseudo-random number generators', *J. ACM*, **36** (1989), 129–141.
[13] J. Boyar, 'Inferring sequences produces by a linear congruential generator missing low–order bits', *J. Cryptology*, **1** (1989) 177–184.
[14] M. Caragiu, R. A. Johns and J. Gieseler, 'Quasi-random structures from elliptic curves', *J. Algebra, Number Theory and Appl.*, **6** (2006), 561–571.
[15] D. X. Charles, E. Z. Goren and K. E. Lauter, 'Families of Ramanujan graphs and quaternion algebras', *J. Cryptology*, (to appear).
[16] D. X. Charles, E. Z. Goren and K. E. Lauter, 'Cryptographic hash functions from expander graphs', *Groups and Symmetries*, Amer. Math. Soc., Providence, RI, (to appear).
[17] Z. Chen, 'Elliptic curve analogue of Legendre sequences', *Monash. Math.*, **154** (2008), 1–10.

[18] O. Chevassut, P.-A. Fouque, P. Gaudry and D. Pointcheval, 'The twist-AUgmented technique for key exchange', *Lect. Notes in Comp. Sci.*, Springer-Verlag, Berlin, **3958** (2006), 410–426.

[19] A. Conflitti and I. E. Shparlinski, 'On the multidimensional distribution of the subset sum generator of pseudorandom numbers', *Math. Comp.*, **73** (2004), 1005–1011.

[20] S. Contini and I. E. Shparlinski, 'On Stern's attack against secret truncated linear congruential generators', *Lect. Notes in Comp. Sci.*, Springer-Verlag, Berlin, **3574** (2005), 52–60.

[21] T. W. Cusick, C. Ding and A. Renvall, *Stream ciphers and number theory*, Elsevier, Amsterdam, 2003.

[22] M. Drmota and R. Tichy, *Sequences, discrepancies and applications*, Springer-Verlag, Berlin, 1997.

[23] E. El Mahassni, 'On the distribution of the elliptic subset sum generator of pseudorandom numbers', *Integers*, (to appear).

[24] E. El Mahassni and I. E. Shparlinski, 'On the uniformity of distribution of congruential generators over elliptic curves', *Proc. Intern. Conf. on Sequences and their Applications, Bergen 2001*, Springer-Verlag, London, 2002, 257–264.

[25] E. El Mahassni and I. E. Shparlinski, 'On the distribution of the elliptic curve power generator', *Proc. 8th Conf. on Finite Fields and Appl.*, Contemp. Math., vol. 461, Amer. Math. Soc., Providence, RI, 2008, 111–119.

[26] J. B. Friedlander, J. Hansen and I. E. Shparlinski, 'On character sums with exponential functions', *Mathematika*, **47** (2000), 75–85.

[27] J. B. Friedlander, S. V. Konyagin and I. E. Shparlinski, 'Some doubly exponential sums over $\mathbb{Z}_m$', *Acta Arith.*, **105** (2002), 349–370.

[28] J. B. Friedlander, C. Pomerance and I. E. Shparlinski, 'Period of the power generator and small values of Carmichael's function', *Math. Comp.*, **70** (2001), 1591–1605 (see also **71** (2002), 1803–1806).

[29] J. B. Friedlander and I. E. Shparlinski, 'On the distribution of the power generator', *Math. Comp.*, **70** (2001), 1575–1589.

[30] A. M. Frieze, J. Håstad, R. Kannan, J. C. Lagarias and A. Shamir, 'Reconstructing truncated integer variables satisfying linear congruences', *SIAM J. Comp.*, **17** (1988), 262–280.

[31] J. von zur Gathen and I. E. Shparlinski, 'Predicting subset sum pseudorandom number generators', *Lect. Notes in Comp. Sci.*, Springer-Verlag, Berlin, **3357** (2005), 241–251.

[32] J. von zur Gathen and I. E. Shparlinski, 'Subset sum pseudorandom numbers: Fast generation and distribution', *Preprint*, 2008, 1-18.

[33] D. Gomez-Perez, J. Gutierrez and Á. Ibeas, 'Attacking the Pollard generator', *IEEE Trans. Inform. Theory*, **52** (2006), 5518–5523.

[34] G. Gong, T. A. Berson and D. A. Stinson, 'Elliptic curve pseudorandom sequence generators', *Lect. Notes in Comp. Sci.*, Springer-Verlag, Berlin, **1758** (2000), 34–49.

[35] G. Gong and C. C. Y. Lam, 'Linear recursive sequences over elliptic curves', *Proc. Intern. Conf. on Sequences and their Applications, Bergen 2001*, Springer-Verlag, London, 2002, 182–196.

[36] C. Günther, T. Lange and A. Stein, 'Speeding up the arithmetic on Koblitz curves of genus two', *Lect. Notes in Comp. Sci.*, Springer-Verlag, Berlin, **2012** (2001), 106–117.

[37] J. Gutierrez and Á. Ibeas, 'Inferring sequences produced by a linear congruential generator on elliptic curves missing high-order bits', *Designs, Codes and Cryptography*, **41** (2007), 199–212.

[38] S. Hallgren, 'Linear congruential generators over elliptic curves', *Preprint CS-94-143*, Dept. of Comp. Sci., Cornegie Mellon Univ., 1994, 1–10.

[39] F. Hess and I. E. Shparlinski, 'On the linear complexity and multidimensional distribution of congruential generators over elliptic curves', *Designs, Codes and Cryptography*, **35** (2005), 111–117.

[40] S. Hoory, N. Linial and A. Wigderson, 'Expander graphs and their applications', *Bull. Amer. Math. Soc.*, **43** (2006) 439–561.

[41] H. Hu, L. Hu and D. Feng, 'On a class of pseudorandom sequences from elliptic curves over finite fields *IEEE Trans. Inform. Theory*, **53** (2007), 2598–2605.

[42] Á. Ibeas, 'On the period of the Naor-Reingold generator', *Inform. Proc. Letters*, **108** (2008), 304–307.

[43] A. Joux and J. Stern, 'Lattice reduction: A toolbox for the cryptanalyst', *J. Cryptology*, **11** (1998), 161–185.

[44] B. S. Kaliski, 'One-way permutations on elliptic curves', *J. Cryptology*, **3** (1991), 187–199.
[45] N. Koblitz, 'CM curves with good cryptographic properties', *Lect. Notes in Comp. Sci.*, Springer-Verlag, Berlin, **576** (1992), 279–287.
[46] D. R. Kohel and I. E. Shparlinski, 'Exponential sums and group generators for elliptic curves over finite fields', *Lect. Notes in Comp. Sci.*, Springer-Verlag, Berlin, **1838** (2000), 395–404.
[47] H. Krawczyk, 'How to predict congruential generators', *J. Algorithms*, **13** (1992), 527–545.
[48] M. Krivelevich and B. Sudakov, 'Pseudo-random graphs', *More Sets, Graphs and Numbers*, Bolyai Society Mathem. Studies 15, Springer-Verlag, 2006, 199–262.
[49] L. Kuipers and H. Niederreiter, *Uniform distribution of sequences*, Wiley-Intersci., New York-London-Sydney, 1974.
[50] J. C. Lagarias, 'Pseudorandom number generators in cryptography and number theory', *Cryptology and Computational Number Theory*, Proc. Symp. in Appl. Math., vol. 42, Amer. Math. Soc., Providence, RI, 1990, 115–143.
[51] S. Lang, *Elliptic curves: Diophantine analysis*, Springer-Verlag, Berlin, 1978.
[52] T. Lange, 'Koblitz curve cryptosystems', *Finite Fields and Their Appl.*, **11** (2005), 200–229.
[53] T. Lange and I. E. Shparlinski, 'Certain exponential sums and random walks on elliptic curves', *Canad. J. Math.*, **57** (2005), 338–350.
[54] T. Lange and I. E. Shparlinski, 'Collisions in fast generation of ideal classes and points on hyperelliptic and elliptic curves', *Appl. Algebra in Engin., Commun. and Computing*, **15** (2005), 329–337.
[55] T. Lange and I. E. Shparlinski, 'Distribution of some sequences of points on elliptic curves', *J. Math. Cryptology*, **1** (2007), 1–11.
[56] H. W. Lenstra, 'Factoring integers with elliptic curves' *Annals of Math.*, **126** (1987), 649–673.
[57] R. Lidl and H. Niederreiter, *Finite fields*, Cambridge University Press, Cambridge, 1997.
[58] V. Müller, 'Fast multiplication on elliptic curves over small fields of characteristic two', *J. of Cryptology*, **11** (1998), 219–234.
[59] M. Naor and O. Reingold, 'Number-theoretic constructions of efficient pseudo-random functions', *Proc 38th IEEE Symp. on Found. of Comp. Sci.*, IEEE, 1997, 458–467.
[60] H. Niederreiter, *Random number generation and Quasi-Monte Carlo methods*, SIAM Press, 1992.
[61] H. Niederreiter, 'Design and analysis of nonlinear pseudorandom number generators', *Monte Carlo Simulation*, A.A. Balkema Publishers, Rotterdam, 2001, 3–9.
[62] H. Niederreiter and I. E. Shparlinski, 'Recent advances in the theory of nonlinear pseudo-random number generators', *Proc. Conf. on Monte Carlo and Quasi-Monte Carlo Methods, 2000*, Springer-Verlag, Berlin., 2002, 86–102.
[63] H. Niederreiter and I. E. Shparlinski, 'Dynamical systems generated by rational functions', *Lect. Notes in Comp. Sci.*, Springer-Verlag, Berlin, **2643** (2003), 6–17.
[64] A. K. Pizer, 'Ramanujan graphs', *Computational perspectives on number theory*, Stud. Adv. Math., vol. 7, Amer. Math. Soc., Providence, RI, 1998, 159–178.
[65] R. Rezaeian Farashahi, 'Extractors for Jacobians of binary genus-2 hyperelliptic curves', *Lect. Notes in Comp. Sci.*, Springer-Verlag, Berlin, **5107** (2008), 447–462.
[66] R. Rezaeian Farashahi, R. Pellikaan and A. Sidorenko, 'The quadratic extension extractor for (hyper)elliptic curves in odd characteristic', *Lect. Notes in Comp. Sci.*, Springer-Verlag, Berlin, **4547** (2007), 219–236.
[67] R. Rezaeian Farashahi, R. Pellikaan and A. Sidorenko, 'Extractors for binary elliptic curves', *Designs, Codes and Cryptography*, **49** (2008), 171–186.
[68] R. Rezaeian Farashahi, B. Schoenmakers and A. Sidorenko, 'Efficient pseudorandom generators based on the DDH assumption', *Lect. Notes in Comp. Sci.*, Springer-Verlag, Berlin, **4450**, (2007), 426–441.
[69] R. A. Rueppel, *Analysis and design of stream ciphers*, Springer-Verlag, Berlin, 1986.
[70] R. A. Rueppel, 'Stream ciphers', *Contemporary cryptology: The science of information integrity*, IEEE Press, NY, 1992, 65–134.
[71] R. A. Rueppel and J. L. Massey, 'Knapsack as a nonlinear function', *IEEE Intern. Symp. of Inform. Theory*, IEEE Press, NY, 1985, 46.
[72] I. E. Shparlinski, 'On the Naor–Reingold pseudo-random function from elliptic curves', *Appl. Algebra in Engin., Commun. and Computing*, **11** (2000), 27–34.
[73] I. E. Shparlinski, *Cryptographic applications of analytic number theory*, Birkhauser, 2003.

[74] I. E. Shparlinski, 'Orders of points on elliptic curves', *Affine Algebraic Geometry*, Amer. Math. Soc., 2005, 245–252.
[75] I. E. Shparlinski, 'Pseudorandom points on elliptic curves over finite fields', *Algebraic Geometry and its Applications*, World Scientific, 2008, 116–134.
[76] I. E. Shparlinski, 'Bilinear character sums over elliptic curves', *Finite Fields and Their Appl.*, **14** (2008), 132–141.
[77] I. E. Shparlinski, 'Pseudorandom graphs from elliptic curves', *Lect. Notes in Comp. Sci.*, Springer-Verlag, Berlin, **4957** (2008), 284–292.
[78] I. E. Shparlinski and J. H. Silverman, 'On the linear complexity of the Naor–Reingold pseudorandom function from elliptic curves', *Designs, Codes and Cryptography*, **24** (2001), 279–289.
[79] J. H. Silverman, *The arithmetic of elliptic curves*, Springer-Verlag, Berlin, 1995.
[80] N. P. Smart, 'Elliptic curve cryptosystems over small fields of odd characteristic', *Journal of Cryptology*, **12** (1999), 141–151.
[81] J. Solinas, 'Efficient arithmetic on Koblitz curves', *Designs, Codes and Cryptography*, **19** (2000), 195–249.
[82] J.-P. Tillich and G. Zémor, 'Hashing with SL_2', *Lect. Notes in Comp. Sci.*, Springer-Verlag, Berlin, **839** (1994), 40–49.
[83] A. Topuzoğlu and A. Winterhof, 'Pseudorandom sequences', *Topics in Geometry, Coding Theory and Cryptography*, Springer-Verlag, 2006, 135–166.
[84] G. Zémor, 'Hash functions and Cayley graphs', *Designs, Codes and Cryptography*, **4** (1994), 381–394.

DEPARTMENT OF COMPUTING, MACQUARIE UNIVERSITY, NORTH RYDE, NSW 2109, AUSTRALIA
E-mail address: igor@ics.mq.edu.au

Titles in This Series

477 **Ignacio Luengo, Editor,** Recent Trends in Cryptography, 2008

476 **Carlos Villegas-Blas, Editor,** Fourth summer school in analysis and mathematical physics: Topics in spectral theory and quantum mechanics, 2008

475 **Jean-Paul Brasselet, José Luis Cisneros-Molina, David Massey, José Seade, and Bernard Teissier, Editors,** Singularities II: Geometric and topological aspects, 2008

474 **Jean-Paul Brasselet, José Luis Cisneros-Molina, David Massey, José Seade, and Bernard Teissier, Editors,** Singularities I: Algebraic and analytic aspects, 2008

473 **Alberto Farina and Jean-Claude Saut, Editors,** Stationary and time dependent Gross-Pitaevskii equations, 2008

472 **James Arthur, Wilfried Schmid, and Peter E. Trapa, Editors,** Representation Theory of Real Reductive Lie Groups, 2008

471 **Diego Dominici and Robert S. Maier, Editors,** Special functions and orthogonal polynomials, 2008

470 **Luise-Charlotte Kappe, Arturo Magidin, and Robert Fitzgerald Morse, Editors,** Computational group theory and the theory of groups, 2008

469 **Keith Burns, Dmitry Dolgopyat, and Yakov Pesin, Editors,** Geometric and probabilistic structures in dynamics, 2008

468 **Bruce Gilligan and Guy J. Roos, Editors,** Symmetries in complex analysis, 2008

467 **Alfred G. Noël, Donald R. King, Gaston M. N'Guérékata, and Edray H. Goins, Editors,** Council for African American researchers in the mathematical sciences: Volume V, 2008

466 **Boo Cheong Khoo, Zhilin Li, and Ping Lin, Editors,** Moving interface problems and applications in fluid dynamics, 2008

465 **Valery Alexeev, Arnaud Beauville, C. Herbert Clemens, and Elham Izadi, Editors,** Curves and Abelian varieties, 2008

464 **Gestur Ólafsson, Eric L. Grinberg, David Larson, Palle E. T. Jorgensen, Peter R. Massopust, Eric Todd Quinto, and Boris Rubin, Editors,** Radon transforms, geometry, and wavelets, 2008

463 **Kristin E. Lauter and Kenneth A. Ribet, Editors,** Computational arithmetic geometry, 2008

462 **Giuseppe Dito, Hugo García-Compeán, Ernesto Lupercio, and Francisco J. Turrubiates, Editors,** Non-commutative geometry in mathematics and physics, 2008

461 **Gary L. Mullen, Daniel Panario, and Igor Shparlinski, Editors,** Finite fields and applications, 2008

460 **Megumi Harada, Yael Karshon, Mikiya Masuda, and Taras Panov, Editors,** Toric topology, 2008

459 **Marcelo J. Saia and José Seade, Editors,** Real and complex singularities, 2008

458 **Jinho Baik, Thomas Kriecherbauer, Luen-Chau Li, Kenneth D. T-R McLaughlin, and Carlos Tomei, Editors,** Integrable systems and random matrices, 2008

457 **Tewodros Amdeberhan and Victor H. Moll, Editors,** Tapas in experimental mathematics, 2008

456 **S. K. Jain and S. Parvathi, Editors,** Noncommutative rings, group rings, diagram algebras and their applications, 2008

455 **Mark Agranovsky, Daoud Bshouty, Lavi Karp, Simeon Reich, David Shoikhet, and Lawrence Zalcman, Editors,** Complex analysis and dynamical systems III, 2008

454 **Rita A. Hibschweiler and Thomas H. MacGregor, Editors,** Banach spaces of analytic functions, 2008

453 **Jacob E. Goodman, János Pach, and Richard Pollack, Editors,** Surveys on Discrete and Computational Geometry–Twenty Years Later, 2008

TITLES IN THIS SERIES

452 Matthias Beck, Christian Haase, Bruce Reznick, Michèle Vergne, Volkmar Welker, and Ruriko Yoshida, Editors, Integer points in polyhedra, 2008
451 David R. Larson, Peter Massopust, Zuhair Nashed, Minh Chuong Nguyen, Manos Papadakis, and Ahmed Zayed, Editors, Frames and operator theory in analysis and signal processing, 2008
450 Giuseppe Dito, Jiang-Hua Lu, Yoshiaki Maeda, and Alan Weinstein, Editors, Poisson geometry in mathematics and physics, 2008
449 Robert S. Doran, Calvin C. Moore, and Robert J. Zimmer, Editors, Group representations, ergodic theory, and mathematical physics: A tribute to George W. Mackey, 2007
448 Alberto Corso, Juan Migliore, and Claudia Polini, Editors, Algebra, geometry and their interactions, 2007
447 François Germinet and Peter Hislop, Editors, Adventures in mathematical physics, 2007
446 Henri Berestycki, Michiel Bertsch, Felix E. Browder, Louis Nirenberg, Lambertus A. Peletier, and Laurent Véron, Editors, Perspectives in Nonlinear Partial Differential Equations, 2007
445 Laura De Carli and Mario Milman, Editors, Interpolation Theory and Applications, 2007
444 Joseph Rosenblatt, Alexander Stokolos, and Ahmed I. Zayed, Editors, Topics in harmonic analysis and ergodic theory, 2007
443 Joseph Stephen Verducci and Xiaotong Shen, Editors, Prediction and discovery, 2007
442 Yi-Zhi Huang and Kailash C Misra, Editors, Lie algebras, vertex operator algebras and their applications, 2007
441 Louis H. Kauffman, David E. Radford, and Fernando J. O. Souza, Editors, Hopf algebras and generalizations, 2007
440 Fernanda Botelho, Thomas Hagen, and James Jamison, Editors, Fluids and Waves, 2007
439 Donatella Danielli, Editor, Recent developments in nonlinear partial differential equations, 2007
438 Marc Burger, Michael Farber, Robert Ghrist, and Daniel Koditschek, Editors, Topology and robotics, 2007
437 José C. Mourão, João P. Nunes, Roger Picken, and Jean-Claude Zambrini, Editors, Prospects in mathematical physics, 2007
436 Luchezar L. Avramov, Daniel Christensen, William G Dwyer, Michael A Mandell, and Brooke E Shipley, Editors, Interactions between homotopy theory and algebra, 2007
435 Krzysztof Jarosz, Editor, Function spaces, 2007
434 S. Paycha and B. Uribe, Editors, Geometric and topological methods for quantum field theory, 2007
433 Pavel Etingof, Shlomo Gelaki, and Steven Shnider, Editors, Quantum groups, 2007
432 Dick Canery, Jane Gilman, Juha Heinoren, and Howard Masur, Editors, In the tradition of Ahlfors-Bers, IV, 2007
431 Michael Batanin, Alexei Davydov, Michael Johnson, Stephen Lack, and Amnon Neeman, Editors, Categories in algebra, geometry and mathematical physics, 2007

For a complete list of titles in this series, visit the AMS Bookstore at **www.ams.org/bookstore/**.